Trusting the Spirit

Trusting the Spirit

Renewal and Reform in American Religion

Richard Cimino

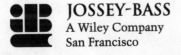

JOSSEY-BASS
A Wiley Company
San Francisco

Jossey-Bass books and products are available through most bookstores. To contact Jossey-Bass directly, call (888) 378-2537, fax to (800) 605-2665, or visit our website at www.josseybass.com.

Substantial discounts on bulk quantities of Jossey-Bass books are available to corporations, professional associations, and other organizations. For details and discount information, contact the special sales department at Jossey-Bass.

 Manufactured in the United States of America on Lyons Falls Turin Book. This paper is acid-free and 100 percent totally chlorine-free.

Library of Congress Cataloging-in-Publication Data

Cimino, Richard P.
    Trusting the spirit : renewal and reform in American religion /
by Richard Cimino.—1st ed.
      p. cm.
Includes bibliographical references and index.
  ISBN 0-7879-5160-9 (alk. paper)
  1. United States—Religion—20th century—Case studies. 2.
Church renewal—United States—Case studies. I. Title.
  BL2525 .C56 2001
  200'.973—dc21
                                              00-011636

FIRST EDITION
HB Printing   10 9 8 7 6 5 4 3 2 1

Contents

Preface

The people I interviewed in researching this book were often curious about why I was interested in the subject of renewal and reform in American religion. They seemed surprised and sometimes puzzled that someone would take an interest in their organizations or movements, particularly if that someone was not a member of or participant in their faith. I usually explained that these groups are important today in forming people's religious identities and in gaining their trust, particularly as many denominational loyalties have faded. Although this is true, it really was not much of an answer. I should have answered that these groups are fascinating and compelling. The people involved are more dedicated and inspired than those one usually finds in everyday life. Sociologist Max Weber had a term to describe many of these renewalists and reformers: *religious virtuosos*—people who are unusually receptive to spiritual things.[1]

Faith and spirituality are more intense among those in renewal and reform groups. The participants want to speak—and argue—about their faith and try to pass it on to others (I had no problem finding willing interviewees). Renewalists and reformers seek to recapture the spirit that formed their particular faiths and traditions and to carry this fervor into their congregations and other institutions. For this reason, these groups clash with the rubrics and conventions of religious life, sometimes causing congregational and denominational schisms.

Despite the importance of renewal and reform organizations in American religion, they have not received much attention. Because of the growing pluralism and divisions within religious bodies, special interest groups—from both inside and outside the institutions—have flourished. This is especially true in the case of groups proposing changes in denominational structures or those challenging the leadership and the laity with their own visions of spirituality, theological truth, and community life. Although renewal and reform functions may be found in one organization, the terms have different meanings. I define groups that focus on spiritual practices and reviving personal faith as *renewal organizations*. Those proposing and working for change in wider structures and leaderships I designate as *reform groups and movements*.

As denominations based on centralized leadership are losing much of their influence among congregations and members, reform and renewal groups have begun to fill the gap, providing participants with spiritual resources and a new sense of community. Although these groups intend to change the larger denominational structure and congregational life, they also increasingly reflect the consumerist and decentralized nature of American religion. They can function as quasidenominations, creating their own literature and means of education, in some cases providing a separate identity for participants.

This book is organized around six case studies of renewal and reform organizations and related movements. Although the groups I selected are among the most prominent in their respective religious bodies and traditions, their weaknesses and failures in efforts of revitalization will be as instructive to the reader as their strengths. The concluding chapter draws on the case studies, as well as research about other groups, and discusses principles and strategies that make for the effective reform and renewal of religious institutions.

Trusting the Spirit will be of interest to religious professionals, academics, students, and laypeople. Religious leaders and clergy will find the accounts of the different renewal organizations and the analyses of the effectiveness of such efforts to be relevant and beneficial to their work. In today's religious environment, clergy and other congregation leaders need to know about these influential renewal and reform organizations in order to work with them to their benefit. Renewal leaders and participants require a greater understanding of how to interact and relate to the congregants and institutions they are seeking to revitalize. Academics and laypeople will profit from the book's portrayal of movements and organizations that are having a noticeable impact in American religion.

The process of renewal and reform consists of a constant interaction between three main actors. At the head of the figurative triangle is the renewal or reform organization, and at the other two points are the congregation (clergy and laity) and the denominations or traditions these groups are working to revitalize. One might suppose that the relationship between the renewal-reform group and the denominational structure—the leadership and bureaucracy—is the most important in understanding this subject. But after a year and a half of studying the literature and speaking with people involved in renewal and reform groups, I am convinced that this is not the case.

As we will see throughout this book, these organizations and the movements related to them are an increasingly influential part of Americans' religious identity. For this reason, the personal accounts of involvement in renewal and reform groups are central throughout the book; the politics and personalities in renewal and reform groups and their respective religious bodies are less prominent. Because this book also seeks to tease out some common themes and principles that can be put to use by people interested in renewal and reform efforts in their own situations, I have tried not to get bogged down in details; indeed, books could be written about each group. My research and interviews were not so much concerned with uncovering the inner workings of these organizations as with studying the participation of laity and clergy in these groups and seeing how that participation has shaped their lives and their involvement in their congregations. From that vantage point, I then looked at the prospects of renewal and reform for these groups within their respective traditions and tried to relate these dynamics to the wider religious scene, on both the personal and denominational levels. (Readers interested in learning more about how the research was undertaken can refer to Appendix A.

I define the phenomenon of renewal and reform somewhat loosely throughout the book. Many renewal and reform groups discussed in these pages do not have formal memberships or other clear-cut boundaries between participants and nonparticipants. Some of the organizations are part of well-organized movements; others are modest operations, with only a magazine or an annual conference as their main tool of renewal. Yet I hope to show how even such low-profile groups are important in meeting religious needs and galvanizing people to causes and movements that change congregations, denominations, and most importantly, participants themselves.

It will become clear early on that what one organization or movement considers renewal another might see as retrenchment or secularization. In the following pages I make no attempt to discern which group or perspective represents genuine renewal (which, given the diversity of the groups under discussion, would be very difficult) or to make theological judgments on their teachings. Rather, I try to understand how the leaders and participants themselves define renewal and reform and then take a look at the results of such efforts and how they may relate to wider patterns and trends in American religion. In the conclusion I examine how the case studies discussed in the book may present readers with strategies and principles that will prove beneficial to those involved in the difficult yet necessary work of religious revitalization.

I would like to thank the following individuals at Jossey-Bass: Sheryl Fullerton for her advice and guidance as this book went through several stages to completion; Chandrika Madhaven for her assistance at crucial points in working on the manuscript; and Sarah Polster for her interest and suggestions when I initially approached her about this project in 1998. I am thankful to James Lewis and the Louisville Institute, which provided a grant that helped me carry out the research for this book. Much gratitude also goes to Gregory Singleton for his comments on the manuscript, and to Reverends Glenn C. Stone and Frederick Schumacher for their comments on the chapter about the American Lutheran Publicity Bureau and the Society of the Holy Trinity. The manuscript's anonymous reviewers provided helpful corrections and suggestions for its improvement.

It is impossible to thank individually the nearly one hundred people I interviewed for this book, but their cooperation, hospitality, and interest were extraordinary. The coordinators and directors of renewal and reform groups deserve mention for the generous time and information they gave me and particularly for the many contacts they provided for my subsequent interviews. They include Carl Nobile, Walter Matthews, Steve Benthal, David Runion-Bareford, Frederick Schumacher, Glenn C. Stone, Judith

Bruder, Brothers Pedro and John of Taizé, Dan and Sheila Daly, Don Wedd, and Rabbi Daniel Siegel.

Although I used pseudonyms for many of the interviewees, that is not always the case. The key to telling real names from pseudonyms is as follows: use of first names only marks pseudonyms; use of first and last names, usually in the case of prominent leaders, marks the real names. I followed a similar principle for congregations and locations: when a congregation's name is cited along with its location, this is the actual name of the church or synagogue.

North Bellmore, N.Y.   RICHARD CIMINO
December 2000

The Author

RICHARD CIMINO is editor and publisher of *Religion Watch,* a newsletter on trends and research in contemporary religion. He is coauthor (with Don Lattin) of *Shopping for Faith: American Religion in the New Millennium* (Jossey-Bass, 1998). He is also author of *Against the Stream: The Adoption of Traditional Christian Faiths by Young Adults.*

Cimino is a freelance researcher and writer who has contributed to publications including *The Christian Century, Religion News Service, American Demographics,* and *National Catholic Reporter.* He received his B.A. in Journalism from New York University and his M.A. in Sociology from Fordham University in New York. He currently lives on Long Island, New York.

Trusting the Spirit

Rekindling the Fires of Faith

The call for renewal and reform seems a constant in most religions, particularly those with modern forms of leadership and complex structures. There has always been a need for rekindling religious fervor and devotion as the original fires that once ignited faiths and forged institutions burn low over time. Any religion that exists for a period of time soon finds itself confronted with followers or leaders who claim that its foundations have been weakened or that new teachings or reinterpretations of existing teachings are necessary in order to meet future challenges or recapture the genius of the founders' vision. Whereas many break away from a church body or tradition that they feel has fallen away from the truth, others remain and try to make changes from within. Many of these reformers would agree with evangelical Anglican theologian J. I. Packer's view that the reformer engages in this effort "because you [the reformers] value the heritage of that denomination and you think it worth preserving and you want to see your denomination alive again in terms of fidelity to its heritage and a renewed experience of the power of Christ in all its activities."[1]

The call to revive one's faith, to return to faith after wandering away from God, fills more pages of the Jewish and Christian Scriptures than any other theme. Judaism was marked by factions and subfactions concerned with purifying and reinterpreting Torah and the Talmudic commentaries. It can be argued that Christianity was viewed by its founders as a renewal caucus within Judaism. As often happens, the teachings and practices of this upstart group grew too radical for the host body. The intended renewal of Judaism by the first Christians moved beyond the walls of the synagogues to transform itself into a new faith with its own structures and its own diversity and tensions. As Christians formed their own churches and Christianity was recognized as an established religion, mystics, ascetics, and others bristling at the new official status ventured into the desert and other remote places to recover the simplicity of the Christian message and experience. Such an exodus gave birth to monasticism as well as to the possibility that reform and renewal need not cause new split-offs from the main church. As new religious orders such as the Franciscans emerged, they brought conflict to the Roman Catholic Church, which only gradually came to accept and value them as sources of intense spirituality and devotion. But other renewal movements with variant teachings—from the Cathars to the Waldensians—met with less acceptance and were either forced out, persecuted, or allowed to leave the church voluntarily.

The Protestant Reformation is the classic case of reformers seeking to remain in their parent church body and work for internal change—up to a point. The efforts of reformers and their followers could be compared to a complex dance in which they took certain actions and then took their cues for their next actions from the responses of Catholic Church authorities. On the one hand, they wanted to remain in the church and retain much of its teachings and practices in their reforms, and therefore they made concessions on certain points or emphasized common ground. On the other hand, they arrived at various conclusions—such as the teaching of justification by faith—that they felt they could not retract. The latter course of action usually resulted in church authorities giving the reformers a period of time to change their mind or modify their views to be in line with church teachings. If the reformer or dissenter did not make the concession or leave voluntarily, church authorities pronounced excommunication.

The multiplication of reformers and new churches born during this period can be explained by many factors, particularly the invention of the printing press, which helped spread new ideas unchained from a hierarchical and established institution. The era from the Reformation until the twentieth century brought a virtual avalanche of new faiths and denominations; it seemed that the idea of staying within an established church and working for change had lost its power. Within each of the Reformation churches renewal movements gradually formed, as for example, the pietist movements and communities developing within the state Lutheran churches of Germany. But even the groups starting out as renewal efforts had a greater tendency to split off from the parent body to form a separate existence. In Europe, renewal groups surfaced not only in Protestantism but also in Orthodox Judaism. Hasidism, a mystical and communal movement, emerged in the eighteenth-century Jewish communities in Eastern Europe. Like Protestant pietism, Hasidism sought a religion of the heart that addressed everyday life, and it too encountered opposition from the religious establishment.

One of the most well-known historical examples of an influential renewal group was the Oxford movement in Anglicanism. The movement, starting around the mid-1830s and led by such figures as John Henry Newman, sought to regain the liturgy and worship of pre-Reformation times as well as encourage efforts toward Christian unity. Many of these recoveries from the pre-Reformation church (such as frequent receiving of communion) were eventually adopted by the wider Anglican church. The Oxford movement also gave birth to religious orders in the church that up to the present day preserve many of the reforms of Newman and his fellow renewalists. As often happens in renewal groups, several of the leaders left the movement in search of greener pastures, some going to Roman Catholicism and others leaving Christianity altogether.

Outside of Roman Catholicism and Eastern Orthodoxy, both of which place sacred value in a larger external religious structure, a Protestant or a Jew faced fewer taboos about going to the next village and starting a new congregation and denomination if things became difficult in the faith of his (or her) birth.

The general Protestant tendency to break off from an institution and form new denominations intensified in the free-market atmosphere of the United States. When religious traditions were transplanted to this country, even the more hierarchical churches often adopted a more congregational style that placed less importance in centralized leadership. One can see the tendency to fragmentation in the many different kinds of Presbyterian, Lutheran, and Baptist groups that have branched out in new forms throughout U.S. religious history.

Newer, indigenous denominations such as the Church of the Nazarene and other Holiness movements started out in the attempt to renew existing Methodist churches, but gradually their adherents became convinced that their witness to new doctrines and practices was not appreciated in their denominations and moved to create their own church bodies. During the nineteenth century, other organizations and movements, from the YMCA to abolitionism and revival crusades, never formed their own denominations but worked within many churches to draw wide support for their causes.[2]

It was also in the late nineteenth and early twentieth centuries, as the nation as a whole was becoming more pluralistic, that internal differences among the faithful became acute. Fired up by the theory of evolution and the influence of European theologians inspired by the Enlightenment, clergy and laity could begin to entertain and embrace views that they felt would renew their respective churches, views that sometimes ran into conflict with creeds, confessions, and traditional beliefs about the inspiration of the Scriptures. The mainline churches—Congregational, Presbyterian, Methodist, and Episcopal—were the bodies most influenced by the continental drifts of liberalism and higher biblical criticism from Europe. Although the presence of liberalism in the churches did not break into the public consciousness until the fundamentalist-modernist controversies of the 1920s, notably in the Scopes trial dealing with evolution, conservatives had formed groups decades before in order to counteract modernist influence in churches.

The early fundamentalists were not separatists but rather members and leaders in good standing in mainline churches and seminaries. In many cases, these concerned churchmen created parachurch organizations (long a staple of American religious life) that united conservative believers of different denominations for specific purposes. Otherwise, they attempted to stay in their church bodies and form associations and, in some cases, parallel structures that upheld conservative teachings. These counterstructures were often seminaries—the entryway for liberal theological influence in denominations—or missionary societies. In the Presbyterian Church, for instance, conservatives started their own missionary society to fight liberal influence. Many times these conservative efforts at renewal resulted in another series of schisms and new denominations coming on the scene.

The denomination building and schisms taking place in American Christianity in the nineteenth and twentieth centuries was also present in Judaism. Reform Judaism, founded in Germany in the mid-1800s, broke from traditional (or Orthodox) Judaism in its attempt to update the religion and gained many adherents among immigrants in the United States. The American-born Conservative movement originated in 1913 and sought to create a middle way between Reform and Orthodox Judaism. The smaller Reconstructionist branch, which taught that Judaism was a civilization rather than a divinely revealed religion, found a following among many American Jews (particularly those in the Conservative branch) starting in the 1920s but did not organize its own synagogues and a seminary until 1968.[3]

Sociologist Robert Wuthnow points out that between 1870 and the end of World War I, the number of congregations—Protestant, Catholic, and Jewish—grew from around 70,000 to over 225,000. This spectacular growth brought a rapid expansion of central agencies. Programs to manage pension funds, establish benevolent institutions, plan evangelism and church planting, publish Sunday school literature, and conduct missionary activity abroad mushroomed during this time. The growth of centralized structures particularly expanded from the 1930s to the 1950s. For instance, during the 1930s, Jewish municipal federations were founded in nearly one hundred new locations. The rise of the modern denomination was a key factor in the formation of renewal and reform movements and ministries. Many American denominations structured themselves similarly to the rest of corporate America in the 1950s.[4]

The 1950s expansion in religious building and organizational life came after a period of decline and cutbacks during the Great Depression and World War II. Like other organizations, churches and synagogues were faced with a flurry of new demands for buildings and services in what has been called a religious boom, but it was more likely a period of catching up on the building of institutions that had been delayed for the previous two decades. By that time, denominations had also become involved in ecumenical endeavors that demanded a higher degree of coordination than would have been possible in the loose associations that went by the name of denominations early in the nation's history. Casting the church leader in the role of corporate executive, charged with handling the ever-widening responsibilities of denominations, made for efficiency but resulted in the growth of bureaucracies and centralization.

As many denominations were centralizing, special interest groups were also expanding throughout American religion. Most of these were nondenominational in character, but new organizations also emerged within denominations. These organizations catered to specific groups, such as women, youth, and ethnic minorities, and addressed new issues coming to the surface in religious life—from world peace to racial and social justice. Special purpose groups often took a mediating role between the local congregation and the larger nationwide structure. Many of these groups may have started out as grassroots movements seeking to counteract the bureaucracy of denominations, only to be later integrated into the denominational structure or to form mini-bureaucracies of their own as they expanded.

In the turbulent late 1960s, these special interest groups became galvanizing forces in the battle on social issues in denominations. Antiwar groups that formed within and between denominations, such as the ecumenical Clergy and Laity Concerned, were met by equally organized conservative groups critical of such a liberal stance by mainline leadership and special caucuses. During the same time, mergers between groups of the same tradition ignited new oppositional groups (and eventually new denominations). Conservative Methodists founded the Forum for Scriptural Christianity in 1966, and evangelical Presbyterians formed the Presbyterian Lay Committee in 1967, both as responses to the new social activism and the growth of theological and social liberalism in these denominations. The influence of feminism and the drive for women's ordination in Christian and Jewish denominations were another impetus in the formation of special interest groups.

All of these groups reflected and intensified the new pluralism growing in many religious bodies. Although official doctrinal statements and social statements may give the impression that they are representing monolithic organizations, today's denominations contain groups and subgroups, unofficial magazines, newsletters, and

Web sites reflecting a wide range of opinions and practices. These groups not only want their voices to be heard and respected, they want to change things in their denominations and galvanize members around their agendas. These groups often have specific aims, whether they be calling attention to persecuted believers in other parts of the world, pressing for the rights of homosexuals to be ordained, or, conversely, seeking to restrict gay rights in their denominations.

Renewal and Reform in the Religious Marketplace

Organizations and movements that have a wide vision of change, as opposed to the specialized groups discussed above, are often referred to as renewal and reform groups. Since the 1980s, these groups can be found in most denominations, whether conservative, liberal, or moderate. They all have in common the aim to transform the religious body and its members through distinctive teachings and practices. That is about where the similarities end for most of these groups, at least at first glance. Some groups attempt to restore traditions and doctrines that are perceived to have been lost or diluted, whereas others chart new ways of faith and practice.

One movement may concentrate on reforming denominational structures through political advocacy and negotiations with leaders; another group may be interested in renewing its denomination or wider tradition through spiritual formation of its members. Many of these renewal and reform groups are not connected to any one denomination or tradition. For instance, the practices associated with the charismatic movement derived from the classic Pentecostal churches but then spread in modified forms into Catholic and mainline Protestant bodies. Studies show that these movements have gained the allegiance of wide numbers of believers, including those heavily involved in their own congregations.

Wuthnow finds that since World War II over five hundred special purpose religious groups have formed. Forty-seven percent of such groups, which range from Bible study to social activist groups, had some form of denominational sponsorship prior to 1960. In contrast, only 32 percent of the groups founded since 1960 have had denominational sponsorship. "In short," Wuthnow writes, "special purpose groups have not only increased in prominence relative to denominations but have also become more distinctly separate from denominations in origins and sponsorship."[5]

Wuthnow cites surveys from the mid-1980s suggesting that vast numbers of Americans are familiar with special interest groups and activities. Approximately one person in four has had some contact with home Bible study groups, a total of about forty million Americans. About one person in ten has come into contact with healing ministries, the charismatic movement, or positive thinking seminars. Wuthnow finds that the number of participants in these special interest groups is comparable to, or maybe even greater than, the number of members of denominations. "Even the 2 or 3 percent involved in antinuclear coalitions, holistic health activities, or the charismatic movement is larger in absolute size than the membership of many denominations."[6]

There is little doubt that the number of renewal and reform organizations has expanded along with special interest groups. The Presbyterian Church (USA) provides an example of how pluralism in a mainline denomination can lead to a pluralism of renewal and reform groups (not including special interest groups focusing on missions or family life in the church). At least fifteen renewal groups are pressing for conservative change in the denomination, and another five or so are devoted to liberal or progressive renewal and reform efforts.

The growth of information technologies such as the Internet, which allows people free expression outside of official channels, will increase the informal discussion forums and fellowships providing free discussion of and alternatives to official doctrine. I have found that renewal groups of all kinds recruit for participants and disseminate their views over the Internet. The recent actions of both Jehovah's Witnesses and ultra-Orthodox Jews in Israel to ban use of the Internet among their members reveal that tightly controlled and regimented groups see this technology as a threat, permitting members too much freedom of interaction.

This new involvement in special interest and renewal groups tends to supersede old religious identities and boundaries and create new bonds between like-minded believers. A participant in the Episcopal charismatic movement may have more in common with a fellow charismatic in the Baptist church across town than with the

Episcopalian worshipping next to her. Not only do these renewal groups attempt to change their respective religious bodies, but they also generate a new kind of ecumenism among people involved in practices and experiences they have in common.

It is no coincidence that renewal and reform groups and movements seem more centered on experience than does the average congregation. Increasingly, Americans, particularly those in the younger generations, are gravitating to experiential forms of religion. Experience need not be limited to ecstatic or deeply mystical definitions; experiential religion can also be found in participation in liturgy that creates a sense of mystery and the sacred, as well as in the feelings of community and solidarity found in small groups. In the same way, seeker-based congregations of all faiths play down denominational doctrine and the importance of religious heritage and try instead to reach the unaffiliated through modern idioms—drama, contemporary music, as well as sermons and seminars based on current or practical concerns, such as child rearing and twelve-step programs.

In *Reinventing American Protestantism,* Donald E. Miller describes the new networks of independent charismatic churches now flourishing, such as the Vineyard Fellowship and Calvary Chapel, as embodying much of the turn to the experiential and postdenominational and thus becoming the major force for renewal in Christianity today. These churches also have decentralized structures that downplay rigid hierarchies and involve the laity in most ministries. Miller calls on mainline Protestants to incorporate the experiential approach, informality, spontaneity, and the antibureaucratic positions of these "new paradigm" churches.[7]

It would be a mistake, however, to think that significant renewal movements will always come from outside the established or mainstream religious institutions. Surveys show that even the most straitlaced denomination contains more pluralism and diversity than one might suspect. As we will see in the pages ahead, many of the subgroups and movements in these denominations are coming to conclusions about decentralization similar to those of new paradigm congregations. It is not yet clear that a postdenominational mind-set will become the norm in the United States. In a recent study by Hartford Seminary, it was found that members of churches with strong liturgical and ethnic traditions, such as Catholics, Episcopalians, and Lutherans, have a higher rate of denominational identity than members of denominations without such distinctive practices and traditions. It was especially the cradle members, those brought up in the faith, who had a strong sense of denominational ties; those who switched to the denominations in adulthood identified with them somewhat less.[8]

Even if the entrepreneurial independent churches (such as the two Miller identifies, Vineyard Fellowship and Calvary Chapel) are currently a major force in American religion, their ascendancy may not continue. Religious change and revitalization move in cycles. Congregations and networks that are considered cutting edge and innovative today will eventually take on the accretions of denominations, bureaucracies, and entrenched leaderships; in fact, leaders of the Vineyard Fellowship are currently wrestling with these very issues. If these ministries do not undergo schisms, their members in the future will consider the age-old possibility of renewing their existing institutions. They will realize that these venerable denominations and networks have generated practices, teachings, and identities that are worth preserving or developing and will gather together to do the work that defines renewal and reform.

Varieties of Renewal and Reform

There are almost as many reform and renewal groups and ministries as there are denominations. Theologian William Abraham identifies a wide variety of renewal efforts that are currently prominent in American religion, efforts centered on community life, education and theology, social justice, missions and evangelism, music and the arts, family life, liturgy and worship, and spirituality.[9]

The six case studies in this book fall roughly into three main categories of reform and renewal that are active today: evangelical and charismatic, liturgical and contemplative, and progressive or liberal. These three camps often overlap; for instance, a liberal group may also be concerned with liturgical renewal. But each group or movement often has a core identity that tends in one of these three directions. Evangelical as well as charismatic renewal is usually marked by an emphasis on experience as well as doctrine. In the evangelical movement, the experience centers around being born again and having a personal relationship with Jesus, as well as acceptance of biblical authority and a concern for evangelism. Aside from the born-again experience, charismatics claim a number of other important experiences, such as being baptized or filled with the Holy Spirit, speaking in tongues, and healing the mind and body. My case studies of the Catholic charismatic renewal and the Biblical Witness Fellowship in the United Church of Christ plant these groups firmly in the evangelical and charismatic camps. But laying aside the theological differences for a moment, one can find a basic evangelical style in traditions outside of Protestantism. The style is marked by a personal, direct, and experiential faith as well by the drive to introduce others to such beliefs and practices.

Evangelical- and charismatic-style faith may be found in Catholic devotion to the Virgin Mary and popular apparitions associated with her, or in the invitation of American Jews to bring the disaffiliated back to synagogue through courses that decipher hidden codes in the Torah. The call for members of the highly successful Opus Dei movement in Catholicism to apply their faith to the workplace, bring friends to the group's seminars, and practice discipline in their spiritual lives has strong affinities to Protestant evangelicalism.

Liturgical and contemplative renewal and reform usually concern worship and the practices of prayer and meditation. *Liturgy* means the "work of the people," as the shape of worship involving prayers, chants, hymns, and actions concerning the sacraments and other rituals should involve the whole congregation. Yet liturgical movements were and continue to be started and mainly supported by clergy and other church leaders. To understand the dynamics of liturgical renewal, we will look at the American Lutheran Publicity Bureau and the Society of the Holy Trinity. Both these groups have a strong theological component, as they seek to recover the authority of the creeds from the early church and confessions from the Reformation era for the modern churches. Contemplative renewal is often driven more by laypeople who seek the mysticism and spirituality derived from meditation and the practices such as chanting and silent prayer. The ecumenical community of Taizé is our case study for this kind of renewal.

Liberal or progressive reform and renewal is a relative concept; what may be liberal to one group is conservative to another. But most progressive groups seek greater freedom within their denominations and wider traditions. They tend to propose changes in both doctrine and practice that are relevant to modern insights, as well as to engage in social action. Progressive reformers are less likely to see their traditions as contained within a book or guarded by a central teaching authority. These groups may be grassroots upstarts that emerged in longtime conservative or even moderate bodies, or they may be holdovers from periods of liberalization in their denominations that eventually come under conservative leadership. Our case studies of liberal renewal and reform will concentrate on Call to Action and the Jewish Renewal.

The following accounts of renewal and reform groups are not necessarily representative samples of this phenomenon. Rather, they can be considered snapshots of people involved in the renewal and reform effort. These efforts are among the most prominent organizations and movements of their kind in their respective religious bodies, capturing the dynamics and dilemmas found in the renewal and reform enterprise.

Some may wonder why I have limited the case studies to Christian and Jewish groups. American religion increasingly includes Muslims, Hindus, Buddhists, and myriads of other believers also concerned about renewing their faiths. The main reason I have concentrated on these more familiar religious expressions is because their institutions have existed long enough for many more renewal and reform efforts to emerge in this country. There are examples of both renewal and reform in new religious movements (one thinks of a significant reform effort in the Hare Krishnas relating to abuses of power by the movement's leadership) and in world religions transplanted to the United States. But I decided to stay within the Jewish-Christian traditions because I am most familiar with them and because I wished to avoid diluting and ignoring important distinctions (in concepts ranging from renewal and reform to denominations) that occur in moving from Western to non-Western contexts.

1

Let the Spirit Move the Structure

Catholic Charismatic Renewal

It's difficult to remain a removed observer when it comes to the Roman Catholic charismatic movement. Charismatics, with their emotional, even ecstatic, worship, their close bonds of fellowship, and their expressive affection, had a way of putting me in the middle of things. Seated in the back row of a large meeting, I was sought out by a prayer team that zeroed in on this visitor with the "laying on of hands." At a prayer meeting huddled in the corner of a huge church in New Jersey, I was ushered into the center of a small circle where praise, prayers, concerns, and testimonies of miracles were exchanged in a casual, matter-of-fact manner.

"This prayer group is a real family. We've been together twenty years. The renewal has sustained us. In this parish, you can get lost in the crowd," said Frank, a veteran of the Catholic charismatic renewal since the early 1970s. Ann, an elderly woman who came to the group more recently, said that since becoming involved in the renewal her faith "has become personal. The Word came alive. It was me and Jesus."

Like that small prayer group dwarfed by its mammoth parish, the Catholic charismatic renewal movement no longer draws much attention in American Catholicism compared to its early days. But the renewal generated a more personalized and informal style of faith that spilled out from the prayer groups and large charismatic conventions to have a significant impact on the contemporary church. When we look at the influence of the various charismatic

and evangelical groups and movements in mainstream denominations, we see that it is the charismatic Catholics who have managed to contain much of the energy of the renewal within their
institution. How have they done that? And what are the costs and
benefits of taming the fires of ecstatic worship and spirituality to
the needs and restraints of a centralized institution?

It Started with Duquesne

Just as the Pentecostal movement emerged out of the Holiness
churches in the early twentieth century and intended to transform
this tradition from within, the mainline and Roman Catholic
churches of the 1960s and 1970s saw the growth of charismatics
in their ranks. Like their Pentecostal siblings, the charismatics saw
their mission as one of infiltration and witnessing from within their
churches about their experience of baptism in the Holy Spirit and
spiritual gifts. As with other evangelical renewal groups mushrooming in mainline Protestant churches, the charismatics felt that
their church bodies had lost their spiritual direction through the
influence of liberal theology and social action. They thought that
once their fellow laypeople and clergy experienced the filling of
the Holy Spirit (also known as the baptism of the Holy Spirit), they
would seek to follow the New Testament Christianity they found
spelled out in the Bible. The charismatic way of church renewal is
not focused much on the political work of activism and electing
leaders into high church positions. Rather, charismatics believe
that true renewal can take place only after people feel the power
of the Holy Spirit.

Catholic charismatics in particular hoped that the renewal
would lead Catholics—both laity and church leaders—into a personal encounter with Christ and the Scriptures. The Second Vatican Council, held in the 1960s, had laid the groundwork for a
more Christ-centered church that involved the laity in new ministries and the study of the Scriptures, a practice not previously
encouraged for fear that individual interpretations of the Bible
might conflict with church teachings. But it was the charismatic
renewal of the 1970s that introduced Catholics to a more intimate
and evangelical style of faith. Although the renewal did not disre-

gard the liturgy and the role of priests and rituals that defined Catholic worship and piety, its leaders argued that believers also needed a more informal and direct encounter with Christ to build their faith and revive the church.

Pentecostals and charismatics believe they have recovered the gifts and infilling of the Holy Spirit described in the New Testament book of Acts. Speaking in tongues, healings, and prophecy are considered signs of being open to the Holy Spirit. The experience of baptism in the Holy Spirit is seen as a key experience that comes after conversion, empowering believers to live the Christian life.

The charismatic renewal in the Roman Catholic Church traces its roots back to 1967, to a group of college students and professors at Duquesne University in Pennsylvania. They had some contact with and knowledge of the Protestant Pentecostal movement that had pioneered in recovering the spiritual gifts described in the New Testament. During a retreat, these Catholics soon began to experience many of the classic Pentecostal manifestations, particularly speaking in tongues. During this time, the charismatic renewal had been seeping—sometimes exploding—into all of the mainstream Christian bodies. Episcopalians, Lutherans, and Presbyterians were all recipients of a new infusion of enthusiasm and ecstasy marked by speaking in tongues, healings, and other gifts of the Holy Spirit.

The Catholic students contacted leaders of other campus spiritual renewal efforts such as Cursillo, a group also based on Bible study and personal spirituality, though without the Pentecostal practices. These contacts helped transmit these strange new practices and teachings around the country. There was enough interest in charismatic phenomena among Catholics during that same year to organize a national conference at Notre Dame University—the first of many such large gatherings that would give the renewal a national and eventually an international presence. But the trademark of the Catholic renewal was the mushrooming of small prayer groups based in parishes and homes. Both the small groups and national conventions were coordinated by diocesan renewal centers and a national coalition known as the National Service Committee for the Catholic Charismatic Renewal (NSC). The committee, which is also known as the Chariscenter USA, did not seek to regulate or control the movement, but rather to act as a resource center, organizing national conferences, publishing literature, and channeling services to diocesan renewal centers.[1]

The history of the NSC reflects the divisions and tensions between Pentecostal origins and Catholic identity present in the renewal itself. The committee was the result of cooperation between new communities, called covenant communities, that were born in the heat of the renewal. Two of the most prominent of these covenant communities—the Word of God in Ann Arbor, Michigan, and People of Praise in South Bend, Indiana—found there was a need to coordinate services and resources to the fledgling movement.

Some leaders saw New Testament–style communal life as an outgrowth of charismatic activity. Renewal leader Kevin Perotta writes that "many participants originally saw the movement as restoring to the Catholic Church some of the miraculous and communitarian character of the early church."[2] The covenant communities sometimes functioned as actual communes, with members living and worshipping together. Many others, however, permitted members to live outside of the communities but required them to make a strong commitment to common life and service in the group. These communities became vehicles for new charismatic innovations in education, publishing, and worship. Leading charismatic periodicals such as *Pastoral Renewal* and *New Covenant* owed much of their inspiration to covenant communities. Several of the prominent communities and the ministries they spawned became ecumenical after a few years, particularly as likeminded communities sprang up among Protestant charismatics.

The NSC was also established to prevent schisms and bring some unity to the growing but unorganized movement. "There was always the potential that the movement might spin out of control," says Walter Matthews, director of the NSC. In fact, Matthews often used this image of things spinning out of control during my interview with him in a restaurant not far from his Virginia headquarters.[3] "You have to integrate religious experience with Catholic practice. If you don't, you'll spin out." He stressed that the renewal lives in a tension that many participants have difficulty handling. "To some, the initial experience [of charismatic worship and praise] is so galvanizing that they want it all the time.

Then they go to Mass and they don't experience it." So they formed enclaves where the charismatic experience was in the forefront of Christian life or left for Protestant churches. "Others resolved the tension by going the other way, by leaving the renewal. They wanted to be Catholic and hid their charismatic experience," Matthews says.

The covenant communities were in the former camp, as they created "little islands" of charismatic purity and intensity on the edges of American Catholicism. In attempting to be ecumenical (or nondenominational, as doctrinal issues pertaining to church unity were not a key concern of these communities), the covenant communities distanced themselves from the church hierarchy. In the 1980s, bishops started investigating and intervening in covenant communities in which members and former members made charges of authoritarianism and other abuses. For example, former members saw the idea of headship, both of the community leader and of husbands toward their wives and children, as one of the covenant community teachings that sometimes led to abuses of power. A recent case of a covenant community moving in authoritarian directions and feeling the hierarchy's discipline, as well as its own members' rebellion, is the Mother of God community in Maryland.

The community started as a prayer and Bible study group during the renewal's beginnings, but in its thirty-year history it evolved into a large community—with over twelve hundred members at its peak in the mid-1990s—with a complex hierarchy of leadership. It was during the 1990s that members and former members made public their charges of a controlling lay-based leadership that regulated and had to approve their careers, finances, marriages, and courtships. When financial discrepancies were reported in the community, the Archdiocese of Washington started investigating the group. Eventually, Mother of God was brought more closely into line with the archdiocesan system, which monitored any further abuses of leadership. Like other communities experiencing leadership breakdowns and reorganization, Mother of God is a shadow of what it once was in terms of membership. Even now, charismatic leaders debate the best course of action for dealing with these communities. Critics suggest that a watchdog organization such as the NSC should oversee these communities.[4]

By this time, the covenant communities had became a source of division within the NSC. One wing of the NSC eventually moved to Ann Arbor with the Word of God community, and the other wing, subsequently to be called the National Service Committee of the Catholic Charismatic Renewal, took a more distant approach to these communities, although it was based at the People of Praise community in South Bend. Matthews, once a member of the People of Praise, said that the NSC wanted to be in the mainstream of the church. "We wanted to be bridge builders to all the expressions of the renewal." There was growing diversity in the movement during this period. There was the emergence of renewal among ethnic communities—particularly the Hispanics—the growth of diocesan renewal offices, parish prayer groups and specialized ministries such as FIRE, an evangelistic organization, and several prominent healing ministries. The covenant communities saw themselves as forerunners of a new kind of religious order and did not have much to do with the charismatic renewal spreading through ordinary parishes. But that was where the renewal was to find its main expression and its greatest influence.

It was in the 1980s that Catholic leaders signed on as strong supporters of the renewal. There appeared to be less opposition to the renewal among Catholic leaders than in most mainline Protestant churches. Fairly early on, the Catholic bishops established a working committee to relate to the movement. One of the first statements from the Bishops' Committee on Doctrine in 1969 declared that "theologically the movement has legitimate reasons of existence. It has a strong biblical basis. It would also be difficult to inhibit the working of the Spirit which manifested itself so abundantly in the early Church [sic]."[5]

A major statement on the renewal issued by the Bishops' Committee in 1984 praised the charismatics for their "efforts to foster the pursuit of holiness, to encourage Catholics to a fuller participation in the Mass and the sacraments, to develop ministries to serve the parish and local Church [sic], to foster ecumenical bonds of unity with other Christians, to participate in evangelization."[6] That last point about evangelization seems particularly important, as the Catholic Church has increasingly sought to rally the many renewal movements and groups to bring about a re-Christianization of the West. Under the dynamic and conservative papacy of

John Paul II, the church has seen movements such as the charismatics, Opus Dei, and Cursillo as agents to revitalize and purify both stagnant church structures and society at large. All of these movements promote loyalty to church teachings while also stressing distinctive personal spiritualities and vigorous outreach to inactive Catholics and non-Catholics. Pope John Paul II has continuously praised the charismatics in such efforts.

In dioceses, bishops often designated a priest to act as a liaison with the movement. In the Rockville Centre Diocese on Long Island, New York, the charismatic renewal office even merged with other renewal ministries and became an official division of the diocese. Most of the other renewal offices are independent nonprofit organizations that cooperate with their dioceses. Although the popes, bishops, and dioceses have to some extent sought to support and harness the renewal for reenergizing Catholicism, it is at the parish level that one finds the strongest charismatic influence.

The number of American Catholics affected in one way or another by the charismatic renewal is impressive. One national survey finds that about 22 percent of Catholics surveyed, or an estimated twelve million of the fifty-five million Catholics, claimed charismatic gifts or self-identified as charismatics.[7] Walter Matthews points out that this does not mean that these large numbers are involved today. A revolving-door phenomenon has affected the renewal for some time, with many becoming involved in and many leaving charismatic groups. A study of the renewal by sociologists Richard Bord and Joseph Faulkner in the early 1980s already showed slower growth rates and suggested that there were other conservative groups in the church and thus "now more avenues for expression of traditional values [in the church] than existed at the time the [renewal] flourished."[8]

Whatever the reasons for the defection rate, Matthews estimates from prayer group figures and informal surveys taken in dioceses that 250,000 to 500,000 Catholics are involved in the renewal today. Of that number, only about one-half are involved on a weekly basis (such as attending prayer meetings). Carl Nobile of the Renewal Office of the Rockville Centre Diocese in New York estimates that about 70 percent of the lay leadership in his parish came from the ranks of the renewal, for example, graduates of Life in the Spirit seminars, an early innovation of the renewal.[9] These courses are usually presented in parishes and serve as a step-by-step introduction to charismatic Catholic teachings and practices. Those who finish such a course usually receive the baptism in the Holy Spirit. Nobile estimates that about 50 percent of lay leaders in the whole Rockville Centre Diocese also emerged from the renewal. He may not be exaggerating. A study of Catholic small groups headed by William D'Antonio of the Catholic University of America found that participation in charismatic prayer groups created a strong interest and involvement in parish life. The 1999 study found that even among charismatic prayer groups that are not an official part of parish life, participants are still very involved in parishes. In a survey of members of charismatic small groups and communities, 67 percent say they have become more involved in parish activities since joining.[10]

Diane and her husband, Ed, who are participants in a Long Island prayer group, demonstrate how the renewal turns out active parishioners with strong involvement in church ministries. When Diane received the baptism of the Holy Spirit, she was in the process of becoming more involved in the church after a long period of inactivity. She was working with the ministry for young married couples and attending Mass regularly when she began to notice a group of worshippers who always sat together in the front of the church. They were in charge of hospitality, welcoming visitors to the Mass, but what really stood out for her was their joyfulness in worship. "I wanted to have what they had. I asked my husband about them and he said they were the charismatics. To me, they just seemed like really alive people. They brought a sense of God to the church," Diane says.

She and Ed started to attend charismatic prayer meetings and eventually a Life in the Spirit seminar held at the parish. When it came time for the leaders and other participants of the seminar to pray over her to receive the baptism of the Holy Spirit, Diane was ready and willing. "It was like an eruption. I burst out in tongues and tears. It was ecstatic but not really driven by emotions. It was driven by God. After that time, I was never the same. God took my heart." Eleven years later, Diane says her spiritual life has been a "roller coaster ride. I feel like I haven't had a minute to breathe." Diane involved herself in ministries that she never thought she could do, especially caring for the dying and ill at hospitals and hospices. She is also involved in a pastoral formation program at her parish. Ed did not have the same ecstatic experience as his wife. He believes that the spiritual experiences he had as a Lutheran youth were the baptism in the Holy Spirit, but even after the seminar and other charismatic gatherings, he has never spoken in tongues. "I don't think it's the only sign of the baptism in the Holy Spirit. The Spirit gives gifts where he will. Some, like my wife and other people at our prayer group, consider it a 'surrender gift.' [They say] if I just yield my life enough to God, the tongues will come." He added that Catholics, unlike Pentecostals, don't necessarily see speaking in tongues as the main evidence of the baptism of the Holy Spirit; other spiritual gifts might be given.

Diane and Ed's charismatic faith brought greater devotion to the Eucharist. Diane takes part in the adoration of the Eucharist daily at a nearby church. But at the same time, she sharply contrasts the church she grew up in with her current charismatic lifestyle of faith and practice. "We were never taught to praise God. We were taught rules and regulations but not the experience of God." She adds that the charismatic movement has "empowered the laity to experience God on a different level. The hierarchy is not as important. Before, you really had to experience God through them. The priests took that role of being in between God and the people. [Now] it's a direct experience." On following church teachings, Diane added that she doesn't "blindly have to follow rules. There's more a sense of God in the community" found in her prayer group or other church gatherings.

On such a divisive issue as women's ordination, both Diane and Ed disagree with the Vatican, saying they see no reason against ordaining women priests. They feel no scruples about attending their more charismatic-friendly parish even though they live within the boundaries of another parish. Diane and Ed are part of a larger pattern of American Catholics shopping for a parish that fits their beliefs and practices, even though Catholics are officially supposed to attend the parish of the neighborhood in which they live.

Even without the strong parish connections, charismatic prayer groups have a unique dynamic that is highly valued by and beneficial to participants. A typical prayer meeting usually starts with a time of enthusiastic prayer and praise. Contemporary praise songs with simple but catchy melodies, often written by composers who share in the charismatic faith, and scriptural lyrics fill the room. Participants raise their arms in a sign of praise and pray silently or aloud.

At one point in a meeting I attended, there was silence, and then the woman leading the service invited everyone to "use their gifts of tongues"—bringing on waves of foreign sounds that sounded like rapid-fire repetitions of word fragments—alamana, alamana, alamana, alamana. During one song, the worshippers left their seats and joined hands while raising them, then danced up and down the aisles, up the front, and around the back of the room. At times the meeting seemed almost to lose control, but then the woman in front would assert some order and move the service along. Shortly after the dancing, she called for "words of knowledge" and "prophecies." These are utterances, usually in English, said to be directed by the Holy Spirit. One woman from the back spoke quietly in the first person: "My children, I love you and I'm with you. Be my witnesses." Then someone else broke forth in tongues—this time, it sounded less like fragments of words and repetitions of vowels and more like an actual foreign language. After the speaker was through, the leader asked whether anyone had an interpretation of this message. A man on the side answered with another brief first-person prophecy: "My children, I am here. I am here. Stay in my love," followed by several people praying in tongues and offering thanksgiving.

The give-and-take between participants prophesying and those interpreting the message did not always involve speaking in tongues. At one point, a man said the image of a bridge and people going back and forth on the bridge came to his mind. A few moments later, an elderly woman stood up and shared a verse about hope and then explained how the bridge image may be showing people how God is bringing them to a new place in the new millennium.

Sociologist Matthew P. Lawson found that the interaction and sharing that takes place in a Catholic charismatic prayer group often has a flow and rhythm to it that is distinct from that of other small groups. When a participant shares a message or scriptural teaching, he or she is confirmed or challenged by the others, as the group seeks to negotiate a unifying theme from the individual contributions. This unified theme—whether it be a new direction for the prayer group or a solution to a member's particular problem—is taken by the participants to be the will of God. Lawson writes that rather than blindly following habitual routines, prayer group participants are taught to be "open to different ways of doing things, and to be attentive to how multiple and sometimes conflicting demands may come together to indicate alternative courses of action." He concludes that "Charismatics, by desiring God's will rather than their own, and by searching for that will by opening themselves to the integrating force of the Holy Spirit, may be practicing skills that help them negotiate their way in a complex society."[11]

A Conservative Renewal?

The sense of lay empowerment and the strengthening of a personal relationship with God was common among all the charismatic Catholics I interviewed. But this new sense of empowerment did not often translate into the questioning of church authority and teachings, as it had for Diane and Ed. D'Antonio and researchers also found in their study of Catholic small groups that charismatic activity led participants to be more conservative. Seventy-three percent of respondents said their involvement in charismatic small groups had "strengthened their attitude toward the pope and the Vatican." When asked whether their actions and beliefs would be guided more by the pope or by conscience, 69 percent tilted toward the pope, whereas only 18 percent stressed the role of conscience. Compare this with the attitudes of small groups found in American parishes in general: only 32 percent would follow the pope, and 55 percent would lean to the dictates of their consciences.[12]

Robert, a sixty-seven-year-old pioneer of the charismatic movement, has strengthened his Catholic identity in recent years—sometimes to the detriment of his charismatic faith. In the early 1970s, he found himself going through a mild depression. Despite a promising career in the aerospace field and a happy family life, he felt an emptiness in his life. When he attended a charismatic prayer service in his parish for the first time, he was impressed by how people "praised the Lord so freely and unashamedly." Robert decided that this sense of freedom and commitment to Christ had to become a part of his life. He attended a Life in the Spirit seminar, and at the conclusion of the course he was prayed over to experience the baptism of the Holy Spirit. "When [the prayer group] put their hands on me, I wept like a little baby. I received the gift of tongues. I also was given a great love for the Word of God. I stayed up nights reading the Bible and getting little sleep—it didn't matter." He was instrumental in starting a prayer group that recently celebrated its twenty-fifth anniversary. But shortly after getting involved in the renewal, Robert found himself drifting from Catholicism and joining a Pentecostal church. He had started fellowshipping with non-Catholic Christians who convinced him that the Bible taught that Catholic teachings were unbiblical.

But a nun whom Robert had known for many years would not give up on him and his need to come back to the church. She gave him a tape of Scott Hahn, a well-known Catholic convert and apologist from Franciscan University of Steubenville, Ohio. "[Hahn] traced Catholic teachings back to the early church fathers. What the early church taught, today's church teaches, and it's all what the Scriptures teach too," Robert says. He made his confession for the first time in eleven years and received communion "with a fervor like I had never received [the sacrament] before. I saw the sacraments, in fact, the whole church in a new light, that there was tremendous beauty in these teachings."

Today, Robert is still enthusiastic about his Catholic faith, often lecturing on his experience and church teachings. His charismatic involvement is less solid. He is not a regular participant in any prayer group, although he occasionally attends charismatic meetings. In fact, he often argues with charismatic Catholics and others in his parish on the importance of obedience and commitment to Catholic teachings. He recently argued with a deacon in his parish who claimed that the belief in purgatory is not required by the church. "Some charismatic Catholics don't believe in all the teachings of the church. They take very Protestant points of view. They don't [consider] that the church's teachings are also from the Bible." But Robert finds that when he is in charismatic settings, he feels the gifts of the Holy Spirit stirred up and revived after all these years, particularly the gifts of prophecy and teaching. He still feels that the charismatic movement is important for stirring up a love for Christ in nominal Catholics, providing them with a place where prayer is "unashamed." The renewal also provides what he calls a "communications link" with many of the Pentecostal churches because both groups of believers share a common experience.

Not many charismatic Catholics have left permanently for Protestant churches, but Robert's experience is far from rare in the charismatic renewal today. Participants have a new appreciation of the Catholic tradition. The peak of the Catholic charismatic movement in the 1980s dovetailed with the emergence of a conservative pope who saw the importance of renewal groups in his program for revitalizing world Catholicism. Pope John Paul II spoke in evangelical terminology, stressing the importance of the "new evangelization." He appealed to Catholic charismatics and other conservatives who were concerned that the spiritual thrust of American Catholicism was being neglected or watered down in the attempt to be relevant and socially active in the years after the Second Vatican Council.

Nowhere is the conservative trend in the renewal more clearly seen than at Franciscan University in Steubenville, Ohio. In the 1970s, the university was a struggling college with a weak Catholic identity and was close to shutting its doors before Father Michael Scanlan and other charismatic leaders came on the scene. They encouraged a strong charismatic revival at the college, as well as bolstering its enrollment and endowments. Gradually, the charismatic emphasis was supplemented by traditional devotions involving Mary and the saints, as well as a strong defense of papal authority. But some observers, including Matthews of the NSC, wonder aloud whether succeeding leaders of Franciscan University will be able to maintain the delicate balance between charismatic practices and conservative teachings that Scanlan set up. Although the university still brings many young people into contact with the charismatic renewal, notably through their huge and popular conferences, they often do so less openly and with more sensitivity to strict conservative and orthodox sensibilities than in the past. A future leader might well marginalize the charismatic renewal even further in the life of this training ground for conservative Catholic leaders.

One should not draw too straight a line between the Catholic charismatics and the conservative revival in the U.S. Catholic Church. The conservatives' remedy to the spiritual maladies of the American church often focuses on the importance of disciplining and even punishing—in the case of such liberal theologians as Hans Küng and Charles Curran—wayward members, clergy, and bishops, as well as rekindling traditional devotions that were swept away after Vatican II (such as the Latin Mass). The charismatics' prescription remains quite different. They insist that the church may well resist renewal even if orthodoxy holds sway among its bishops, theologians, and priests. The Catholic charismatic values of openness to spiritual experience—that God may be doing a "new work" at any time, a theme heard at most prayer meetings; the importance of healing body, mind, and spirit; and freedom and expressiveness of emotions and the body in worship—find little common ground with either traditionalists or political activists. Although we have seen that Catholic charismatics have found new value in such traditional practices as Marian devotions and adoration of the Eucharist, they do not champion what some might call a return to the tradition in the same way as many conservatives do. "Traditionalists often speak about tradition as it existed just before Vatican II," says Steve Benthal of the Rockville Centre Diocese Renewal Office. "But tradition includes the Acts of the Apostles also."[13]

Bringing Charisma to the Parish

In 1992, Bishop Paul Cordes, the Vatican-appointed representative to the Catholic charismatics around the world, issued two challenges to the renewal movement. The first was to take a strong role in the "new evangelization," and the second was to help bring about a renewal of the sacraments of initiation (baptism, confirmation, and Eucharist). These two challenges are important in understanding how a decentralized movement like the charismatic renewal is able to function in the hierarchical Catholic Church.

Renewal leaders have long stated that the charismatic renewal was not necessarily foreign to the Catholic tradition. Although the Pentecostals may have been the ones to recover the charismatic gifts and baptism of the Spirit, these originated in the early church, which was the starting point of Catholicism. In other words, Catholics may have been among the original Pentecostals. It is a bracing claim for these latecomers to the Pentecostal experience, but recent research does find interesting similarities between the modern-day charismatic phenomenon and Catholic practices from earlier eras. Kilian McDonnell is the most prominent of scholars seeking to integrate charismatic renewal with Catholic theology and practice, and has written with theologian George Montague the book *Christian Initiation and Baptism in the Holy Spirit.*

This research was later presented to charismatic and other church leaders at an NSC conference in 1990 and summarized in the booklet *Fanning the Flame.* The work claims that the New Testament and subsequent writings by the church fathers taught that baptism by the Holy Spirit was the same thing as Christian initiation, involving water baptism, confirmation, and acceptance into the Christian community through partaking of the Eucharist, and not an invention of classic Pentecostals. Such church fathers as Tertullian and Cyril of Jerusalem taught that spiritual gifts (or charisms), including speaking in tongues, prophesying, and healing, were a natural outgrowth of water baptism and the other sacraments of initiation. Some of these early theologians even referred to there being two baptisms, one by water and another one that would be a fuller realization or "release" of the first baptism.[14]

But it is another matter whether these teachings and new interpretations can find a place both among the charismatic rank and file and in Catholic parishes. The popular Life in the Spirit seminars that introduce people to charismatic experience and practices are now being reworked to include the revisions found in *Fanning the Flame* and other scholarship, and eventually to delete the Pentecostal-oriented "second-blessing" language of the earlier courses. The second-blessing teachings hold that baptism in the Holy Spirit is a distinct experience apart from conversion and water baptism. There is, however, a major obstacle in the attempt to reconceptualize the Catholic charismatic experience. The new scholarship tends to debunk the idea that speaking in tongues has historically accompanied the baptism in the Spirit.

Even though Catholic charismatics have not assigned speaking in tongues as the principal sign of the baptism in the way that Pentecostals (and many charismatic Protestants) have, many in the renewal view this gift as a sign of the believer's surrender to the working of the Holy Spirit. Among the charismatic Catholics I interviewed, there was the prominent claim that speaking in tongues is a "surrender gift." Sociologist Meredith McGuire's extensive study of Catholic charismatic prayer groups also found that participants highly valued speaking in tongues as an indicator of one's spiritual commitment and depth.[15] Matthews himself says, "If that wedge was ever driven [between those who see speaking in tongues is an important by-product of the charismatic, spirit-filled life and those who do not], the renewal would collapse."

Matthews adds that *Fanning the Flame* has been met with a "mildly positive response," although not enough (especially from the theological community) for the church to begin implementing its proposals of integrating charismatic practice with the liturgy and sacraments in dioceses and parishes on a large scale. "You're dealing with a two-thousand-year[-old] institution. It's going to take time for these insights to be absorbed," Matthews says. Part of the problem is that for all the influences and vitality that the renewal has imparted to wider American Catholicism, few parishes are visible showcases of the renewal. When the NSC sent out a survey to parish prayer groups a few years ago to find out how many "renewed parishes" there actually were, it found only a few parishes that fit the bill. Matthews adds that the problem with the survey was that many Catholic charismatics still conceive of a renewed parish as being one in which everyone raises their hands in worship or people speak in tongues during the Mass. "We identified a renewed parish [as] being one where there was openness to the Holy Spirit and the Spirit's gifts. We know there are many priests who have been through the renewal." Matthews points to regular conferences at Franciscan University introducing priests to the renewal that regularly drew up to thirteen hundred people, and not simply the same crowd attending every year.

The problems start when the priests—who are influenced by the renewal at different levels—come back from such conferences and try to introduce their parishes to the charismatic experience. "Most do a terrible job of it," he says with frustration. Matthews recalls one priest making people raise their hands when they sang. The Episcopal Church has done a better job of permitting renewed parishes to be formed, he notes. The church allows (through its own renewal organization) a matching of churches interested in charismatic renewal with priests influenced by the renewal. Individual Episcopalians who have a commitment to or interest in charismatic renewal can also gravitate to parishes of similar orientation with little difficulty.

Most Catholic parishes are still based on geography, with members of a given neighborhood attending a specific church. Although the mobility of Catholics to parishes of their choice has been growing since Vatican II, there is still the idea that a parish has to serve all the people of a given area. This means that parishes and pastors are hesitant and sometimes opposed to catering to specific movements (not a wholly negative tendency, Matthews adds). Hampered by a traditional sense of reserve between pastors and parishioners and a frequent shuffling of priests from one church to another, charismatic renewal may well be allowed but not encouraged to spread into the mainstream of parish life.

Having a charismatic pastor tends to make the integration of charismatic practices into parish life less difficult. The Reverend Chris Adrias, pastor of St. Margaret of Scotland in Selden, Long Island, New York, was a veteran of the renewal when he came to the parish several years ago. He received the baptism of the Holy Spirit when he was a young seminarian in the early 1970s, a time when charismatic practices were viewed as strange and foreign by priests and parishioners. Adrias was the first priest to be assigned as a liaison to the charismatic renewal in the Diocese of Rockville Centre, and his concern to mesh charismatic experience with Catholicism has followed him to St. Margaret's parish. "It hasn't been all that difficult," he says. "Maybe it's because I'm a pastor; a parish priest may have more difficulties. Language is very important. Sometimes the language used [for Catholic charismatic practices] has been Protestant, such as getting the 'second blessing'—that thing you need to be 'saved.' Our language is sacramental and incarnational. It's part of the skin."[16]

Adrias teaches the baptism of the Holy Spirit as part of the sacraments of initiation. A new parishioner is viewed as having received the baptism of the Spirit when he or she has been introduced to the faith through water baptism, communion, and other rites of initiation. The parishioner may not manifest any gifts at that time. In fact, such gifts as speaking in tongues, healing, and prophecy may be experienced only as the member moves deeper into parish life—and not only into the charismatic prayer group. "I see all this as normal, as part of the Catholic experience, and treat it as such. If you treat it as this small group has something that this larger group needs, then you've failed." Adrias now views the deliberations that may come out of an ordinary parish meeting as a possible form of prophecy. Charismatic songs have blended in with other Christian contemporary music at the Masses. At the end of many Masses at St. Margaret's, a deacon will ask for those who need healing to come forward for prayer. Even speaking in tongues need not be controversial or unusual, Adrias adds. "I explain that it's like children's talk. We present it as a fact. If you talk about it with nonchalance, then people don't mind."

Adrias admits that all this mainstreaming of charismatic gifts and practices could dull the "prophetic edge" of the renewal that was intended to challenge the routines and cobwebs of institutional Catholic life. But that is a danger that all movements face as they move into maturity and gain a measure of influence and acceptance, he adds. An equally pressing problem may be what Matthews and several other leaders and participants I interviewed called the "graying of the renewal." It was evident in the prayer meetings I attended that the majority of participants were over the age of fifty. Matthews is convinced that the renewal is following the trajectory of other social movements, such as the labor movement, that have existed over thirty years.

He cites the three phases the renewal has undergone in the last three decades. The first decade for any movement is the period of growth, with leadership that can be described as innovative and visionary. The second decade stresses building the organization and is when the movement reaches a peak of growth. The third phase, the "operational" phase, is characterized by the motto "We've always done things this way." In this phase, the movement hits a plateau, though sooner or later it may go on a downward path or, if changes are made, show new signs of growth. The charismatic renewal is deep in this third phase, and Matthews expects that the holding pattern will give way to noticeable signs of decline if changes are not made. The most important problem to be resolved is that the renewal has not given the younger generation the chance to lead. "If you go to the prayer meetings around the country, you'll see that the same people are in leadership for twenty or more years. There's a real problem of entrenchment and struggles for power in some groups," he says.

Matthews adds that it is the new ethnic Catholic charismatics who show the most vitality as well as the most integration into parish life. The numbers are impressive: about one-fifth of Hispanic church members are or have been influenced by the charismatic renewal (totaling close to six million people), and 20 percent of the one million Haitian Catholics in America are said to be charismatic, according to Monsignor Joseph Malagreca, the coordinator of Hispanic and Haitian charismatic ministries for the NSC.[17] Charismatic growth among Koreans and Filipinos in the United States is also strong. Malagreca says that the difference between many "Anglo" charismatic prayer groups and the ethnic ones are clear right from the beginning. "The Haitians and Hispanics usually start the meeting by praying the rosary. It's very sacramental." The other noticeable difference is the strong presence of youth, especially among Hispanic Catholic charismatics. Like other charismatic prayer groups, the ethnic ones often make up the backbone of a parish. It is not unusual for these prayer groups to draw up to four hundred people to their meetings. Although the renewal has affected the clergy to a lesser extent, Malagreca estimates that over 50 percent of ethnic lectors, Eucharistic ministers, and other lay leaders in parishes have been touched by the renewal.

A New Chapter for Catholic Charismatics?

It seemed like a typical charismatic prayer service, with the opening session marked by ecstatic prayer and contemporary Christian praise songs. But the speaker's message about miracles would be most controversial and most illuminating in showing how the renewal movement continues to walk a tightrope between compliance with the Catholic institution and openness to new spiritual currents. "There's a revival people are speaking about that many people are skeptical about," she said. This revival is bringing about "new manifestations," such as "holy drunkenness" and "holy laughter," as well as reports of miracles of gold teeth and gold dust appearing to participants. Just the other day, two of her friends reported finding new gold teeth after attending charismatic meetings in Philadelphia.

The nun was referring to the latest turn in the unpredictable drama of the charismatic movement. The holy laughter phenomenon was first reported at meetings in a charismatic church in Toronto. The congregation, called the Airport Vineyard Fellowship, swelled to thousands as worshippers and bystanders claimed to come under the Holy Spirit's power, laughing uncontrollably and falling into trancelike states—they encountered what had come to be called the Toronto blessing. This phenomenon, which then spread to England and Florida, was unique. It seemed to be based in certain key congregations, such as an Assembly of God church in Pensacola, Florida, where tens of thousands would visit to receive a unique visitation of the Holy Spirit. The phenomenon became controversial enough in Pentecostal and charismatic circles to get the Toronto church expelled from the Vineyard Fellowship. But the manifestations were felt in many such churches.

One of these churches is the Presentation of the Blessed Virgin Mary Church (Presentation BVM) just outside Philadelphia. Since 1994, revival services have been held in this Catholic parish. The services may at first resemble many charismatic prayer groups, with worshippers raising their hands, speaking in tongues, and conducting healings. But it is during the "praise times," when the sanctuary is filled with people speaking in tongues, that the laughter begins. "First a lone woman laughs loudly, then others join her until many are holding their stomachs and laughing out loud," according to one report. Monsignor Vincent Walsh, pastor of the parish, explains, "This is charismatic revival. It is the next step beyond charismatic renewal."[18]

From the mid-1970s, Walsh had been a representative and facilitator of the charismatic renewal in the diocese. After his four years in this position, 160 of the 300 parishes in the diocese had charismatic prayer groups. But the rapid growth of the charismatic movement in the 1970s slowed considerably in the next decade. Even in a fast-growing charismatic Catholic center such as Philadelphia, the prayer groups stopped growing. When he was assigned to pastor the Presentation BVM parish, Walsh started to develop contacts with Protestant charismatics and Pentecostals. In 1994, he went to a camp meeting in Kentucky led by Rodney Howard Browne, who was instrumental in introducing the original Toronto blessing. He saw for himself the holy laughter and other new phenomena at the meeting and realized that this was the new move of the spirit for which he had been waiting.

Walsh took videos of the services back to his parish, and holy laughter began to break out during the prayer meetings. The numbers attending the weekly prayer meetings began to rise again, from twenty-five meeting in a living room before the revival hit in 1994 to four hundred by July of 1997. Many of those coming to the services live outside the Philadelphia area. Making the pilgrimage to a special place being used by the Holy Spirit is a key ingredient in the phenomenon—a practice that is not foreign to Catholics, who have historically trekked to holy places in search of miracles.

Reaction to Walsh's revival has been mixed. Some, like Carl Nobile, a charismatic leader in the Rockville Centre Diocese, find that the revival rubs them the wrong way. "It's the emphasis on laughter. When I was in Philadelphia, I saw priests pushing people down [to receive holy laughter]. I thought, wait a minute, that's fundamental Pentecostalism. That's not from my church." On the other hand, like many charismatic Catholics, Nobile doesn't want to close himself off from this new current if it is a work of God. "I don't want to do what the hierarchy did with the renewal thirty years ago, just hope it would go away. That's what happened—the people went away to other churches."[19]

Although the NSC has not taken a position on the revival, Walter Matthews is skeptical about viewing the phenomenon as the next phase of the renewal. He distrusts the strong emphasis on group experience in the revival as opposed to the blending of the personal and the group that is found in the charismatic mainstream. Although he has experienced holy laughter himself, Matthews says that these manifestations take place only in large group meetings and can be manipulated to tend toward a sort of mass hysteria. The emphasis on the experience is also disconcerting. "People who go to Philadelphia talk about getting 'it.' But the Holy Spirit isn't an 'it.' Saint Theresa had a similar experience [of holy laughter], but she said you shouldn't seek it. The fact that people take buses to Philadelphia shows that they're looking for a spiritual experience and then they have to defend the experience. When you do that, you start spinning out."

The other problem Matthews has with the revival is that it can be traced to one man—Rodney Howard Browne, the Pentecostal who fomented the Toronto blessing. "It's not happening anywhere else in world Catholicism," he says. Of course, the revival presents a larger dilemma to the charismatic renewal as a whole. Even if it becomes widely accepted among Catholic charismatics, the more extreme and controversial manifestations may scare off the church hierarchy—at a time when the renewal has gained acceptance and leaders are working to integrate charismatic practice with sacramental life.

Ecstasy and Religious Institutions

Sandra describes her early involvement in the Catholic charismatic renewal with the vividness of a recent day gone by, even though close to thirty years have elapsed. When she first got involved in the charismatic renewal, it was an underground phenomenon at her parish. The pastor would not allow the strange prayer group to meet in the parish buildings, so they had to gather outside in the adjacent yard. That did not stop crowds from attending or a courageous priest from taking the group under his wing. Those early meetings struck visitor and devotee alike with unusual force. "The meetings would start with intense prayer with people praying in tongues. It was really beautiful. There was a sense of holiness there. Everyone would start singing 'Alleluia' over and over again with their hands raised, and that could last for twenty minutes. There [were] no restraints or attempts to control it."

Speaking in tongues and receiving prophetic messages were common back then, says Sandra, as was dancing and being "slain in the spirit," the phenomenon of falling to the ground in ecstasy after being prayed for with the laying on of hands. Many youth attended the meetings along with others of all age-groups, and a crop of young men who came out of the prayer meeting felt called to the priesthood. Like so many others, Sandra drifted away from the prayer meeting in the 1980s. It was only a few years ago that she visited the prayer group again, and she was not prepared for what she saw. "It was so tame. The meeting began so dryly and routinely. There was no real prayer or sense of enjoyment. They [the prayer meeting organizers] had a little group of people who they designated as the ones who would speak in tongues and another group who would interpret the messages. I remember when everyone could speak in tongues or interpret or both. It was like they had the Holy Spirit in this box, and he would be allowed out of the box at some times but not others. I cried. I had to leave early."

Like Sandra, most of the Catholic charismatics I spoke with agreed that the renewal's emotional peak has passed, although some participants might welcome today's more sedate and structured environment. One study finds that the Catholic charismatic movement has often been "subordinated to institutional subgroups and cliques, with little widespread effect on traditional religious structures."[20] Leaders acknowledge that the renewal has not directly challenged or changed structures in the church, aside from encouraging parishes and dioceses to integrate charismatic practices into the sacraments of initiation. Some parishes in which the covenant communities held sway over the renewal may have been more radically restructured. In the heyday of these communities' influence in the 1970s, charismatic leaders tried to make covenant communities more central to parish life. Such a restructuring would have challenged leadership in the church, as priests and other leaders would emerge from the communities rather than be appointed by the diocese.

Of course, the charismatic renewal in Catholicism could have taken another route altogether. Like some of the covenant communities that eventually broke off from the church, the charismatics could have joined their counterparts forming the many independent congregations and networks that have attempted to arrange and rework their structures around the charismatic experience. Donald Miller calls these congregations "new paradigm churches" in that they stress decentralization of power, the importance of experience over doctrine, and the use of contemporary idioms in worship and outreach.[21] Although many features of the new paradigm are found among denominational charismatics (the new paradigm's use of the body in worship is even more evident in the charismatic liturgical churches with their blend of sacraments, ritual, and charismatic practices), they have opted for a churchly style that does not move toward the fragmentation and decentralization of much of American Protestantism.

Monsignor Malagreca of the NSC says there is still something of a disconnect when the charismatic style of leadership encounters the leadership mode of the official church and its bureaucracy. "Charismatics bring with them an attentiveness to people and their gifts, and praying [over the issues]. That can rub against the style of the bureaucracy where there's favoritism and the importance of connections."[22] If the charismatic "gifts" style of leadership presents a refreshing contrast to the slow grindings of bureaucracy, it is not clear how the charismatics—or any spiritual renewal group—can change the church's structure to reflect these concerns.

We have seen that the charismatic movement has experienced an entrenchment of leadership (the graying of its prayer meeting leadership), instability, a drop-off in participation, and what has been called an institutionalization of charisma. To avoid institutionalization, a movement or group has to choose and plan intentionally which direction to go once its initial fervor has decreased. Where raw energy and inspiration once seemed sufficient to propel things, the movement now requires structures.

As the history of the NSC demonstrates, the Catholic charismatic renewal—and most other charismatic movements within mainstream denominations—made an early commitment to work within church structures and to reaffirm and strengthen participants' Catholic identity. That commitment gave the renewal security, but it also tended to blunt the edges of the movement, making it difficult to form a cadre of church leaders who will implement a distinct charismatic approach to church structures and leadership. The charismatic movement will have to accept its minority status within a pluralistic American Catholicism in which renewal has many meanings and expressions.

On the parish level, the future is far from pessimistic. The presence of a charismatic pastor or at least leaders friendly to the renewal can create innovation in a parish, whether it be the formation of a strong healing ministry, a more personal approach to the sacraments of initiation, or most important, an energized group of lay leaders that may help mitigate the Catholic Church's shortage of clergy.

Yet any type of ecstatic renewal movement runs the risk of alienating as much as energizing members of a congregation. The tendency toward elitism is perhaps greater with these kinds of groups and movements than with other forms of renewal. The claim of an experience of an emotional, ecstatic encounter with God can lead the recipient to conclude that those who have not had such an experience may be deficient in faith. Multiply the belief of that one person by ten or twenty other congregants, and there is the potential of an in-group of the supposedly spiritually adept stirring up bewilderment and even hostility among the rest of the members.

Such a conflict is all the more likely to happen when specific signs and manifestations, such as speaking in tongues or even distinctive gestures or vocabulary, are closely associated with the experience of personal renewal. I do not mean to suggest that those experiencing ecstatic and other kinds of spiritual renewal are responsible for most of the major conflicts in congregations. Those engaged in any renewal movement usually run up against opponents who make things difficult largely because they do not want to move in that new direction, even if such a change would be beneficial to all concerned. Proponents of charismatic and other ecstatic renewal have the added disadvantage of engaging in practices that may be off-putting and seem strange to the uninitiated, giving naysayers another reason to close their minds to the potential changes. The road to feuds and church splits is lined on both sides with offensive proponents and closed-minded and bitter opponents of renewal.

Renewalists represent a challenge to a congregation and its leaders. Congregations are faced with the question of how and to what extent the practices and experiences of these spiritual pioneers can mesh with their beliefs and culture. Every congregation has a culture—ways of interacting, expectations, traditions, and memories—as well as beliefs that have to be integrated with any new directions that are introduced into this ecosystem. New pastors and priests usually realize that they have to introduce congregations to their distinctive style and other innovations very gradually, with a lot of input from the congregants themselves. Charismatic renewal in the Roman Catholic context may have fared better than in other church situations because Catholicism has had a long experience in containing different styles of piety without causing the schisms and divisions so common in American religious history. But all those who seek charismatic and other ecstatic renewal have to ask themselves how they can import their particular gifts to their congregations in ways that build on the strengths of these cultures without stirring up the toxins and other negative energies that are ever-present in any congregation or community.

2

Grassroots Protestant Renewal
Biblical Witness Fellowship

The Reverend David Runion-Bareford of the Biblical Witness Fellowship (BWF) calls himself a "renewal food fighter," though he does not look the part.[1] His friends and associates say that his learned and friendly manner stands up even in tense debates with liberals, as he argues that their denomination, the United Church of Christ (UCC), is on the brink of apostasy. Under Runion-Bareford's leadership, BWF has become a case study in aggressive and proactive renewal.

Runion-Bareford has even mapped out a "stealth" strategy for evangelical lay members to slip renewal into liberal congregations right under the noses of clergy. He advises evangelicals to start with intercessory prayer. Then, without challenging the pastor or fighting church boards or councils, with a few other like-minded members, he suggests they pick one area of the church that no one cares about—whether it be missions or Sunday school—and establish a strong evangelical beachhead there.

Both friends and foes agree that Runion-Bareford does not have an easy job as director of the leading evangelical renewal organization in the United Church of Christ, with its 1.3 million members. The UCC has been among the most liberal mainline denominations in the United States, both in theology and in social action. The emergence and growth of BWF in the church brings to mind a difficult question: How is it possible to renew and reform a denomination when, as many observers claim, denominational affiliation is of little importance to church members? Church members no longer place much confidence in the larger structures that connect and govern congregations; many seekers join churches more for the services they provide than for their denominational heritage. Nowhere is this more evident than in liberal Protestant churches, and perhaps no denomination embodies liberal Protestantism better than the UCC.

Recent studies show that the UCC has had particular difficulty in generating a sense of belonging and denominational identity among its members. A City University of New York survey that asked Americans to identify their religious affiliations found a particularly low response among UCC members. Researchers suggested that many members may still identify with the predecessor denominations and traditions (such as the Congregationalists) that make up the UCC today.[2] A more recent study by sociologist Nancy Ammerman and a team of researchers found that, compared to members of congregations with strong liturgical and ethnic heritages, such as Episcopal, Lutheran, Catholic, and Eastern Orthodox, fewer UCC members said that denominational affiliation was important in deciding which congregation to join.[3]

Evangelical Renewal in Mainline Churches

Among the many special interest groups and caucuses seeking renewal and reform in American denominations, few have attracted the high degree of popular support and proliferated as much as the evangelical groups like BWF. Something in the very nature of evangelical Christianity calls out for the revival and revitalization of denominations, congregations, and individuals. In the past, groups attempting to revive spirituality, theological orthodoxy, and evangelistic fervor within larger structures often gave birth to new denominations. John Wesley's Methodist movement started as an evangelical renewal group within the Church of England. Wesley and his followers viewed the established church as spiritually tepid, failing to encourage holiness in its members.

As has happened in other renewal movements, members of Wesley's movement grew restless and dissatisfied with the progress of renewal in the established church—while church officials grew impatient with the fervor of Wesley and his followers—and there was a parting of the ways leading to the birth of Methodism. Similar groups have sprung up throughout U.S. religious history. But the growth of theological liberalism in the nineteenth and twentieth centuries was a key factor in bringing evangelical renewal groups to the surface. These groups exploded onto the scene in the 1960s and 1970s, when there was a perception that mainline church bodies were increasingly liberal in doctrine.

In the Presbyterian, United Methodist, Episcopal, and other mainline denominations, renewal mainline caucuses emerged that challenged the leadership on issues ranging from doctrine to politics. The fact that these denominations were in the midst of sharp declines in the 1960s bolstered the claim of evangelical renewalists that their churches had taken a wrong turn in embracing policies and teachings that sought to revise and reinterpret the faith to address modern society. Even nonevangelical scholars agreed that mainline religion, which was so formative of American culture, had lost a strong supernatural dimension that generated a sense of meaning for members.

Confessing the Faith

By the end of the 1970s, basic questions about the value and meaning of life, and the purpose of the family and sexuality became rallying points in the battle between conservatives and liberals in the mainline denominations. The conflicts were to be just as acrimonious as the clashes over doctrine and biblical inspiration in the preceding decades. BWF emerged out of the heat of battle over issues of sexuality in the UCC in 1978. The UCC had issued a sexuality report that sought alternative views on a wide number of issues, from homosexuality to traditional language about God. As usual, the UCC had been years ahead of other churches in pushing the envelope on issues that were later to cause skirmishes in the culture wars. The denomination, which was the product of a 1957 merger between the Congregational Christian Church and the Evangelical and Reformed Church, was respectably liberal before liberalism was respectable.

The sexuality report, issued by the Board of Homeland Ministries, explored the possibility of accepting homosexual relations as well as premarital sexual relations as valid expressions of love and questioned the doctrine of God's fatherhood. The document created strong division in the church. Even though it was passed at the 1977 General Synod, more than a third of the delegates voted against it. The minority, led by laywoman Barbara Weller and the Reverend Martin Duffy, filed a dissenting report, which was adopted by the synod. But that was not the end of the matter. Weller and other members took their concerns to the UCC president and other heads of denominational ministries.

Weller and company argued that the denomination did not take into consideration their views, which they claimed represented the majority of members. One member of the group was told that the Board of Homeland Ministries had never taken its direction from congregations and had no plans to do so in the future. The meeting was instrumental in causing frustrated dissenters to organize. A conference on sexuality was organized by the dissenters in Philadelphia, but the discussion turned to other areas of church life. As BWF official Gerald Sanders writes in a historical account of the group, "One thing that became clear there was that the issue before the UCC was much larger and more important than the problem of human sexuality. The real issue was the question, What will be the ultimate authority for the faith and practice of the United Church of Christ?"[4] The organizers unquestionably felt that the authority and infallibility of the Bible in matters of faith and morals should be the guide for the denomination; through the subsequent formation of United Church People for Biblical Witness (UCPBW), which later became BWF, they sought to put pressure on the denomination to bring the church to that realization.

The organization went right to work, seeking to intercept the unfolding of liberalization by the time the next General Synod would begin in 1979. Weller and other volunteers started a newspaper entitled *The Witness*, compiled a book that provided a conservative response to the sexuality document, and then mailed this material to every pastor in the UCC. Again, however, UCPBW organizers were stymied at the synod. They charged that the denomination regularly stacked the deck against them on contested issues. Rather than each church having a say in the content of such a statement, a denominational committee was formed that would deliberate on these questions. UCPBW leaders and members argued that the democratic nature of the church was being stymied by the formation of these special interest committees mainly made up of church officials. The shelving of the UCPBW's critique of the sexuality document during the synod convinced renewalists that the unity between the local church and the national offices did not exist.

The problem for BWF was how to insure some kind of orthodoxy and evangelical fervency in a body that allowed its congregations and regional synods a large degree of autonomy. But for Sanders and other BWF leaders, congregationalism in church governance was not the key problem. "What the UCC needs is a reformation in which the Synod [sic] becomes more representative of the local churches. When delegates are elected by conferences and associations, the people electing them seldom know where these candidates stand on the issues," Sanders writes.[5] The concern over congregational representation is likely to be intensified as the UCC embarks on the "covenant" model of church governance. This model calls for a closer relationship among congregations, conferences, and the denomination's national office.

Becoming a Fellowship

A more drastic stance of resistance and challenge to renewal took place in 1983, when the Dubuque Declaration was issued by UCPPW. The document called for a "confessing fellowship" that would publicly proclaim the orthodox faith and draw the line between authentic faith and apostasy and false faith. The document sought to ground its claim in the confessional founding statements of the UCC, thereby avoiding charges of novelty or fundamentalism. A new, less political approach to the issues was also seen in the UCPBW's change of name to BWF in 1984. As the word *fellowship* implies, the new organization sought to work for renewal by "beginning in the local churches and then letting the effort impact other areas of the Church [sic]. This differed from the work of the UCPBW, which had been directed primarily at the level of the General Synod," writes Sanders.[6]

This more grassroots approach appeared to strike a chord: in BWF's first six months of operation, membership grew to forty thousand financial supporters. The focus of BWF was now providing support and resources to evangelical UCC churches. For instance, congregations not wanting to rely on the denominational pastoral placement and referral program and seeking to secure theologically orthodox pastors were provided with names of such clergy by BWF. The growing dilemma of the loss of seminarians to more evangelical denominations was another concern of BWF. Leaders of the group would regularly visit UCC seminaries to encourage students to remain in the denomination. They formed caucuses of evangelical students in seminaries and also provided scholarship aid to seminarians who were supporters of BWF. The same sort of channeling was provided by BWF's mission work: those seeking to serve in conservative evangelical missions or desiring to support such ministries went to BWF to locate these mission endeavors in the UCC. Local chapters were founded across the country, bringing laity and clergy together to deliberate on church-wide issues and to foster theological and spiritual renewal.

Early on, BWF maintained that it sought to work strictly within the UCC. BWF's leaders and board members encouraged churches and clergy to remain in the denomination; in fact, membership in a UCC congregation was a necessary condition for joining BWF. Although the relationship between membership in the UCC and involvement with BWF has been drastically redefined in recent years, this early emphasis on the loyalty of BWF members to the denomination was made often because church officials accused the group of promoting schism and division among members and congregations. And there were signs that BWF was having a unifying impact (at least on the surface) on UCC denominational life, providing a haven for disaffected evangelical churches. Before BWF was formed, the number of congregations leaving the UCC in protest of its liberalism in the 1970s was at a high of approximately forty churches a year with approximately thirty thousand members. In the years after BWF started, the number of churches splitting from the denomination decreased to twelve a year.

During this time, BWF helped congregations involved in evangelical renewal, providing pastoral referrals, counseling (particularly for those considering leaving the denomination), and other resources. Runion-Bareford says that a distinctive kind of "renewal church" developed during the 1970s and 1980s. These congregations, particularly those in New England, were often pastored by graduates of the evangelical Gordon-Conwell Theological Seminary in suburban Boston. These churches were open to currents influencing evangelicals nationally; they often blended Reformed doctrine with an openness to the charismatic movement. They also had a strong "social gospel" component (coming from the liberal Congregational tradition) that called for involvement in their community and in missions, and they often had contemporary styles of worship.

Most of these churches also suffered splits as evangelical renewal was introduced into their congregations. Runion-Bareford estimates that 250 UCC congregations became renewal churches due to the ministry of BWF. Another important facet of BWF was and continues to be mission work. The organization sends out more missionaries than the UCC proper, as it connects congregations that are dissatisfied with missionaries assigned to them by the UCC with missionaries (both UCC and interdenominational) that are evangelical in belief.

The attempt to create an evangelical presence in the national and local church structures faced its greatest challenge in 1991, during the meeting of the Ohio conference. A measure before the assembly called for churches to adopt a policy, known as the "Open and Affirming" policy, that would lift restrictions on homosexuals participating in church life, including the ban on ordination. Ohio was known as the Bible Belt of the UCC, and BWF sprang into action to mobilize churches in voting against the measure. The Ohio BWF chapter sent representatives into every church to speak out against the resolution. To the shock of BWF members and other conservatives in the UCC, the conference passed the Open and Affirming measure by a ratio of two to one.

To many, this decision effectively ended the drive to reform the UCC church structure. "We ended hope of politically ending liberal rule," says Runion-Bareford. After the Ohio ruling, BWF itself seemed to be in danger of folding. Its local chapters were dissolving. In the 1990s, the rate of churches leaving the UCC had picked up again to the pre-BWF, 1970s figure of forty per year. Another major disappointment to evangelical renewalists stemmed from a dialogue with then–UCC President Paul Sherry. BWF and other evangelicals thought their concerns had been heard, but they were disillusioned when the denomination did not follow up on these dialogues.

Turning to a Postdenominational Approach

Conservatives in the UCC began to look for alternatives after 1991. Convinced that their leaders abdicated leadership in maintaining orthodoxy in the denomination, conservatives often sought new kinds of oversight. One proposal was made to let these disaffected members join the Calvin Synod, a nongeographical UCC conference consisting of Hungarian Reformed churches. The Calvin Synod is strongly conservative and confessional and, as a body that existed prior to the UCC merger, has considerable autonomy within the denomination. But denominational officials strongly opposed any such affiliation, even proposing to break up the synod and put each of its churches under the oversight of its geographical conference if such action took place.

A new diversity of bodies and renewal groups was also emerging during this period. A small dissenting group called the Renewal Fellowship was formed that allowed both UCC and non-UCC congregations to join—a foreshadowing of the policy that BWF was to adopt—but few congregations signed up. UCC charismatics had been active in Focus Renewal Ministries since the 1970s, and they increasingly joined forces with other renewal groups, such as BWF.

Meanwhile, moderates concerned with returning the denomination to a more confessional, historic Christian identity while maintaining involvement in ecumenism and social action formed the Confessing Christ movement in 1993. Most unique is the genesis of the Association of Evangelical, Reformed and Congregational Christian Churches in 1997. Its name is an amalgam of the denominations that merged to form the UCC. The Evangelical Association, as it is known, is different than the usual schismatic group in that it seeks to include both those who have left and those still in the UCC. Although it has only forty congregation members as of 1999, its "both-and" character fits in with what has been called the "new paradigm."[7] This denominational model stresses the role of decentralized networks that deliver services to and provide connections between congregations rather than the centralized and hierarchical structures of previous models. Denominations are seen as service providers for a network of like-minded congregations rather than structures that unite and represent churches.

In fact, the diversity and a loosely held sense of denominational identification within the UCC appear to have strongly influenced its evangelicals to be in the forefront of creating decentralized strategies and networks. This is most clearly seen in the new face of BWF under the leadership of Runion-Bareford since the early 1990s. When asked about the future of the UCC, Runion-Bareford is candid: "It's heading toward fragmentation. The future is uncertain." He is also convinced that working for change within the structure of the church is doomed to failure. "The goal is not to take over and restore the hierarchy in Cleveland [the UCC headquarters] or recoup the money. The goal is to renew the six thousand churches [in the denomination]." He is convinced that evangelicals are not "intentionally political" the way that mainline church leaders and activists are and says that he is part of a second generation of renewalists who understand the denominational leadership's mind-set.

In one way, the fifty-year-old Runion-Bareford has come full circle in his career. In the 1960s, he was a social activist involved in antiwar protests. He was also a student and admirer of Saul Alinsky, whose confrontational tactics attempted to put a wrench in the workings of the political structure. After serving a number of years as a UCC pastor, he sees himself as renewing his activist-strategist role in BWF, even if the fellowship has only two staff members and a budget of $100,000 a year. Of his strategy, Runion-Bareford says that he's "following the '60s approach of asking, 'What can we do with little time or cost that will cost the denomination great time and money?'" This strategy is evident in BWF's letter-writing campaigns that attempt to scramble the signals sent out by the denomination's leadership.

When the denomination sent its churches a letter on the controversial Fidelity and Marriage statement, describing its liberal policy allowing the ordination of homosexuals, BWF sent out a letter criticizing the statement to every UCC church; the UCC posted both letters on its Web site. Other actions, such as proposing resolutions at synods, are attempts to interrupt business as usual and ignite theological debates. BWF alerts the press to controversial events, such as a feminist gathering, providing reporters with its own spin about what it refers to as the "unorthodox" goings-on at such meetings. Runion-Bareford clearly enjoys his pranksterlike work and the protests it has caused among church officials. "We don't care. We're laughing a lot. We aren't angry. We're not afraid of what [officials] say because they've said it already. They've been less critical since we've been more uppity."

BWF's noninstitutional approach to renewal was most clearly spelled out in a Winter 1998 issue of its newspaper, *The Witness*. The issue was devoted to the postdenominational "new paradigm," with reports that many UCC congregations are finding the services once provided by their liberal denomination elsewhere. Popular interdenominational evangelical hymnbooks such as *Praise and Worship* have replaced the need for those provided by the denomination. New organizations that serve an ecumenical function— such as Vision New England and Churches United for Global Mission—are providing congregations with connections and resources, such as pastoral recognition, education, pensions, health insurance options, and referral networks.

One article notes that although these new associations may be replacing denominations for many conservative UCC churches, they do not usually provide these congregations with a new identity. "In fact, most if not all of these associations will assume that participating churches will retain their historic denominational affiliation. It will be a both/and rather than an either/or alternative."[8] As for ecumenism, Vision New England has three thousand member churches from eighty denominations with common evangelical beliefs increasingly working together in evangelism, discipleship, and social ministry. The organization is facilitating a new alliance between evangelicals and Catholics in New Hampshire. More controversially, it has also convened what it refers to as multidenominational "ecclesiastical councils" of respected pastors throughout New England for mainline pastors to hold services ordaining members of their own congregations. These services would conflict with the UCC practice of conference leaders and pastors conducting ordinations. Runion-Bareford says that this issue of *The Witness* provoked a good deal of concern among church members and officials. Not least among their concerns was BWF's claim that it plans to cooperate with and include former UCC congregations in its programs.

The Reverend Edith Gussey, secretary of the UCC, says that the opting-out strategy of the evangelicals at BWF, such as using non-

denominational Sunday school literature, is not necessarily forbidden; the "denomination has always supported the autonomy of
the local congregation. But ideally, we would like to see congregations [using UCC resources and working within the church struc-
ture]. It's part of our covenant with them."[9] By using the term
covenant, Gussey is referring to a recent church policy that calls for
a new, closer connection and more accountability between the
churches and the denomination's leadership. Runion-Bareford
and other evangelicals, by contrast, tend to view the connections
between the congregation and the denomination as what they
term an "association," with local churches determining the degree
to which they will relate to the UCC.

That 1998 issue of *The Witness* made clear that BWF had
changed its philosophy as well as its strategy of renewal. Gone was
the earlier concern to show UCC leaders that BWF was faithful
to the denomination and did not encourage schism. Runion-
Bareford says that in counseling pastors, he no longer stresses that
they remain in the UCC. "A lot of times, being UCC is a burden to
churches as they minister to their communities," he says. He adds
that "at a time of decreasing denominational loyalty, denominational officials are going around calling people to loyalty. It doesn't
make sense." With new ecumenical arrangements between the
UCC and such denominations as the Evangelical Lutheran Church
in America, Disciples of Christ, Presbyterians, and the Reformed
Church in America, Runion-Bareford sees new alliances forming
between conservatives in each group. "The beauty in this is that
each church should be able to choose from a cafeteria of options."
Hence, theoretically at least, a conservative UCC church could
select a conservative Presbyterian minister if no UCC candidate in
the area fits the bill.

Runion-Bareford sees the intensification of a period of fragmentation and erratic coalition building as only a transitional state.
Eventually, groups of like-minded churches with similar traditions
will naturally move together. Until that happens, BWF plans to
"develop as many ties as possible," even to such "rival" denominations as the Conservative Congregational Christian Conference,
which has attracted many disaffected evangelical UCC congregations. Runion-Bareford and other BWF leaders stress that the
renewal group does not plan to become a denomination, and it

will go out of business when it no longer sees the need for major renewal in the UCC.

Evangelical clergy and participants in the UCC appear to agree—although on a more modest level—with Runion-Bareford's prognosis of greater fragmentation and denominational disloyalty. The charismatic renewal group Focus Renewal Ministries—note the absence of the designation *UCC* in its name—has developed strong ties to other charismatic renewal groups in Catholic and mainline denominations. Focus Renewal Ministries leader Vernon Stoop says, "On the one hand, UCC has passed the point of no return. On the other, hope is on the local level. You [can see] churches that are faithful and individual lives changed." Stoop says that he has often received what he calls the "left foot of fellowship" from denominational officials but is no longer very offended by such rejection. "It no longer bothers me because I have so many other friends. I can always find some fellowship. I feel sorry for younger pastors who don't have that. I think a lot of them will [take up] the party line to belong. They'll act like they believe things, but they really don't."[10]

Pastor Michael, a forty-seven-year-old minister of a small Connecticut congregation, sees a "major realignment of Christians in the next twenty-five years," as congregations join local associations and disassociate from national bodies over doctrinal issues. He did not always feel that way. Ordained in the Presbyterian Church (USA), Pastor Michael was involved both in his denomination and in renewal groups to increase evangelical influence in the church. Then he accepted a call from a UCC congregation. At first, he participated in denominational life. He attended the regional UCC conference gatherings and volunteered to take part in conference activities.

"When they sent me a letter asking me if I wanted to serve, I said I was willing. But they never asked me to do anything. It seems [the conference] didn't want me. I felt like I was increasingly discouraged. The other pastors seemed skeptical about me [as an] evangelical. They didn't want my voice," says Pastor Michael. Then he became active in BWF for a while. With other participants in a local chapter, he tried to elect an evangelical as head of the regional conference, but their candidate was ignored. Although still a supporter of BWF—his congregation gives more money to the group than to the UCC—Pastor Michael has grown weary of trying to reform the UCC.

He no longer goes to conference meetings, nor does he have any contact with the national church body. He has recently purchased new hymnbooks from an evangelical publisher for the congregation; he did not even consider buying the denominational hymnals. Pastor Michael is part of a local association of evangelical pastors in which he finds close fellowship, and he conducts his youth ministry in cooperation with three non-UCC congregations from this group. Every week he meets with two other non-UCC evangelical pastors who help hold him "accountable" and provide the oversight and spiritual support that he doesn't find in his denomination.

Pastor Michael's noninvolvement in the UCC holds up even when it comes to criticizing the church body. He hardly ever criticizes the denomination or speaks about his major disagreements with UCC positions on homosexuality and abortion. "I just focus on the gospel and spiritual issues, not the things the UCC focuses on. I'm not confrontational." When asked why he does not simply withdraw from the denomination, he says that the congregational church structures give him enough freedom and that officially leaving would be more bother than it is worth. Interestingly, his distance from his denomination has made him increasingly less involved in such efforts as BWF. "I think they do great work. But I'm investing my energy in other things," he says. Perhaps if the prospects for evangelical renewal were greater, he would be more involved in BWF and denominational affairs. He adds that even more troubling than the liberal stands on abortion and homosexuality is the way the denomination "discourages honest dialogue, the way they cut off the evangelical voice."

Renewal Congregations Making Their Own Way

Just as the pastors I interviewed appeared alienated from their denomination, the members of the evangelical UCC congregations were largely uninterested in their wider church affiliation. A pastor has to deal with denominational matters, even if it is an unpleasant task, but most laity have the option of ignoring structures beyond the congregation. Andrew, a longtime member of

First Congregational Church in a small New Hampshire village, was part of the church before it was evangelical and involved in BWF. The congregation was a "community church" existing in the center of town and drew most of the church-going residents in the area. The pastor delivered sermons of moral uplift and social action. "It was more like a Lions Club than a church. We had prayer and hymns, but it seems like the pastor didn't have a personal relationship with Christ."

Marge, another veteran member of the congregation, says, "There was no connection between believing and how you should live different. It seemed that Jesus didn't affect everyday life." There were a group of "seekers" in the congregation who wanted more of a spiritual emphasis in the congregation. They began praying for greater spirituality. When a new pastor arrived, there was a marked change in the preaching. Members were being called to repentance and personal faith in Christ. Andrew recalls how a core group of leaders was almost immediately offended by the new evangelical tone of the preaching. They called a meeting to oust the new pastor but found that he had the groundswell of support among the congregation. They had no other option but to leave the congregation. This in effect cleared the way for First Congregational Church to become fully evangelical with little opposition and resistance. "Because of that, there wasn't the residual negativism you find in many renewal churches that still have a remnant [of resisters]," Andrew adds.

In the mid-1980s, the congregation had another decisive meeting—this time concerning the question of leaving the UCC. As often happens in evangelical renewal congregations, it was the members rather than the pastor who brought up the motion to split from the denomination. The congregation was strongly divided (and remains so on this issue) but decided to stay in the denomination, stipulating that it also join BWF; First Congregational Church became one of the first churches to join as a congregation. One of the members had gone to a BWF meeting in another state and reported favorably on the group and how it could provide a way to stay in the denomination. To this day, the bulletin of the church says the congregation is in the UCC and BWF. Its BWF affiliation is a way of saying that First Congregational Church should not be strictly associated with the UCC and its reputation of liberalism, that the congregation also has an evangelical identity. But the tie to BWF has not necessarily reconciled the members of this church with their UCC identity.

"Most of us would say we're Congregational if we had to list our denomination," Andrew says. The laity I interviewed did say they appreciated the autonomous style of church government (known as congregational) in their tradition. But aside from that, they did not show much interest in or knowledge of the UCC and its history or heritage. When I asked laity whether they would look for a UCC congregation if they relocated or went on vacation, all of them agreed that this would be far down on their list of concerns. Most said they would look primarily for a church that was evangelical and dynamic in its faith. The most extreme and negative views among the laity about the UCC were actually from the newcomers to renewal congregations. "It's straight from the devil," says one member of the UCC who is active in pressing for his congregation to leave the denomination.

As we saw earlier with the evangelical UCC pastors, the preaching in the evangelical renewal congregations is centered on matters of personal faith, exposition of the Scriptures, and Christianity's implications in everyday life. Addressing controversial issues in the UCC would add up to negative preaching—something most of the pastors and lay members I interviewed tended to avoid. Preaching or teaching about the UCC and its need for renewal "wouldn't provide spiritual feeding. It's all about what you're supposed to be doing, rather than what you're not supposed to be doing," says Marge.

Church Conflict and Culture Wars

Joined to BWF's decentralized, postdenominational strategy is a stress on a wider culture war dividing society and the churches. In this view, issues such as abortion and gay rights are only the tip of the iceberg of a cultural collision between secularism and the values and institutions built on a biblical foundation. Runion-Bareford espouses the controversial theory that gay activists particularly targeted the UCC because it was such a bastion of mainline America. If they could gain control of this "blue-blooded" and influential sector of American society, then they would have a toehold in other religious and cultural groups. Every issue of *The Witness* newspaper makes connections between the de-Christianization of the United States and the liberalism in the UCC and other mainline churches.

Articles with headlines such as "Church Women United Plans Pagan World Community Day" and "UCC AIDS Curriculum Puts Children at Risk" are intended to be attention-getting devices, but they also show how BWF's original concern with theological issues in the UCC has expanded to embrace social issues that resonate well with American political conservatism. These concerns are not unique to BWF; most of the other mainline renewal groups have also increasingly used culture wars imagery and references, viewing the struggle to renew mainline churches as involving societal and political as well as theological issues.

But even congregations sympathetic to BWF expressed discomfort with the emphasis on contentious social issues. Pastor Richard and his associate, Pastor Joan, at a Congregational church in Connecticut have been longtime supporters of BWF. At the same time, they have supported other renewal ministries and groups that are far removed from the UCC. Their primary involvement is with a Protestant version of the Cursillo movement. The movement, which was founded by Catholics, is based on intense Bible study and prayer, with little attention to denominational doctrine or heritage. Although he pastors a multiethnic church with a strong social action program, Pastor Richard was increasingly disconcerted by the way social activism became the central issue in the church. "At the conferences, they're always telling government what to do, but never telling themselves what to do. The basis of social action was not on Jesus." Pastor Richard and Pastor Joan see BWF and similar groups as a way of prodding the denomination to being more centered on Christ.

At the same time, their congregation feels uncomfortable with BWF's focus on such issues as abortion and homosexuality. Pastor Richard says if he wanted to hold renewal meetings in his church, he would not contact BWF. "They may want to come here and make sure no homosexuals were here," he said. He finds that BWF and other renewal leaders "keep trying to nail me down for not dealing with these sexual issues. I usually tell them, 'Look, you can do the stuff on sex and leave me with issues like housing.' But the focus always seems to come back to abortion and homosexuality." A BWF board member admits that the focus on these issues can cause some to draw away from evangelical renewal in mainline denominations. "Our primary concern is not with the culture war stuff but with the gospel. We [need to help] people believe that we're not against gays or women. It's all part of a larger issue of what type of people we're going to be."

How to Renew a Congregation

The mainstream characteristic of Congregational churches in New England, with their white-steepled buildings often found in the center of town, appealed to the clergy with whom I spoke. It gave them a sphere of influence in their communities that they would not have if they opened an independent church in a storefront on the edge of town. But at the same time, the establishment status of these churches often made renewal among the laity a difficult enterprise.

When Pastor Frank was called to a small liberal UCC church, only two or three people there had any understanding that he was bringing a very different message to the congregation. The previous pastor had left abruptly after originally promising to stay for a longer period. The people were "burned" and wanted to make sure their next pastor was more committed; Pastor Frank's conservative theology and preaching based on the Bible suggested to members that he was serious. "It was a nice church with nice people. They wanted peace and harmony. But I preached the gospel, where people were radical sinners who crucified Christ. I was going to wear them out [until they converted]." A small nucleus of members who experienced conversion eventually swayed the congregation. In looking back on those first few controversial years in the congregation, Pastor Frank counsels clergy to "know their strengths. People sensed my confidence, that I was sincere."

He wanted to show members that he was not bringing some exotic, strange faith to the church but was rather restoring biblical orthodoxy and returning the congregation to its roots. Pastor Frank had come across the century-old church constitution documenting the church's strong Calvinistic beliefs. "I surrounded myself with that background, and it touched many," he adds. But a segment of the church felt that the new pastor's conservative faith and ministry clashed with their more liberal and tolerant Congregationalism. At first, as he preached an evangelical message every Sunday, he said that some tried to ignore the changes being made and "believe what they wanted. But it [didn't] work." In frustration, the treasurer soon quit the church, and others followed, either dropping out of church altogether or moving to more compatible churches.

The church eventually became a leading evangelical congregation in Connecticut—so evangelical, in fact, that after Pastor Frank retired it eventually left the UCC over its liberalism. But Pastor Frank says that most churches undergoing evangelical renewal do not end up as strictly evangelical congregations. "There's an ebb and flow. A congregation may first want someone to preach the Bible. Then they become disoriented [by this change] and would call a liberal the next time."

Old First Church, a historic UCC church in a small Massachusetts village, has made a commitment to stay in the UCC and work for change. Here, unlike at several other churches I visited, it was the laity who steered the congregation into renewal. When the social activism of the mainline churches was tied to allegedly radical and Marxist causes by major media in the 1980s, the laity of Old First Church were the first to sound the alarm, even calling for the church to leave the UCC. Since then, the church does not give to any denomination program, channeling most offerings to BWF and other nondenominational ministries and missions. But members are still seeking to have some influence in the UCC from within. One member who is concerned about abortion serves on a regional church committee on the issue.

The large and growing congregation of Old First Church sees its main role as encouraging other evangelical pastors to move into liberal parishes. The church's pastor, Pastor Kevin, says that since it is located near a large evangelical seminary, the church acts as a liaison between evangelicals and the UCC congregations in the area. Hence he views his own affiliation strategically: his congregation and BWF in general provide evangelical pastors with an access to liberal UCC churches that they would not normally have. And like BWF, the church and its pastor, a founding member of

BWF, do not view changing the structures of the UCC as a realistic or even desirable goal. "Our job is very simple, educating and informing churches about how to go to back the Bible. We don't have to reinvent the wheel," Pastor Kevin says. Like other BWF supporters, he has a pragmatic and localized understanding of renewal: the structures may come and go; it is more important to restore vitality to the local congregation. He adds that people can come to his church for years and not even know it is part of the UCC. "Denominational issues have evaporated as about half of our congregation comes from Catholic backgrounds; what would they think if we were always complaining about our denomination?"

If renewal and reform seems an increasingly dim prospect, and if the renewal organization itself no longer places a high priority on staying in and working for change within denominational structures, then what is to keep groups from withdrawing to form independent associations and programs for ministry? America's spiritual free marketplace provides denominations and associations that may be more in line with the beliefs, goals, and practices of renewalists. I asked some of the evangelical renewalists I interviewed whether there was anything about the UCC that they liked, aside from the challenge of renewing old-line liberal congregations. Their answers were often steeped in personal memory of the predecessor denominations or in church history as they recalled the glories of New England Congregationalism and the German or Hungarian Reformed traditions.

Pastor Michael says that however disenchanted he is with the UCC, he "value[s] the Congregational tradition. It's a great heritage that the UCC moved away from." Like other UCC evangelicals, he found that the local autonomy of the congregation (known as congregational church government) remained an appealing feature of the church. When I asked the same question of one BWF board member in Connecticut, he also looked to the past and the heritage of the UCC. "These churches are ours!" he said adamantly. "Jonathan Edwards, the Puritans, the Great Awakenings—that belongs to us. The Unitarians had no right to the buildings. The Congregationalists belong here [in New England]." A Hungarian Reformed UCC pastor in New Jersey looked back to the founding of the denomination in 1957 and remembered his expectations about the merger. "I thought the Congregational Church had social concern and a membership with a responsible sense of stewardship. And I thought the Evangelical and Reformed Church would contribute the theological foundation absent in Congregationalism. It hasn't happened."

Without a larger vision of renewal for the whole church, it will be difficult to enact change beyond the congregation. Evangelical renewal in the UCC mirrors the pluralism in the denomination itself, making sweeping reform an unlikely prospect. The disdain for churchwide structures among evangelical renewalists will tend to marginalize them in the denomination and its decision-making process. A BWF board member says the only alternative to unofficial forms of withdrawal is for evangelical churches to band together and form their own association that would provide them with voting power at the synods and the regional conferences. But for that to happen, there would have to be significant change in denominational structures to allow new forms of organizing and associating that may clash with the leadership and national policies at any given time. The leadership fears that if BWF gets voting power, then any other special interest group will claim similar rights, thus weakening the unity in the church.

But the case of BWF and the UCC in general shows that fragmentation happens, regardless of official church policies. A denomination built on theological pluralism from its founding is not likely to command strong allegiance even if the leadership tries to strengthen its national role and the church offices take clear and definable stands on social issues. Add to that the laity's growing disenchantment with and distance from their denominations, and things really begin to look depressing.

Because of the UCC's institutional structure, evangelical or any other type of outside reform is difficult in the denomination. Yet on the local level, it is a different story. The renewal churches remain among the largest and fastest-growing in the denomination. Ironically, the many new church ties that these congregations have developed—even with charismatic Catholics—makes them more ecumenical than many traditional UCC churches. Although the postdenominational paradigm may not apply to all American denominations, it appears to be a reality in the UCC. Thus, BWF and its kindred congregations may well be in the vanguard of creating new forms of oversight and association. But it remains to be seen whether or not such innovations will take place in a denomination called the United Church of Christ.

The Ties That Unbind

In one way, BWF and other evangelical renewal caucuses in mainline bodies could be described as beautiful losers. They do not seem to be succeeding in changing leadership and structures in their respective denominations to reflect evangelical beliefs and concerns. There have been few success stories of conservatives turning around liberal denominations. Even in a denomination like the Presbyterian Church (USA)—with many thriving renewal groups and conservative-led legislation to ban gay rights—the mood is one of discouragement and disappointment, as seen in recent calls by some evangelicals to leave the denomination. The sort of denominational housecleaning and political activism needed to turn things around in most bureaucracies may well exceed the concerns of many evangelicals. But this tendency is not inevitable. The United Methodist Church's General Conference in 2000 saw a number of conservative rulings passed, such as restricting gay rights in the church and the firming up of other orthodox theological teachings, mainly due to the influence of renewal and reform groups. Groups such as Good News and the Confessing Movement are reported to have galvanized church members to action through regional conferences, thus leading to greater conservative influence among delegates to the General Conference. But even sympathetic observers note that liberals remain in positions of influence in church agencies.[11]

As we have seen, many evangelicals are less interested in taking over the structures as they currently exist than they are in carrying out evangelism and missions. Whereas liberals tend to place importance in institutions and structural change both in secular politics and religious institutions, conservatives have concentrated much of their energies on personal change, whether through personal discipline and the work ethic in the secular sphere or being born again. The liberal and moderate denominations were in the vanguard of building institutions and incorporating a managerial style into their structures in the mid-twentieth century. Anthony

Robinson writes that the UCC in particular has become a "procedural church," putting its energies into fine-tuning its structure to achieve its goals as an "inclusive" and "multicultural" church body. The denomination defines itself through coalitions, caucuses and other political frames of reference rather than through theological concerns, Robinson writes.[12]

The conservatives tend to be more in tune with the decentralizing currents affecting all institutions, particularly as they have invested less in bureaucracies to begin with. Of course, conservatives can inject themselves into secular and religious politics and gain power to change leaderships and structures as much as any liberals; the conservative takeovers of the Southern Baptist Convention, the Lutheran Church–Missouri Synod, and the Roman Catholic Church during the last two decades prove that point.

The evangelicals in the UCC may be losing the battle to turn their denomination into an evangelical institution, but they are "beautiful" in that they are doing so well on the local level. BWF's claim of renewing 250 congregations is impressive, even when we consider the unpublicized failed attempts at renewal that may have also resulted. There were resisters and even some church splits in congregations under renewal, but the preaching and teaching of these renewal pastors made the evangelical presence a force to be reckoned with. The evangelical message is both attractive and empowering.

In the churches I visited, evangelically renewed members soon became the most active in their congregations, and liberals and nominal members were consigned to an endangered minority. Walk into most evangelical congregations in America today and you can find a bulletin crammed with announcements for Bible studies, prayer groups, mission drives, and youth activities. Evangelical congregations ask much, such as tithing and regular attendance, of their members, but they also provide strong bonds of fellowship, a sense of identity, and direction. The fact that mainline churches have suffered less steep declines in church attendance in recent years may be due to the presence of these evangelical congregations. In fact, sociologists Rodney Stark and Roger Finke find that those United Methodist and Presbyterian congregations tied to evangelical renewal groups have the highest rates of growth in their denominations.[13]

The UCC renewal churches in the Congregationalist tradition particularly have revived their genius for grassroots organizing and activism and have created and discovered resources that provide many of the functions of denominations. They are not agonizing much over whether to stay in and work for renewal or leave a main-line denomination—a conundrum that in the long run just ends up taking up more red tape and causing further painful church splits along the way. With organizations such as BWF and the new Evangelical Association, congregations can remain in the denom-ination and receive new forms of support and ministry from fellow evangelicals of other traditions and backgrounds—from pastoral referrals to Sunday school literature. With the Internet and desk-top publishing, BWF and similar organizations can critique the actions and statements of denominational leaders and saturate churches with their ideas.

The congregational nature of the UCC makes these evangelical churches pioneers in postdenominational renewal, but the same trends are being felt across the denominational spectrum. Even in the hierarchical and centralized Episcopal Church, conservatives are forming new alliances with more traditional church leaders from Third World countries and sidestepping traditional connections with their dioceses and denominations. This tendency was dramatically played out in the winter of 2000, when two priests who are leaders of a U.S. Episcopal renewal organization called First Promise were consecrated as missionary bishops to the United States outside the denomination by bishops from conservative Anglican churches in Africa and Asia. The Anglican bishops and churches in the Third World are more traditional than those in Europe and the United States, and American conservatives have been forming new ties with these increasingly influential church leaders.

The news of the consecration of these missionary bishops alarmed Episcopal Presiding Bishop Frank Griswold and Arch-bishop of Canterbury George Carey, who condemned the conse-crations as invalid. Particularly offensive to Griswold was the way the new bishops were designated as missionaries to help spiritually revive the liberal Episcopal Church in the United States. Whereas liberal church leaders said this unprecedented action would cre-ate more schisms in the church, conservatives saw it differently. "Our calling is to minister to those congregations who believe that the authority of Scripture and the historic creeds are central to our faith, conduct, and unity as Anglicans. We are committed to lead the church, not leave it," said one of the new bishops, the Reverend Chuck Murphy III. In other words, to its supporters, the unofficial consecration of the bishops was less an effort to discard Anglican tradition or heritage than an effort to reconfigure it by establishing new lines of authority and support from fellow Anglican conservatives, even if they worked outside official denominational channels.[14]

In the Presbyterian Church (USA), both liberals and conservatives have formed parachurch and renewal organizations that are beginning to fulfill many of the same functions that the larger denomination once provided. Pastoral referrals, Sunday school literature, missions, and ecumenical arrangements are available from these unofficial structures. That the evangelical renewal groups generate new forms of cooperation and association was demonstrated early in the year 2000, when the National Association of Evangelicals (NAE) changed its bylaws to allow mainline churches to affiliate with the organization as well as with the National Council of Churches. Previously, the NAE had only permitted congregations from evangelical denominations to join the cooperative agency, which was started in 1942 as an alternative to the mainline National Council of Churches. The change allowing for dual membership was part of an effort by the NAE to recognize the work of evangelical renewal movements within the mainline denominations.

This arrangement, as well as the new independence of renewal groups, suggests that Runion-Bareford's prediction of increasing fragmentation and new alliances in the mainline denominations may be on target. It is possible for a congregation to officially remain in a denomination, draw support from a renewal group, and, at the same time, establish close ties with other evangelical churches through the NAE and other networks. We have seen that evangelical and other conservative renewal organizations are likely to model the new forms of decentralized organization earlier and to a greater degree than their more liberal host denominations. This sets the stage for new kinds of organizational conflict—aside from the ideological and theological divisions—and will add more fuel to the ever-present potential for schisms and new denominations that exists within all renewal movements.

3

Return to the Source
Two Conservative Reform Groups

It all started that Lenten season in 1997 when Pastor John Hannah announced to his small inner-city Lutheran congregation at Trinity Lutheran Church in the Bronx that "There will be no more pastor's classes." The classes are a staple in Lutheran and other Protestant churches seeking to draw in new members. Instead, Trinity embarked on the ancient initiation rite called the adult catechumenate. The catechumenate was an initiation process used by the early church to help nonbelievers make the transition into the Christian church. As its name implies, it is often based on catechisms, which use a question-and-answer format to teach the faith.

Every Sunday, Pastor Hannah preached particularly to the candidates for initiation into the church, and then, as tradition dictated, dismissed them before communion began. Then Maria, a lay leader, would shepherd candidates through discussions of the Scriptures and the catechism. By the time Easter arrived that year, Trinity Lutheran was about to double its small membership.

On Easter, eight adults were baptized or confirmed. They gathered around the baptistery with lit candles to sing and speak the ancient liturgy. Then they spoke their vows and promises to the church, with the small congregation reaffirming their approval of the new members and initiates into the Christian faith.

The beret-wearing Pastor Hannah has become a missionary for the adult catechumenate, speaking to interested parishes in his denomination, the Lutheran Church–Missouri Synod, and the larger Evangelical Lutheran Church in America. "Why try to be a Baptist in a Lutheran church? Lutherans don't make very good

Baptists," he quipped, referring to the growing influence of the church growth movement in the Lutheran Church–Missouri Synod, which tends to downplay the historic Lutheran liturgy and sacraments in favor of contemporary services that try to reach the unchurched seeker.[1]

"The catechumenate has been a godsend, and it works. It's the answer to the church growth people. Unless evangelical catholics embrace the adult catechumenate—and we have to do it quick— we'll have problems keeping people in the church," he added.

If Hannah protests against the influence of Baptists and other evangelicals on Lutheranism, he has fewer quibbles about the impact of Roman Catholicism. Like many other Lutherans, he refers to himself as an evangelical catholic, using the word *catholic* in its original sense to mean "universal." Evangelical catholics seek to recover the liturgical and confessional heritage of Lutheranism in continuity with the broad tradition that includes Anglicans, Roman Catholics, and the Eastern Orthodox, and emphasizes the sacraments and liturgy.

Recovering the Confessions and the Church

The evangelical catholic movement is based on the teaching that Martin Luther and the early reformers did not intend to jettison the liturgy, church order, and other traditions of the historic church, much less establish Protestantism. Luther was a Catholic monk who fought mainly to reassert the biblical teaching of justification by faith as central to the church. When this doctrine was rejected by Rome and Luther was excommunicated, the split that resulted in Western Christianity was a tragic necessity, but one that would eventually be mended, according to evangelical catholics.

But Lutheranism developed distinctive teachings and practices apart from Roman Catholicism as it swept across Northern Europe and was eventually transplanted in North America by immigrants and early settlers in the nineteenth and twentieth centuries. In the United States, much of Lutheranism was distinctly Protestant in worship and belief, even if it had liturgical overtones. Whereas Lutherans in Europe retained some evangelical catholic practices (for example, in Sweden, crucifixes, bishops, priests, and other Roman Catholic holdovers are the norm), American theologians and clergy had to reintroduce liturgy and practices of the pre-Reformation church into Lutheran congregations in the mid-twentieth century. This reform was often expressed as a way of returning to one's roots and the original intentions of Martin Luther and the confessional documents of the Reformation. The evangelical catholic movement has always been about recovering classic Lutheran theology as expressed in keystone doctrines such as justification by faith (the belief that one is saved apart from good deeds), as well as in liturgy and worship. This usually means that preaching on the classic themes of sin and grace is balanced with celebration of communion and liturgical and historic church music, including a generous number of Bach chorales.

Attempting to return to the roots of one's religious heritage is a difficult endeavor, largely because of the distance between the present and past and the transformations that take shape in the interim. How do these Lutherans manage this task, especially in our do-it-yourself religious climate that tends to forget the past and reinvent structures and churches every few decades? How do the evangelical catholics go about introducing the Protestant Lutheran rank-and-file members to rituals and teachings, many of which may be unfamiliar and likely to clash with the practices with which they grew up?

A Liturgical Resurgence

The Lutherans are not the only ones to experiment with liturgical renovations and reform. The evangelical catholics were influenced by what became known in the nineteenth and early twentieth centuries as the liturgical movement. During this period, many responded to the Protestant churches' growing emphasis on individualism and rationalism on the one hand and their stress on religious experience or pietism on the other by seeking out the worship patterns of earlier—usually pre-Reformation—eras. Liturgical reformers proposed a third way based on a corporate religious life and the catholicity or universal character of the church. They wanted a return to the sources of the tradition, sensing that believers must return to the founding vision or original mission of the tradition and dust away the accretions and distortions that had accumulated with time. The Oxford movement in England in which Anglicans sought to return to pre-Reformation forms of worship and piety was a major example of the liturgical reform. In the United States, Catholics were leaders in the liturgical reform movement, with one center being St. John's Abbey in Collegeville, Minnesota.[2]

There was and remains a restorationist character to liturgical reform, as it includes the effort to recover forms of worship that may have been less tainted by rationalism. But other factors had a part to play. Increased participation in and access to the liturgy, particularly in democratic North America, is a goal of many liturgical reformers in all religious traditions. This attempt to include the whole congregation and parish (rather than just the priest or minister) in worship was prominent in the Protestant as well as Catholic churches. In fact, many of the new or restored forms of liturgy were developed in informal cooperation and consultation between different denominations, according to Eugene Brand.

As denominations worked to revise and update hymn and worship books into more contemporary language (for instance, addressing God as *you* rather than *thou*) in the 1960s, a new kind of ecumenism based around worship developed. The Second Vatican Council and its far-reaching liturgical changes and innovations served as a model for this kind of liturgical reform. Brand points out that the whole range of new liturgical books—in the Roman Catholic, Lutheran, Episcopal, Reformed, and Methodist traditions—issued in the last three decades have more similarities than differences, a remarkable occurrence considering the theological divisions that still remain between these churches.[3]

A Renewal in the Making

On the frigid January afternoon I met Reverend Frederick Schumacher at his parish in White Plains, New York, it seemed that he was running a one-man renewal movement—both locally and nationally.[4] A pastor friend had just brought him some kneeling benches; like many evangelical catholic pastors, he had recently inaugurated the practice of individual confession in his parish. In his crowded office, he showed off with some pride a fine engraved medallion he had designed to honor Katarina von Bora, the wife of Martin Luther, on the five-hundredth anniversary of her birth;

he planned to distribute the medallions nationally to encourage the Lutheran denominations to celebrate the event. As executive director of the American Lutheran Publicity Bureau (ALPB), a pan-Lutheran renewal organization, Schumacher produced, with another editor and a band of church volunteers, *For All the Saints,* a four-volume prayer book that has run through three printings with over twenty thousand copies in circulation. Schumacher noted that the ALPB's main publication, the *Lutheran Forum,* is the largest independent magazine in American Lutheranism.

The history of the ALPB speaks volumes about the way a renewal movement can move from the margins to the mainstream of religious life and sometimes back again. Like evangelical catholicism itself, the ALPB never intended to become a renewal organization in Lutheran denominations. Originally, the organization was founded in New York in 1914 to help immigrant German Lutherans make the transition to American church life, including the use of English in parishes. As its name implies, the bureau also served as a public relations vehicle for Lutherans to communicate with the wider American society about their faith and traditions. It was this concern to overcome parochialism and reach a wider public with the theology of Martin Luther that led the ALPB and its magazine, the *American Lutheran,* the predecessor to the *Lutheran Forum,* to include evangelical catholic liturgical renewal in its coverage on American Lutheran life.[5]

Such subjects as the importance of baptism and communion, as well as coverage of trends in worship and liturgy, featured prominently in its pages. All this was new to most Lutheran congregations, which celebrated communion only monthly or quarterly and considered preaching the central focus of every service. The differences were often expressed in the terms *high church* (meaning "liturgical") and *low church,* usually referring to informal worship. Evangelical catholic reformers argued that the Lutheran confessions and Luther himself, not to mention the historic Catholic tradition, had favored more frequent reception of the sacrament.

During the 1950s and 1960s, there was a new impetus for Lutheran unity in the United States. Ironically, this came at a time when new fault lines were developing in American Lutheranism. During most of the 1960s, evangelical catholics were prominent in the conservative Lutheran Church–Missouri Synod, with their influence felt in plans revealed at its 1965 convention to create a common Lutheran liturgy and hymnbook. These plans for a common service book came to fruition with the creation of the *Lutheran Book of Worship* in 1977, by which time the Missouri Synod had withdrawn from involvement in Lutheran unity due to its concern about the liberalism in other church bodies. By then, a conservative change of guard had taken place in the Missouri Synod after a lengthy battle with more liberal members in the late 1960s and 1970s.

Such issues as the use of historical criticism of the Bible and the inerrancy of the Scriptures drove a wedge within and between congregations, seminaries, and even families. Those pressing for greater liberalization left the Missouri Synod or were forced out, eventually forming their own denomination, the Association of Evangelical Lutheran Churches. Although the ALPB was primarily geared to the Lutheran Church–Missouri Synod in its early years, the organization and its publications began to take a broader approach, not least because many of its leaders were part of the more liberal or moderate wing that left the church during this controversy.

The ALPB dealt with the issues uniting Lutherans who in the past had little to do with one another. The force of assimilation made ethnic differences between the various Lutheran synods fade into the background, while such issues as inner-city ministry, social action, ecumenism, and new currents in theology came to the fore. In the early 1970s, the bureau started publishing *Forum Letter*, a newsletter that became known for its feisty, independent commentary on and coverage of Lutheran affairs, particularly under the editorship of Richard John Neuhaus, then a young inner-city pastor and activist in Brooklyn.

The 1970s were a time of growing engagement with American and international Lutheranism for the ALPB. Under the editorship of Glenn C. Stone, the *Lutheran Forum* made a special effort to cover the connections between Lutheran churches, society, and culture—with reports on Lutheran life in India and Iceland, reviews of operas, and in-depth coverage of Lutheran social involvement, particularly in the field of racial relations. Although the ALPB retained a strong evangelical catholic identity, it featured theologians, lay leaders, and clergy from diverse perspectives in its publications. The bureau sponsored inter-Lutheran conferences featuring such scholars and leaders as church historian Martin Marty and sociologist Peter Berger.

All in all, the ALPB and Lutherans in general viewed the future with cautious optimism during the 1970s and much of the 1980s. Evangelical catholic liturgical innovations and recoveries such as weekly communion, the celebration of the Saturday vigil before Easter, and common liturgy drawing on Western Catholic forms of worship through the new cooperative Lutheran text, the *Lutheran Book of Worship,* found their way into the Lutheran mainstream.[6]

All this was taking place as the Lutherans' old nemesis, the Roman Catholic Church, appeared to be less and less of a nemesis. The Second Vatican Council had opened Catholicism not only to the outside world but also to its "separated brethren" among Protestants. Observers of Vatican II note that Lutheranism had a good deal of impact in these Catholic reforms; the use of the vernacular in the Mass, the greater role for the laity, and the use of the Bible in the church all had their roots in debates unleashed by Martin Luther four hundred years earlier, not to mention the influence of more modern Lutheran theologians. The new closeness between Lutherans and Catholics resulted in a historic dialogue between the two traditions; in 1999, this led to a joint statement on the doctrine of justification by faith, in which both traditions claimed new convergences on this doctrine even amidst continuing differences.

The ALPB did not look like a typical renewal or reform organization before 1988, probably because Lutheranism had retained a moderate quality that often diffused the conservative or liberal polarization that had marked the rest of mainline Protestantism. Since the late 1960s, steep declines in membership had plagued much of liberal mainline Protestantism; in the same period, conservative evangelical churches were mushrooming. Critics accused these liberal church leaderships of being out of touch with their more conservative constituencies as they concentrated their energies on social action and neglected spirituality and biblical teachings.

Due to its ethnic particularities and its roots in classic Reformation confessions that stressed historic Christian doctrines, American Lutheranism had managed to keep an identity distinct from other Protestant denominations, even as its more moderate and liberal branches remained open to such innovations as women's ordination and ecumenical involvement in the National and World Council of Churches.

Of course, conservatives were dissatisfied with what they saw as liberal tendencies in the major Lutheran bodies (and there were liberal and radical protests within the same denominations), but hope was high among Lutherans that their future would be different as the major denominations—the Lutheran Church in America, the American Lutheran Church, and the Association of Evangelical Lutheran Churches—made plans to merge in 1988. Even if the conservative Missouri Synod was not to join a united Lutheran church, this impending unity, supporters argued, would consolidate the strengths of Lutheranism and add weight to its presence and prestige in American society. The new church would be, after all, among the largest denominations in the United States.

Shelter in a Storm

The merger of the American Lutheran Church, Lutheran Church in America, and the Association of Evangelical Lutheran Churches was the largest church merger to take place in decades in American Christianity. Overnight, two moderately sized denominations and one small one had consolidated to become the third largest Protestant church in the United States, with approximately five million members and over eleven thousand clergy. But the year 1988 serves more as a painful reminder of the beginning of decline rather than of achievement for the evangelical catholics associated with the ALPB. Where they thought the formation of the Evangelical Lutheran Church in America (ELCA) would extend their influence, they claimed that the newly merged denomination marginalized them, driving some of their leading lights out of Lutheranism altogether.

To evangelical catholics and other conservative critics, concerns were apparent months before the merger. An affirmative action policy that stipulated that minorities and women make up one-third of leadership was bitterly opposed by evangelical catholics and other conservative Lutherans. Such a policy was viewed as enforcing a pseudo-catholic church structure that placed more value on political power relations than on choosing leaders by the gifts and guidance of the Holy Spirit. The quota system was part of a general program of inclusiveness, an attempt to diversify the church from its Northern European base to include particularly African American, Asian American, and Latino minorities. This was seen in the churchwide drive to raise the minority membership of denomination to 10 percent within ten years. Related to the stress on diversity were feminist concerns for inclusiveness not only in membership but in liturgy, theology, and language.

Issues of sexuality were ever present in the conflict between evangelical catholics and the ELCA. In 1994, the ELCA issued a statement calling for liberalization on sexuality, including premarital sex and homosexuality (later to be modified). The generally pro-life evangelical catholics, at least as they were represented by the ALPB, registered fervent protests against the ELCA for providing abortion coverage in employee and clergy health plans. As the ELCA moved closer to other mainline bodies, there was widespread concern among evangelical catholics that the church was moving Lutheranism away from its mission of being a reforming movement in the catholic tradition—in Anglicanism, Roman Catholicism, and Eastern Orthodoxy. For many, this was confirmed in the ELCA's 1997 agreement with the Presbyterian Church (USA), the United Church of Christ, and the Reformed Church in America to enter into full communion. The agreement, which allowed the churches to celebrate communion together and to interchange clergy between congregations, was criticized for giving short shrift to the Lutheran teaching of the real presence of Christ in communion and pandering to ecumenism of the lowest common denominator.

Evangelical catholics were convinced that these changes and developments were symptoms of a more pervasive problem: a wholesale accommodation to contemporary culture and its individualism by the mainline Protestantism of which the ELCA was now a part. Such critics charged that the denomination was driven by agendas rather than theology. The ELCA agenda was shaped by an ever-growing bureaucracy that sought to meet a wide range of needs rather than act as a believing community.

Resistance and Opposition

The changes in the ALPB, specifically the *Lutheran Forum,* provides a documentary account of how external forces turned a broad and open theological and liturgical movement into a more self-contained and opposition renewal group. The writers and others gathered around the *Lutheran Forum* freely admit that the evangelical catholic movement changed after the formation of the ELCA. Upon assuming the post of editor in 1993, Leonard Klein wrote:

> [The] publications of the ALPB have been a lively voice for
> moderate confessionalism. In the past, that viewpoint meant the
> freedom to be a cheerful, high-spirited gadfly, tweaking torpid
> and overly cautious church leaders, arguing for renewal in liturgy,
> education, stewardship and evangelism; except for some rare bad
> moments, the relationship to the denominations and the institu-
> tions of the church was a friendly one. . . . I assume the editorship
> in a different climate. The last generation has been a disaster for
> anything like moderate confessionalism. And so our little journal
> has found itself much farther out on a limb and more critical for
> the Lutheran future than ever before. No longer a progressive
> gadfly to stodgy denominationalism, we now find ourselves at the
> head of the effort to reclaim any kind of confessionalist center in
> American Lutheranism.[7]

The increasing references to confessionalism and the confessions in the *Lutheran Forum* sought to provide a source of authority for ELCA Lutherans, particularly as writers made the claim that their church body had gone astray. The confessions' teachings, as found, for example, in the Augsburg Confession, conveyed basic Christian doctrine as well as Lutheran teachings on the gospel and the sacraments, providing a source of Lutheran identity to those unsure of their leaders' orthodoxy.

The *Lutheran Forum*'s decline in circulation from 5,200 in the late 1960s to about 3,200 in the mid-1990s illustrates how the magazine changed from a pan-Lutheran publication that covered a wide range of issues appealing to a broader range of Lutherans into a more polemical mouthpiece for self-defined evangelical catholics. The number of articles in the magazine written by or for laity also dropped sharply during this period. Only about 20 percent of the current subscribers to the *Lutheran Forum* are laypeople. When we consider that there are approximately sixteen thousand clergy in the ELCA and the Lutheran Church–Missouri Synod, we see that the ALPB's publications are reaching only about one-sixth of their potential clergy base.

From the 1960s to the late 1980s, the journal served as an open forum of contemporary American Lutheranism, discussing issues from a wide variety of perspectives. After that period, it highlighted a particular liturgical and confessional aspect of Lutheranism. The change could be seen even in the journal's advertising. Before 1988, the *Lutheran Forum* carried advertisements for books on a wide range of theological subjects—from liberation theology to popular evangelical titles. The scope was narrowed in the post-ELCA phase to books and other products in sync with evangelical catholic sensibilities. The signs of a stance in opposition to the ELCA stared out at the reader from almost every page of the *Lutheran Forum*.

Charges of the ELCA's apostasy, the influence of neopaganism, and preaching another gospel became commonplace in the journal's pages. It was not only that the bureaucracy was drastically losing the faith, critics wrote, but seminaries with their strong feminist programs and influence were also breathing in this air and becoming infected. A frequent target of *Lutheran Forum* writers was the church growth movement; they stressed that congregations involved in the effort to use contemporary music and discard the traditional liturgy were losing their Lutheran identity. The polemics reached a fever pitch with a sustained attack on Protestantism: the problem was not that Protestantism was distorted or had become apostate; rather, the problem was Protestantism itself and the way it cut itself off from catholic tradition to embrace individualism and freedom from any authority. Much of this critique dovetailed with Leonard Klein's indictment of the ELCA for its policy of paying for abortions in its clergy and employee health plan, as he charged that "real churches don't kill babies."[8]

This is not to say that the ALPB and evangelical catholics did not also have concrete ideas about denominational reform. Before the formation of the ELCA in 1988, both the *Lutheran Forum* and the *Forum Letter* devoted many articles to the future structure and ministries of the new denomination. In the years prior to and just after the merger, prominent evangelical catholics called for active involvement in the ELCA structure. Aside from discarding quotas and scaling down the bureaucracy, the most common proposal involved increasing the voting influence of bishops and clergy and decreasing the voting power of the laity to less than its 60-percent majority. The prevalent view of the writers was that majority voting and democratic procedures should not decide questions of doctrine and practice. In such matters, a magisterium or a central teaching authority consisting of bishops should be the ones to decide such crucial questions.

Before and after the merger in 1988, evangelical catholic critics also added that their proposals were driven not so much by the fear of the laity as by the realization that most of the lay delegates are selected by political criteria, such as quotas. Yet in the *Lutheran Forum* and other evangelical catholic strongholds, there is the common sentiment that the ELCA, and the Missouri Synod for that matter, are not going to be changed anytime soon by political means. Rather, reform will most likely take place in the parishes and, to a lesser extent, at the synod level.

In interviewing evangelical catholic pastors who support the ALPB, I found that their relationships with local leaders and bishops were often shaky, even in synods with orthodox and evangelical catholic bishops. ALPB Director Reverend Frederick Schumacher is engaged in a serious conflict with the Metropolitan New York Synod over a statement entitled "Reconciled in Christ" adopted at the synod's 1998 annual meeting. The statement called for acceptance of gays in all congregations. Schumacher publicly challenged the statement, saying it was imposing an agenda of gay rights and acceptance of homosexuality on the churches. Although he supports the document's call to love and minister to all people, including those with homosexual orientations, Schumacher said it divorced love from biblical teachings. He found little support for his protests and soon took another route: his congregation suspended giving to the synod and the ELCA, channeling money to orthodox Lutheran causes instead.

Another pastor said he has not been giving any money to the ELCA—either locally or nationally—for several years. Now he is taking a more radical step. He said he is opting out of the ELCA pension and health plan in order to protest the approval of abortion as an option in the denomination's health coverage. In April 1999, *Forum Letter* editor Russell Saltzmann wrote a short article giving readers details about how they could opt out of the ELCA health plan and transfer to the plan of a new smaller orthodox Lutheran denomination.

Congregations have commonly withheld funds from larger structures as a means of protest in American churches, both conservative and liberal. The trend dovetails with a more general pattern of decreased giving to benevolences outside of congregations, which is often interpreted as a sign of disenchantment with centralized leadership and bureaucracy in general among churches.

Alternative Voices

If the ALPB serves a smaller and more self-defined group of Lutherans today than it did before 1988, the organization and its publications also hold a greater value for participants and readers. The ALPB is unlike many renewal groups in that it doesn't have large lay and clergy memberships, regular meetings, and affiliated congregations. ALPB leaders intentionally sought to avoid fostering a party spirit, which would set evangelical catholics off as a definable camp within the church, separated from other Lutherans. The bureau acts as a clearinghouse and resource center where evangelical catholics can find the theological and pastoral support for their ministries and concerns about their denominations. This loose-fitting and modest role may not serve as much of a counter-cultural bulwark against the forces that evangelical catholics see as assailing their churches, but the flexible and ad hoc nature of the ALPB has its own strengths. As one pastor said in an interview, before the formation of the ELCA, he never read ALPB material. He was generally satisfied with the material and support he received from the American Lutheran Church. After the merger, however, he found the independent and critical voices in the ALPB and its publications—particularly the *Lutheran Forum*—a source of sustenance and encouragement.

The ALPB still does not hold a party line on Lutheranism aside from an adherence to confessional Lutheranism and the maintaining of the traditional liturgy. Some members of its seventeen-member board of directors see Lutheranism as a movement that should go out of existence and gradually merge with Catholicism or Eastern Orthodoxy. Others see the Lutheranism as a permanent fixture on the religious landscape, even if it celebrates intercommunion with other churches. Some may be strong supporters of a closer relationship with the Episcopal Church, including accepting the historic episcopate (the practice of consecrating bishops in a historic line of succession going back to the apostles); others are more critical of this ecumenical relationship.

The bureau publishes a full range of tracts on Lutheran basics, ecumenism, the confessions, sexual ethics, and liturgy in accessible language and style. The tract ministry was scaled down in the 1980s due to the similar publications published by the denominations and publishing houses. Today, however, more tracts are being issued, as evangelical catholics and other Lutherans have less confidence in ELCA-sponsored literature. It is not unusual to see a rack of tracts in evangelical catholic church vestibules, with ALPB material outnumbering ELCA and Missouri Synod literature.

The four-volume prayer book *For All the Saints* was often viewed by pastors as the most lasting legacy of the ALPB. Before the volumes came out, most evangelical catholic–inclined clergy would use Roman Catholic books that had daily prayers and readings according to the church calendar. The use of *For All the Saints* helped make formal daily prayer a more Lutheran phenomenon. It appears that the books got pastors praying more frequently, and that eventually spilled out into parish life. Daily prayer services, usually held in the morning, are increasingly held in evangelical catholic parishes, and the laity are starting to join in, according to Schumacher. The *Forum Letter* likewise serves as an alternative to the publications of ELCA and the Lutheran Church–Missouri Synod (LCMS). Both evangelical catholics and others concerned with the dominance of official publications in American Lutheranism appreciate this independent source of news.

One ELCA pastor in New York says: "The ALPB is a nuanced, sane, and balanced voice of the church. I read the *Lutheran Forum* and other publications without the cautionary red flags popping up when I read other things." Supporters of the ALPB repeatedly cite trustworthiness as the key feature of ALPB material and express a strong distrust of denominational material. Almost none of the clergy I interviewed distributed the ELCA's magazine, *The Lutheran*.

One pastor said he is "sheltering parishioners against the malarkey" by boycotting official publications, which he calls "propaganda." At the same time, he recommends ALPB material, especially the *Forum Letter,* to his members. The pastor, like other clergy and even ALPB officials, admits that the *Lutheran Forum*'s highly theological material may go over the heads of laypeople, but he is uncertain about making the magazine more accessible because he likes the theological challenges presented in its pages.

As a resource organization, the ALPB does not draw unqualified support from evangelical catholics. Pastor Anne, a suburban New York executive-turned-pastor, said she finds a disturbing tendency of some evangelical catholics gathered around the ALPB to state "official positions and not give people the other side of the issues. They seem too simplistic. What's at issue in a lot of things are pastoral [in nature]. You have to know where people are rather than just saying that something is totally wrong." She used the example of introducing laity to liturgy and other evangelical catholic practices. "We need to remember that we are dealing with God's people. Even if we feel strongly about something, we may have to backpedal and not force our agenda on people." Other Lutherans who call themselves evangelical catholics take a more liberal approach to theological and moral issues than do the editors of the *Lutheran Forum.* For instance, some congregations that identify themselves as evangelical catholic are also part of the Reconciled in Christ movement, which calls for the full inclusion of homosexuals in the church and its ministries.

Despite the sharp polemics and anti-ELCA position of many evangelical catholics that are associated with the ALPB, I found that the negativity was not being returned at church headquarters. "The evangelical catholics have an important part to play in the ELCA," the Reverend Randall Lee, executive assistant to the secretary of the ELCA, explained in one of the organization's conference rooms at its plush headquarters near O'Hare Airport in Chicago.[9] He sees the ELCA leadership as being "in dialogue" with the evangelical catholics gathered around the ALPB and the *Lutheran Forum.* Lee views the evangelical catholic influence running on a parallel track to, and in the opposite direction from, the church growth–seeker movement in the denominational leadership. The division is expressed in the more evangelical catholic influence found in the Division of Worship and the evangelical church growth influence in the ELCA's evangelism office. This means that whereas the evangelism offices may be providing material on contemporary and seeker services, the worship division may issue liturgical statements drawing on Roman Catholic and Anglican sources.

Lee acknowledges that the *Lutheran Forum*'s influence is powerful: its editors' stand against the concordat between the ELCA and the Episcopal Church was decisive in the defeat of that measure in 1997. Lee added that such measures as the 1999 Episcopal Church–ELCA concordat (endorsed by the *Lutheran Forum* editors and passed), the Lutheran-Catholic agreement on Justification by Faith in 1999, and an earlier ELCA document on liturgy and worship practices all serve to extend evangelical catholic influence. But Lee sees many evangelical catholics as overly romantic and naive about denominational realities in regard to some issues. For instance, many at the ALPB and the *Lutheran Forum* support the idea that the activities and statements of the various church offices should be subject to veto by voting delegates of the churchwide assembly, an idea that Lee calls "unrealistic."

It is also misleading to portray the ALPB as only a conservative renewal organization in American Lutheranism. In the Missouri Synod, the ALPB has served as a channel for protesting increasingly conservative policies, such as the enforcement of closed communion (allowing only Missouri Synod Lutherans to receive communion), restricted roles for women, and a curtailment of ecumenical involvement. Although the Missouri Synod has historically been congregational in government, President Alvin Barry increased the forces of centralization in the denomination during the 1990s, giving the executive office new powers of discipline and enforcement of teachings and policies. The ALPB also published the book *Different Voices, Shared Vision,* written by LCMS women calling for greater equality between the sexes in the church (though stopping short of support for women's ordination).[10] The ever-present desire for unity between LCMS and ELCA Lutherans is still a live issue for the ALPB, as demonstrated in past events bringing together leaders from both communions to speak at inter-Lutheran conferences.

A Priestly Society

"Though some of my fellow pastors may not share this view, I believe I was chosen and set apart for the ministry from birth," says Pastor Mark at his ELCA parish in a working-class neighborhood of Brooklyn. "He chose me to be Christ's representative on earth. On the date of my ordination, I ceased being a mister and became a pastor. I have to be a cut above the person in the pew," he added.

The high view of the ministry expressed by Pastor Mark is common among evangelical catholics. The condition and role of the clergy is a central concern among most conservative liturgical renewalists in the various denominations, who believe that the ministry is a high office set apart for preaching God's word and celebrating the sacraments. This emphasis on the clergy is the one reason the ALPB finds its main support among members of the clergy and also illuminates the founding of the Society of the Holy Trinity (STS for its Latin name)—one of the first religious orders for Lutheran pastors in North American history.

The STS emerged in Martin Luther–like fashion when evangelical catholics issued a document similar to their founder's ninety-five theses to the leadership of the ELCA in 1996. This time it was only the *9.5 Theses* and was drawn up by ELCA pastors in New Jersey to protest modern theological and ecclesiological trends in the church. The document attacked the use of inclusive language that obscures the traditional understandings of God and the Trinity, the growth of political activism and ideologies that take precedence over the spiritual mission of the church, the elevation of democratic procedure to replace the role of pastors and bishops in teaching the faith, the breakdown of liturgical order in the church, and called for a common liturgy.

The trigger for the formulation of the document was a proposal made at an assembly of the New Jersey Synod to study the possibility of using alternative formulas for the Holy Trinity, replacing the words *Father, Son, and Holy Spirit* with *Creator, Redeemer, and Sanctifier.* The trend of using inclusive language, including gender-neutral, feminine, and masculine imagery, had been growing in all the mainline churches. In this case, some pastors felt that resistance was necessary.

Unlike Luther's theses, the document did not cause much of an uproar in the church body it criticized. Newly elected ELCA presiding bishop George Anderson stated that the document's concerns were being addressed and that there was no need for its signers to meet with church leaders. Other church leaders ignored it, or charged its signers with being divisive and encouraging a tendency toward schism, said its organizer Reverend Phillip Johnson. He and other pastors became convinced that going the political route of confronting church leaders with problems in the larger structure would not be effective.

They called for a society that would support pastors in their struggle for theological, spiritual, and liturgical faithfulness to the Lutheran tradition. Started in 1996, the STS is modeled after the societies and other institutes for clergy in the Anglican and Catholic traditions that come into existence during a perceived period of crisis in churches. "They are regarded with skepticism at first but then are recognized by the church as serving a purpose," said Johnson, the head or senior of the STS.[11] Although the STS uses the *9.5 Theses* as its founding document, its cornerstone is its rule that requires members to engage in regular prayer, such as praying the divine office, including Matins (morning prayer), Vespers (evening prayer), and Compline (prayer at the close of the day). Other requirements include regular retreats, individual confession of sins, and mutual pastoral visitation.

The requirement of mutual pastoral visitation best illustrates the specific kind of clergy-based renewal the STS—and much of evangelical catholicism—promotes. A member will receive visits by other members or by the head of a local STS chapter. Such visits will bring up matters of personal accountability, confession, absolution, and other ministerial concerns. Johnson adds that such visitation "opens up a ministry of learning. The focus is on parish ministry." One leader of the STS in Chicago says the society provides members with a "moral theology. In seminary we learned about ethics, but not moral theology. We didn't learn about dealing with confidentiality in confession and practical things like that."

The growing theological pluralism within the ELCA and the conflicting agendas of the various special interest groups have left the clergy adrift, many STS members say. "The diversity in the ELCA has gone beyond diversity and is now incoherence,"

Johnson adds. Mutual pastoral visitation provides a means of oversight that members claim is in short supply in the official church structure of bishops and specialized ministries. "Bishops are supposed to be doing it, but they're not. Much of the work the bishop does in the ELCA is administrative," added Johnson. "Bishops are only bishops in name. They provide no spiritual care," said another STS member.

This alternative form of oversight and fellowship found in the STS is already having a practical effect in parish life. Parishes looking for an evangelical catholic, confessional pastor can turn to the STS for referrals about eligible candidates—and in the process, override the usual protocol of seeking the bishop's guidance on the matter. "This happens all the time. If a church is tied to Lutherans Concerned [the Lutheran gay rights organization], they try to get a pastor sympathetic to gay and lesbian concerns. It's a game everybody plays," said Johnson. The laity are also using the STS as a way of finding evangelical catholic, confessional congregations. For instance, a family would be referred by their home pastor to a fellow STS member pastor in the area to which they are relocating.

Although the STS, with some two hundred members, does not seek directly to address the volatile culture war issues, such as gay rights and abortion, that are embroiling the ELCA and other mainline bodies, deans of local STS chapters and Johnson himself have stepped into conflicts between member pastors and their bishops. For instance, when one synod passed a measure to encourage member congregations to join Lutherans Concerned, the STS expressed its support for a dissenting pastor. Randall Lee of the ELCA said the denominational leadership has two potential difficulties with the STS. First, mainly because of its inter-Lutheran character, the group has no definite mission (or apostolate) to a wider church body and could become isolated. Secondly, it could become a holding pen for disgruntled Lutherans railing against the ELCA or the Missouri Synod. Johnson admits that many current members see the STS as a last resort before they leave the Lutheran church altogether.

The STS seeks particularly to address the formation and character of the pastoral office. Johnson is troubled by the number of seminarians he has seen who view the ministry as a helping profession. Like the Anglicans, Roman Catholics, and Eastern Orthodox, evangelical catholics tend to view the ministry as a priestly calling that is distinct from the laity. Clergy in more Protestant settings see their calling in more functional terms. In practical terms, the more Protestant-oriented clergy may not wear their clerical garb when not in church on Sunday, whereas the catholic-oriented clergy would be more likely to do so. As the founding statement of the STS says, "When the distinctiveness of the Ministry of the Word and the sacraments is obscured by a culture-bound egalitarianism, by anti-clericalism, or by pastoral loss of nerve, then the training and work of pastors loses its focus and center."[12]

Catholic Altars, Protestant Pews?

In my interviews with clergy, I found that those who were brought up in the Lutheran church said they always considered Lutheranism as a liturgical church that had more in common with Roman Catholic rather than Protestant worship and teachings. Those who converted said they adopted the church because of the liturgy and catholic identity of Lutheranism.

Take the case of Pastor Wayne, age forty-seven. He grew up in the Wesleyan Church, which is an evangelical church stressing the born-again experience and preaching. During high school, he wrote a report on Martin Luther and the Reformation, and he became curious about the Lutheran Church. "When I attended a Lutheran service, I thought the liturgy was catholic. Someone from a pietist background could see that this was obvious." For Wayne, reading the *Lutheran Forum* and such evangelical catholic theologians as Arthur Carl Piepkorn reinforced this view of Lutheranism.

Pastor Joseph was brought up in the Roman Catholic Church. But he sensed an inflexibility, an attitude of "it's my way or the highway," that led him to consider leaving the church. He also had problems with the Protestant churches he attended. "Any opinion seemed to count. There was nothing that held them together [except] the pastor." He investigated both the Episcopal Church and the Lutheran tradition because they both retained a sacramental and catholic approach to worship and doctrine. He finally decided to join the Lutherans because they "were more precise about things. The confessions, such as the Book of Concord, spelled out norms and standards."

History bears out the close affinity clergy have for liturgical renewal. In his historical study of the Church of England, sociologist John Shelton Reed finds that one of the reasons the high church Anglo-Catholic revival (another name for the Oxford movement) swept through nineteenth-century Britain was its appeal to the young clergy. During this period the clergy's secular influence and importance were decreasing due to the growing availability of higher education and the professions for educated young men. The rituals and lofty nature of the Anglo-Catholic priesthood rehabilitated the status of this calling from one that was simply based on preaching and lecturing. In restoring the confessional, the priests' central function in consecrating the Eucharist, and other priest-led Catholic sacramental practices, the Oxford movement gave these young clergy a "view of the priesthood as a calling like medicine or the law, with its own special (indeed, divinely ordered) authority and abilities."[13]

The emphasis on the importance of the pastoral office found among evangelical catholics and other conservative liturgical reformers today comes during a period of similar change and upheaval. The therapeutic and feminist revolutions have challenged and changed fundamental tenets of the ministry. Training in concepts and techniques drawn from therapy and the helping professions puts the accent on clergy meeting the individual's personal needs rather than on administering the mysteries of a holy and transcendent God. The influence of feminism and women clergy in general on the churches has challenged traditional hierarchical notions of congregational leadership (though there are women clergy in the ranks of evangelical catholics).

The presence of women clergy in congregations has tended to expand the role of the laity; this in turn allows decision making based more on relationships than on leadership from above. To go against these strong currents in ministry will be difficult, and this may be a reason why such an order as the STS was deemed necessary. Such groups provide a counterculture in which more traditional styles of ministry are preserved and cultivated.

The opening account about Pastor Hannah of Trinity Lutheran Church in the Bronx and his work in promoting the adult catechumenate also illustrates the difference between clergy and laity when it comes to evangelical catholic reform. Pastor Hannah stressed the value of the adult catechumenate as establishing new Christians and new church members in the rhythms of the liturgical year. Church member and lay leader Maria, however, emphasized the way the catechumenate made new members feel welcome and provided them with mentoring and individual attention. These views, though not necessarily contradictory, suggest that the laity view liturgical and confessional renewal in more pragmatic rather than theological terms. This clergy-laity gap was pronounced on several issues.

Only a small minority of the laity I interviewed had knowledge of the evangelical catholic criticisms and concerns about the ELCA or the Missouri Synod. It was not that the members disagreed with their pastors on various issues, but rather that they had not thought much about the national expressions of their denominations. Most said they rarely heard their pastors speak about their denominations; they came to their conclusions about such matters as gay rights, quotas, and feminism only after I pointed out church statements on these issues. This may seem surprising, given the fervent protests and criticisms of these denominations by evangelical catholic clergy. But most of the pastors admitted that even though they may publicly criticize the ELCA or the Missouri Synod in church gatherings and in print, they rarely bring these concerns into the pulpit on Sunday mornings or even discuss them in adult education programs.

"I have a passion to preach the gospel and administer the sacraments. I never wanted to use the worship service as a setting to be wrestling with these church issues. It may be that I've taken the cowardly path of not talking [about such matters]," says one pastor in Chicago. It may be part of the ethos of evangelical catholics that they do not bring up the more political and divisive denominational issues, given their concern about the primacy of worship and the spiritual mission of the church.

The small minority who did speak of these issues came from parishes where pastors were more outspoken or were educated in theology themselves. Cynthia, a businesswoman in her forties, was introduced to the ALPB and the effort to renew Lutheranism when she was a delegate to the synod convention of the Lutheran Church in America, a predecessor denomination of the ELCA. Although Cynthia found the large worship services inspiring, she was dismayed that a liberal political agenda dominated the proceedings. "I didn't think the church should be advocating on either side of an issue like nuclear disarmament. It seemed that people were using the church to advance their own political position."

The ALPB had a table at the convention hall, and Cynthia found their literature "very sensible," in that it criticized such a social agenda by the church. Never enthusiastic about the formation of the ELCA, Cynthia became more negative about the state of the denomination after serving as a delegate at one of the national conventions. "Anything that suggested that we were Lutheran was [replaced] by the need to be inclusive; I mean there were Shinto dancers! There didn't seem to be any strong leadership. Everyone's opinion counted equally—whether it was an Indian who had been Lutheran a few months or a professor from the seminary. Even the bishops didn't want to be seen as leaders. They did a great job of it too. They acted more like they were at the Kiwanis Club. I wasn't in awe of them at all."

Most of the pastors I interviewed readily admit that they have met and continue to meet resistance on the liturgical changes they have introduced into parishes. When I asked one pastor whether I might interview some of his parishioners, he sharply discouraged it. The members would have no understanding of my questions about liturgy and sacraments, let alone evangelical catholicism. Although he had been at the church three years, he said it would "take many years of modeling" for his parishioners to catch on to an evangelical catholic sensibility. "The weekly Eucharist is where it hit the road," he said about his arrival at the "run-of-the-mill" Missouri Synod Lutheran church. "There was a group that would sit it out and not commune." Parishioners would later comment to him after sermons that it was the first time they heard preaching about the sacraments being integral to the Christian life.

The struggles that pastors cited ranged from conflicts about introducing weekly communion to the presence of the paschal candle, the candle lit during the Easter season to symbolize Christ's resurrection. Pastors sought to acclimate parishioners to these changes through a gradual process of education and preaching on evangelical catholic themes. One church I visited featured regular messages in the bulletin pointing out the nuances of observance of the liturgy and the church calendar. As my interviews with the laity suggest, even when liturgical renewal is fully implemented in churches, there is often a gap between clergy and laity in their views on the importance of such rituals.

Take the case of Mary, an eighty-three-year-old member of a leading evangelical catholic parish in New York. She was baptized in the church and fondly recalls when it was in the center of a thriving German neighborhood, an area that is now cosmopolitan and highly pluralistic. Mary remembers a different church too. Aside from a much larger congregation, there was little of the "fanfare" that marks worship at the church today. The minister wore a plain black gown, and "it was a simple service with a sermon; I was raised on that. Communion was once a month. As long as you went up [to receive communion] once a year, you were still a member in good standing." All that changed in the 1970s when an evangelical catholic pastor arrived at the church. "Liturgy became more important than the sermon," Mary said.

When communion was celebrated every week, she and other members at first "resented it. I hesitated about it. But then when everyone around you went up to receive and you were the only one seated there, you did it too. Now it's a tradition." Yet Mary still finds herself more comfortable with a low church service based around the sermon. If she had to relocate, she said she might even join a Baptist church. "The Baptists lean to the old-fashioned style. It's more simple. All I ask is that a church sticks to the word of God."

Jack and Eileen are a couple in their sixties who have been deeply involved in church and denominational affairs since their youth. Jack took a leadership role in committees and organizations in his local church and in Lutheran men's organizations on a national level. But their involvement in their small ELCA congregation in southern New Jersey has become more problematic since a new evangelical catholic pastor arrived. She introduced a number of changes that bother Jack and Eileen and some other members, both young and old. In contrast to the laid-back informal services they were accustomed to, more liturgy and weekly communion at all services have become the rule.

The new pastor encourages the congregation to make the sign of the cross; she had planned to dispense ashes on Ash Wednesday until she met with protests from members. "Having communion every service cheapens it. It becomes rote, once it becomes a habit.

You don't think about what it means. It's all these ceremonial and symbolic things—the robes and liturgies. Now some churches are calling their service Masses. It's catering to the Catholics," Eileen says. Both are particularly troubled by the undemocratic way that these innovations have been brought into the life of the congregation. "They're trying to make all the churches alike. It's pressure from above," Jack said of the regional synod of the ELCA.

Those more receptive to evangelical catholic renewal—such as commitment to the sacraments and the liturgy—often received their initial exposure to Christianity in such liturgical settings. The dramatic conversion stories of John and Emily are something of an oddity in Lutheran parishes, but their receptivity to many evangelical catholic practices and teachings may be more typical. John, thirty-nine, was born Catholic but said he never absorbed much of the faith during his childhood and youth. Emily, thirty-five, was a cradle member of the Lutheran Church but during her early years only attended sporadically. Both got heavily involved in drinking and drugs during the 1970s and 1980s. When they married and became parents, they made repeated attempts to get off alcohol and drugs.

"I was a crack head and began to realize I couldn't do it on my own. I remember pulling my car off the road and falling on my knees. I needed someone stronger than myself," Emily said. The couple turned to the local Lutheran church for help. "We liked how it was part of the community, like in having a food pantry. When you asked questions [of the pastor], you got answers," John said. Today, they view receiving communion frequently as important and the liturgy as preserving the faith of the early church. "Receiving communion is a cleansing. Once a week, I'm getting God into me. We're more Catholic than Protestant. Martin Luther was a Catholic priest. Lutherans put Jesus first, while [Roman] Catholics added a lot of laws. So the Reformation reformed Catholicism and brought it back to the Bible and the fathers of the church."

The account of Lucille, a fifty-five-year-old homemaker who belongs to the same church as Eileen and Jack, is probably more common among those who have resonated to the teachings and practices of the evangelical catholic movement. She grew up in a Lutheran church and always appreciated liturgy as compared to an informal, casual service. Lucille was happy with the changes the new pastor made in the services, since it made the church "less pastor-centered. We didn't just sit there and observe, but participated in the liturgy." She is referring to the new roles that laity have in the liturgy in the ELCA—such as assisting ministers, deacons, and lectors who read the scripture lessons during worship. She adds that the "Word" (or the sermon) and the sacrament should not be separated, and she welcomed the change to receiving communion at every service.

The restructuring of the liturgy along more Roman Catholic lines—such as chanting the liturgy, the commemoration of the saints, and even making the sign of the cross—has an ecumenical meaning for Lucille. "There are a lot of people who grew up Catholic in the church and maybe seeing us making the sign of the cross makes them feel more comfortable." On commemorating the saints, Lucille said, "It's important to know that there are examples of the faith for us and that [they] didn't have to be Lutheran. The liturgy incorporates all of us into worship. It's important for all Christians to have a common bond."

Matthew, a forty-four-year-old New York investment analyst, grew up in the Wisconsin Evangelical Lutheran Synod, a strongly conservative denomination that forbids fellowship with other Lutheran churches, not to mention non-Lutheran denominations. Matthew eventually became involved in planting a Wisconsin Synod congregation in New York. When that project fell through, he gravitated to an evangelical catholic ELCA parish. He was used to a less liturgical and sacramental form of Lutheranism; where Matthew grew up, the minister wore a black gown, and parishioners would never cross themselves or use kneelers, because they were considered too "Roman Catholic." But he started studying the liturgy and church history and found that Lutheranism "was part of the Western Catholic tradition." Today, he feels that his church's link to other historic communions, such as Roman Catholicism and Eastern Orthodoxy, has made his faith "more universal and less provincial" in contrast to his Wisconsin Synod beginnings.

Throughout my interviews, it was evident that even though evangelical catholic practices may become accepted as traditions in a church, members do not necessarily understand or agree with the theological underpinnings that pastors provide. Cynthia, the businesswoman who has also been involved with the ALPB, says that there is a split between the pastors who have strong catholic attachments and sensibilities and laypeople who define themselves as Protestant. Although she supports the ALPB and evangelical Catholic efforts at reform, she sees some evangelical catholics as "[Roman] Catholic wanna-bes. There's nothing wrong with the Lutheran tradition. We don't need to become more Roman Catholic or Eastern Orthodox. We just have to be Lutheran."

One Chicago ELCA pastor says that for many cradle Lutherans, evangelical catholic practices have an "added-on quality." He cites one example of his older parishioners who have ties to the Moody Bible Institute, an institution preaching conservative evangelical Christianity. They have not forsaken their evangelical past and piety but have come to a new appreciation of weekly communion in their congregation.

Will the Last Evangelical Catholic Leaving Turn Out the Lights?

Despite the Advent wreaths, candles, rich red carpeting, incense, and chanting, there was a melancholy undertone running through the service at Immanuel Lutheran Church in New York that December evening in 1998. The event commemorated the twenty-fifth anniversary of the death of Arthur Carl Piepkorn, the leading Lutheran scholar who to a large degree launched the evangelical catholic movement in the United States. The service brought together Piepkorn's former students from Concordia Seminary in St. Louis, Missouri, and others who were deeply influenced by his writings and teaching. As one hears often among evangelical catholics, the preacher lamented that "fifteen years ago it seemed that we had won the day" in Lutheranism. But things had changed by 1998. In fact, the gathering could have been mistaken for a meeting of Lutherans in recovery.

The main speaker was Robert Wilken, a leading historian of Christianity who converted from Lutheranism to Roman Catholicism a few years ago. Another speaker was prominent theologian Richard John Neuhaus, a Lutheran pastor (and past editor of the ALPB's *Forum Letter*) turned Catholic priest. The celebrant and preacher for the night was yet another newly minted Catholic who was until recently the longtime pastor at Immanuel. A respondent to the lecture was a pastor of a parish where the assistant had become an Eastern Orthodox priest. The roll call of ex-Lutherans was not confined to the clergy. The Reverend Gregory Fryer, pastor of Immanuel, later told me that three key lay leaders of the congregation had recently become Roman Catholics.

Conversion to Roman Catholicism and to Eastern Orthodoxy has become fairly common in evangelical catholic circles. Several of the contributors and editorial associates of the *Lutheran Forum* and ALPB have converted, including three prominent woman pastors. Jaroslav Pelikan, the renowned Yale University historian of Christianity, had only a year earlier converted to Eastern Orthodoxy. The reason many of these individuals give for having sought a new church home often touches on the view that the ELCA has drifted beyond the point of renewal. Official church structures gave no support to maintaining an evangelical catholic identity, these converts argue, whereas the Roman and Eastern churches have maintained their catholic structure, teachings, and authority.

When Neuhaus converted in 1991, he even went so far as to say that the Reformation had run its course. The reforms of Vatican II and subsequent changes—teaching the priesthood of all believers, and a greater emphasis on grace rather than works in salvation—signified that the concerns posed by Martin Luther had found a hearing and even a following in Rome. In this view, the place for evangelical catholics was now in uppercase Catholicism. The departures bring to mind those of the Oxford movement in the nineteenth century, when under the leadership of theologian John Henry Newman a steady stream of young men left the Church of England to embrace Roman Catholicism.

As we will see throughout this book, renewal and reform movements often have a high rate of turnover and defection. Much of this leave-taking is not difficult to understand. When reformers' and renewalists' efforts to enact changes in the larger structure are met with repeated setbacks, frustration sets in, sometimes even among the most committed. There comes a point when the reformer eventually looks around and sizes up the gains and potential gains of his or her toil and decides whether it is worth the effort in the long run. As one Lutheran pastor who had become an Eastern Orthodox priest said, "It was the problem of being a minority.

You have to raise kids and pass on the faith. It's [difficult] to perpetuate that kind of Lutheranism."

Discovering Conservative Ecumenism

That service at Immanuel Church, however, also demonstrated the new kind of ecumenism found in many renewal movements today. It was only a few decades ago that Lutherans or Episcopalians converting to Catholicism said goodbye not only to their churches but also to their colleagues and, in some cases, their friends and families. The thought of an ex-Lutheran Catholic convert preaching or leading prayer in a Lutheran service would have been considered scandalous then—by both Lutheran and Catholic. Even if laypeople were unfamiliar with many of the evangelical catholic positions, they now appreciate the sense of closeness to other churches that they have found in following a common church calendar, commemorating the saints from other traditions and gaining an appreciation of the width of the catholic tradition.

It may be argued that this sort of ecumenism goes only in one direction—toward the Anglican, Catholic, and Orthodox churches—and away from other Christian traditions that are less liturgical. It is true that most evangelical catholics feel more at home with other liturgical Christians; this is evident in the ALPB's lack of involvement with other types of evangelical renewal groups. But the evangelical catholics also attempt to mine other traditions for their catholic elements. For instance, the 1997 "full communion" agreement with the Presbyterian and Reformed churches was dismissed out of hand by only a few pastors I interviewed. Most said that there are catholic tendencies and even movements in the Reformed denominations that they would gladly approve. The catholic factor thus serves an ecumenical function that compels evangelical catholic Lutherans to venture beyond denominational boundaries to establish new, and often ad hoc, bonds of fellowship and unity with other Christians.

The most obvious example of this is the closeness between Missouri Synod and ELCA evangelical catholics. Even though the official denominations show few signs of rapprochement, it is very difficult to tell ELCA and Missouri Synod evangelical catholics apart (apart from the latter's prohibition of women pastors). The types of ecumenical involvement among evangelical catholic parishes are of the informal variety. One ELCA church on Long Island holds joint retreats and prayer services with the neighboring Eastern Orthodox parish and has close association with a nearby Missouri Synod parish. This ELCA parish has little to do with two nearby churches in the same synod, mainly because they have contemporary services and are influenced by the church growth movement. Another pastor in his early forties would like to see evangelical catholics accepted as a new order in Roman Catholicism. "We should busy ourselves for this particular destiny [of being an order within the Catholic Church]. If you look back at church history, you'll see other examples of this, such as the Franciscans or Dominicans," the pastor said.

These pastors represent a younger generation of evangelical catholics who often find closer bonds of unity with Roman Catholics, Orthodox, and Anglicans than with fellow Lutherans. The older generation (those over fifty) tend to believe that there will most likely always be an orthodox Lutheran church, even if it is no longer in the ELCA. The *Lutheran Forum* now has Roman Catholic and Eastern Orthodox priests as ecumenical advisors. The ALPB has recently become more active in ecumenism in its association with the Center for Evangelical and Catholic Theology, based in Northfield, Minnesota. That organization issues the journal *Pro-Ecclesia*—which is published and distributed by the ALPB—and holds conferences on a wide range of subjects, from reform of the papacy to biblical interpretation. The center serves as a think tank for this new kind of ecumenism, drawing together evangelicals, Catholics, Orthodox, Lutherans, and other mainline Protestants who look to the "great tradition" of the church built around the early ecumenical creeds and liturgy as providing the model for theology and Christian life.

The Future of Liturgical and Confessional Renewal

"I've been at this for thirty-four years, and it's getting harder every year," said Pastor Schumacher seemingly out of nowhere during my interview with him about the ALPB. "Now people are out shopping for churches, looking for music that we just can't do. How do you instill a sense of the Lutheran tradition to younger generations, the liturgy, the beautiful music?" Schumacher was touching on a problem shared by others attempting to renew religious bodies and congregations based on retrieving traditions and historic doctrine and creeds. Americans are increasingly shopping for faith based on practical matters like child care, music, and the quality of a pastor's sermons; meanwhile, they ignore denominational concerns and doctrine.

The evangelical catholics gathered around the ALPB and the STS, as well as most other confessional renewalists, would be the first to admit the problems they have in extending their influence in their denominations. When one asks these renewalists about the future of these organizations in their denominations, the answers are far from upbeat. Many see increasing marginalization and opposition of their ministries; some may well be planning escape to greener pastures, even as they express allegiance to their current tradition and congregations.

One remedy for this alienation is to follow the decentralizing example of the Biblical Witness Fellowship and encourage new informal and formal networks of association. When Paul Hinlicky was editor of the *Lutheran Forum* during the stormy years of the early 1990s, he urged the formation of an ecumenical alternative synod that would gather together orthodox believers of a catholic orientation from many denominations. Even if such a synod were not to become a separate church, he wrote, Lutherans should treat their own "denominational machinery as lacking ecclesial density, as nothing more than a mechanism for pensions, charity and other necessary temporal goods and services."[14]

In the ELCA, the commitment to quotas and the policy of inclusiveness makes it difficult for those who come from outside this system to make significant changes or form new caucuses with wide influence. The Missouri Synod is run on more democratic procedures, but the growing centralization of a conservative leadership leaves little room for renewal organizations and clergy and laity to work for changes. Because renewal organizations are, by their very makeup, more extreme or single-minded in their agenda than pluralistic and pragmatic denominations, they are sometimes viewed as a threat by leaderships.

But from a historical perspective, the evangelical catholic effect in Lutheranism is impressive. The once-unusual practice of weekly communion in American Lutheranism has spread to many ELCA congregations—whether or not they call themselves evangelical catholic or agree with the opinions expressed in the *Lutheran Forum*. Approximately 25 percent of ELCA congregations now have weekly communion. With the broad use of texts such as the *Lutheran Book of Worship* (LBW) and, for the Missouri Synod, *Lutheran Worship,* the evangelical catholic vision is no longer the province of any one group or tradition. Other innovations such as the observance of the Easter vigil, inner-city parish ministries, and ecumenical relations with Roman Catholicism and Eastern Orthodoxy have also spread far beyond the evangelical catholic borders within which they emerged.

Under the editorship of Ronald Bagnall, the *Lutheran Forum* appears to be entering a less polemical phase, with the majority of articles addressing liturgical and theological concerns rather than critiquing denominational policy and teachings (although the *Forum Letter* still focuses on these issues). Now that several of its editors have strongly supported and helped bring to fruition the 1999 ELCA concordat with the Episcopal Church, it is not difficult to imagine the evangelical catholics finding a more favorable position in the church, at least on matters of liturgy and ecumenism, if not on confessional doctrine and ethics.

Other conservative liturgical renewal groups have exerted a significant influence in their church bodies. The Anglo-Catholic wing of the Episcopal Church has introduced liturgies and practices, such as weekly communion and Easter vigils, that are now an integral part of parishes far from high church. The more sacramental and liturgical wing of the Presbyterian Church (USA) introduced a service book that follows historic liturgies in stressing the sacraments and the church calendar. Of course, many of these developments took place because liturgical reformers had influence over a long period of time in their denominations—something that evangelical catholics, Anglo Catholics, and others say they no longer have in their current church situations. It could be that these conservative liturgical and confessional renewalists win many battles within their traditions but ultimately lose the war; they do not gain predominant influence in their leaderships.

The attempt to return denominations to their confessional roots faces a number of obstacles, particularly in the mainline traditions. The pluralism of beliefs and theologies in mainline bodies suggests that no single overreaching theology will define mainline denominations in the future. The growth of special interest groups and caucuses both within and on the periphery of denominational life will work against unity and a strong sense of connectedness among members.

Religious experience, ranging from having a born-again conversion to finding enlightenment through meditation, is increasingly what draws seekers to congregations and regular spiritual practice. Traditional doctrines and confessions often take a backseat to the feelings of mystery and awe that ancient forms of worship such as the Roman Catholic Latin Mass or the poetic and majestic liturgy of the Anglican Book of Common Prayer provide. But those drawn to these mystical experiences may eventually seek out the teachings and doctrine behind the rituals, as evidenced in the growth of conservative Catholic religious orders as well as conversions to Eastern Orthodoxy and Orthodox Judaism.

In fact, recent research suggests that church members respond favorably to congregations with a strong denominational identity. Sociologist Nancy Ammerman and a team of researchers from Hartford Seminary, Hartford, Connecticut, found that 55 percent of congregations consider themselves "strong standard-bearers of their denominational heritage." These congregations consciously try to highlight denominational doctrines and traditions to create religious identities for their members; cradle members rather than those not born into these traditions are usually the most receptive. Ammerman found a high rate of denominational identification among the Lutherans, Episcopalians, Catholics, and others with strong liturgical and ethnic heritages.[15]

The conservative liturgical and theological renewalists have the resources to address the widespread hunger for roots and community in America. As much as the evangelical catholics and others may want to distance themselves from the consumeristic, experiential tendency of today's religious seekers, their liturgical services and stress on the sacraments bearing the presence of God speak to the seekers' spiritual needs. Of course, the liturgical and sacramental religious elements do not appeal to all church members and could be a stumbling block of conflict and controversy as much as a channel of spiritual revitalization. As we have seen from the interviews, some people view the concentration on the liturgy and ritual as a distraction from evangelism and the practical reality of living the Christian life.

Such dissenters feel that new liturgical practices, however historic or orthodox they were intended to be, are being imposed on them without their consent. Just as most of the evangelical catholic clergy were drawn to liturgy early in their lives, many of the laity who are opposed or indifferent to liturgical renewal were raised on less formal modes of worship. Because liturgical renewal in parishes most often moves from the top down, flowing from the liturgically trained pastor and assisting ministers to the untutored laity often raised on a different kind of piety, its progress will continue to be difficult and slow. But in order for confessional and liturgical renewal to survive and prosper, its teachings and sensibility must find a place among the laity.

Evangelical catholic Lutherans and others of a similar persuasion have come to the conclusion that it is easier and more edifying to concentrate on fellowship and cooperation with like-minded believers wherever they find them and to nurture their own congregations than to expend resources and energy in attempting to reform denominational structures. Although the evangelical catholics and other conservative liturgical and theological renewalists are opposed to theological and liturgical pluralism, believing it compromises the concern for truth and unity, they may be forced to make peace with this new diversity. John Shelton Reed writes that the early Anglo Catholics seriously sought a unified and orthodox "Catholic" Church of England. But the doctrinal pluralism sanctioned in the Church of England eventually worked to protect the Anglo Catholics from an imposed uniformity that would be at their expense and provided toleration for their distinctive practices and beliefs.[16]

In the same way, the new pluralism, with all of its problems, can create the space for alternative institutions, like the ALPB and the STS, to flourish and present their own visions for renewal of the wider church. Of course, religious pluralism is difficult to defend as a theological virtue in most congregations and denominations—a matter we will explore in the conclusion of this book.

4

The Quiet Revival
Taizé

The first Taizé service I attended opened with a recording of French chants, which I later learned were sung by the brothers of the Taizé community in France. It was difficult to know actually when the service started, though refrains of songs and chants sung by the twenty people present cued me in that something was going on. These songs were simple in lyric and melody but also poignant and striking—maybe because the verses were often repeated. A verse such as "Lord, be our light in the darkness" repeated about twenty times tends to stay in the memory.

The room was dark and shimmering with the lights of candles illuminating an icon of the cross up front. We heard no sermon or announcements. The songs and chants were interspersed with scripture readings and followed by a long period of silent prayer. Spoken prayer petitions were voiced spontaneously; some of the participants then knelt around the cross and lit candles. After more chanting and singing, some participants filed out of the room, while others remained in silence. When the recording of the French Taizé brothers began again, I guessed the service was over and made my exit.

After my time with the evangelical catholics and their tendency to engage in deep theological discussion, coming upon the Taizé services was a culture shock. Where the Lutherans are highly articulate about their faith, the Taizé services are marked by silence. Where theological differences are played up and vigorously argued among the evangelical catholics and other evangelical believers, the sharp edges of conflicting beliefs and practices are softened in

Taizé. Culture war issues, such as abortion, feminism, and gay rights, are not openly addressed in Taizé services.

Part of this peacefulness is due to the open-ended and noninstitutional approach of the Taizé community; one does not find the investment of years and money that members put into congregations or the tensions between clergy and laity that mark ordinary congregational life. There are no membership rolls (except for membership in the monastic order in France); there is no bureaucracy in the organization. Taizé is an example of how renewal and reform efforts do not necessarily have to be the sole province of highly organized movements. Taizé remains what it was started as almost sixty years ago: a monastic community for both Protestants and Catholics that has a special ministry with young adults. Without borrowing notes from church growth specialists, the community has managed to tap into the decentralized and postmodern mind-set of many congregations, clergy, and laypeople in the religious marketplace in the United States. Taizé does not want to change denominational structures or even congregations. Rather, it does its work of renewal by creating spaces of prayer, silence, and reflection on spiritual and social concerns within existing institutions and then letting that new source of spiritual vitality influence and inspire others.

Ecumenical Monasticism

Taizé may be distinctive now for its blend of monastic piety and youth appeal, but it was one of many new religious communities that emerged from the Protestant churches in the period after World War II. Like similar groups such as Iona in Scotland and the Evangelical Sisterhood of Mary in Germany, it was influenced by a liturgical renewal that sought to recapture monastic life, sacramental worship, and the disciplines of meditation and contemplation that had been obscured by Protestant opposition to these Catholic practices since the Reformation. Monastic life in particular, with its practice of celibacy and isolation from the outside society, for centuries aroused popular suspicions and accusations of fostering elitism and a spiritual class system.

The Protestant teaching on the priesthood of all believers was often interpreted to mean that religious orders and monasteries were detrimental to vital faith because they taught that only the elect members of these groups could attain Christian perfection. Monasticism was accused of giving the sacraments and silent contemplation more priority than the preached word. Protestants held that all work and occupations could be vocations, ways of serving God; thus, isolating oneself in a monastery was unnecessary. It was only centuries later that some theologians and church leaders gained the distance from the heated battles of the Reformation to reconsider some of these practices that had been discarded in the effort to purify the faith.

Taizé's founder, Brother Roger Schutz, was instrumental in fostering this rethinking on monasticism that was to gain a place in Protestant churches. He was born in Switzerland into a devout Protestant family in 1915. The conflicts and hopelessness of World War II convinced Schutz that the Christian life should be a continual process of reconciliation with other people. He left Switzerland in 1940 at the age of twenty-five to settle in France, where the war was raging. It was in the French town of Taizé that he felt led to start a community, as well as to help in resistance efforts. In 1949, he and several other men who had been attracted to Schutz's vision of a community, made lifelong monastic commitments to celibacy, acceptance of the leadership of the prior, and sharing material and spiritual goods. Brother Roger saw the order as embodying a "parable of community"—a phrase that is central to Taizé's identity.[1] By living and worshipping in this community, he hoped to create a model of how the church and the world itself should be—a global community.

Although the first brothers were from Protestant churches, Roman Catholics increasingly joined. Brother Roger found his order in the middle of strong criticism and opposition. The Roman Catholic Church opposed the Protestant leadership of the group; Protestants condemned the adoption of what had come to be seen as Catholic practices—monasticism, celibacy, contemplative prayer—as well as the ecumenical openness to Catholicism. Brother Roger tried to break out of the restraints of historic Protestant-Catholic animosities, although he seemed to find the most inspiration (for example, in monasticism and frequent observance of communion) in the Catholic tradition.[2]

Taizé was soon in the vanguard of ecumenical progress. The community became a meeting place of church leaders from

Catholic and Protestant traditions years before ecumenical organizations, such as the World Council of Churches, brought these
traditions together. The advent of the Second Vatican Council was
an important event in the life and identity of Taizé. Brother Roger
was an advisor and guest of the council, and he saw the event as
embodying many of the teachings and principles that marked his
community. The community was adamant that members retain
their membership in their respective churches and bring the
strengths of their traditions into the order; Taizé has always maintained that it was not starting another church or even a movement
that paralleled other churches.

Beyond the Monastery Walls

Before the late 1960s, Taizé consisted of the community of brothers
praying and worshipping in a small Romanesque church. Occasionally, they welcomed a handful of people from the region for
retreats. By the efforts of work camps of volunteers, the order
expanded its building to include several bedrooms. The brothers
had been noticing a steady stream of young visitors, and in 1966
they started convening youth events. These meetings drew ever-
larger crowds from a wide spectrum of people, with visitors from
forty-two nations by the late 1960s. Most visitors were between the
ages of eighteen and twenty, and the numbers of participants at
the meetings had reached eighteen hundred.[3]

At a time of growing crises involving youth around the world—
student unrest and protests over the Vietnam War in the United
States and violence in the Middle East and Europe—Taizé began
to recognize its special ministry. In 1968, the community opened
a Council of Youth that was intended to create new lines of communication and dialogue with youth on moral and spiritual questions. With this vague mission and an admittedly improvisational
nature, small groups of people in the council gathered around the
Taizé community met to discuss and pray about a way to present
and live the gospel to the world. The council was not limited to
those who visited Taizé.

Brothers and participants began spreading the Taizé message
outside of the walls of the French monastery. Their advice to pilgrims and others interested in taking the spirit of Taizé outward

was simple: start cultivating an "inner life" through prayer and contemplation and then become a "sign of contradiction" to the world by practicing reconciliation between different people, working for unity and nonviolence, and battling injustice.[4] Pope John Paul II adopted the phrase "sign of contradiction" as a theme of his papacy and has borrowed other concepts from the community.

The growing gap between the rich and the poor, between the Northern and Southern Hemispheres, became a prominent area of concern to Taizé. The community's theme of reconciliation and peace between Christians spilled beyond the monastery's walls to become a message of world peace and justice, although Taizé itself did not provide a specific platform or agenda. Nevertheless, Taizé's social conscience was in line with the progressive social action outlined by the optimistic post–Vatican II Catholic Church and, to a lesser extent, the World Council of Churches and the emerging theologies of liberation.

"We have been born into a world which for most people is not a fit place to live," intoned a letter from the youth council. "A large part of mankind is exploited by a minority enjoying intolerable privileges. Many police-states exist to protect the powerful. Multinational companies impose their own laws. Profit and money rule. Those in power almost never pay attention to those who are voiceless."[5] Brother Roger and other members of the community traveled to Asia, Africa, and Latin America with delegations of young people to live with the poor and engage in dialogues and encounters with the indigenous people. Small celebrations were organized around the world by people involved with Taizé, and local churches explored the connections between spiritual practice and social action.

Such living examples of social and spiritual reconciliation were called by the brothers the "church of the future"—living the gospel among the poorest and most neglected and attempting to "talk of hope without seeming to consent to a passive resignation or a fanatical activism."[6] By the late 1970s, there was concern by people outside the community that Taizé would be seen as competing or overshadowing the work of established churches and their social ministries; thus it was emphasized that all these cell groups and initiatives were not supposed to use the name *Taizé* or the designation *Council of Youth* and should eventually meld into existing initiatives in local churches. By this time, many Taizé brothers had left the community in France—at least temporarily—and established communities (or fraternities, as they are called) in several poor areas of the world. The brothers have resided in tin huts in Africa, on refugee boats in China, and in a ghetto in New York as part of their vision of sharing the suffering of the poor.

Brother Roger did not so much expect to turn out a cadre of young activists as to set up what he called a "community of communities" that modeled reconciliation and unity for the wider society. The effect of such communities would not be limited to youth because they would encourage an "encounter between the generations . . . [where the] particular gifts of each age group [could] be brought to light."[7] In other words, the church had to put itself in order and find unity before any global unity could be even a possibility.

A typical Taizé prayer service demonstrates the ecumenical identity of this community. The emphasis on Scripture or the "Word"— whether in chanting or reading or praying—is a Protestant feature. The presence of icons and bodily prayer, as in lying prostrate before the cross, as well as the notion that beauty should be a central theme of worship, is clearly derived from Eastern Orthodoxy (a component becoming ever more important in Taizé's work in Eastern Europe). The stress on the Eucharist and the importance of believers being reconciled to one another has the imprint of Roman Catholic teaching stressing confession and the universality of Christianity.

Another concrete ecumenical concept was Brother Roger's early urging that Christian unity would need the ministry of a "universal pastor"—in other words, the pope. In a 1979 Taizé document, he called for prayer for the "transfiguration" of the ecumenical ministry of the Bishop of Rome so it would be more acceptable to non-Roman Catholics.[8] This had long been a theme of Brother Roger's ecumenical thought. As he said in a 1971 address in New York, "Every local community needs a pastor, to gather together the flock always inclined to fragment and scatter. Can we really hope to see the Church gather in unity unless it has a similar pastor for its universality?"[9]

It was his long association with the irenic and ecumenical Pope John XXII and the Second Vatican Council that convinced Brother Roger that such a ministry was necessary for Christian unity. But he added that for this to happen, the Catholic Church would have to accept Christians in such a way that they would not have to convert to Roman Catholicism and deny their traditions and origins in order to belong to the universal church. Such changes as making ecumenism a priority and inviting non-Catholics to participate in Vatican II led Brother Roger to think that a universal and unified church might not be far off. It was only after the death of Pope John XXIII that his hopes were tempered, partly, he felt, because his fellow Protestants did not actively seek greater unity and accept the possibility of the ministry of the pope for such a unified church.[10]

Although modesty and unpretentiousness are a Taizé hallmark, the community has had significant impact in world Christianity. Many of its ideas about ecumenism have filtered into such precincts as the Vatican and the World Council of Churches. Brother Roger's early—and unheard-of—view of a transformed role of the pope as the universal pastor of one reconciled yet diverse Christian church found a larger hearing when Pope John Paul II, long an admirer of Taizé, proposed a very similar concept in his 1997 encyclical on ecumenism, *Ut Unum Sint* (That they may be one). The pope's practice of hosting massive youth gatherings around the world is said to be loosely modeled on Taizé gatherings.

The Taizé style, with its silent vigils of worshippers holding candles, actually helped shape the mass protests in East Germany before the Berlin Wall fell in 1989. The East German churches had been holding Taizé services and were in touch with Taizé brothers in the period before the protests gained world media attention. Taizé's influence is most likely to be felt in Eastern Europe and the former Soviet Union in the future. The number of pilgrims from these countries to the community in France has dramatically increased in the years since the collapse of communism. With the community's use of Orthodox worship elements, chanting, icons, veneration of the cross, and bowing, Taizé could serve as a bridge between the Christian East and West.

How Not to Build a Movement

Taizé pilgrims are urged to go back and work in their own communities and parishes for change and renewal. They are also told not to replicate the Taizé community in their own environment.

The brothers did not foresee that the pilgrims would seek to renew their congregations and parishes primarily by bringing home the contemplative style of prayer they had discovered in France. In the United States, the name *Taizé* gradually grew to encompass much more than the religious community in the little French village.

To describe Taizé as decentralized in its operation would be an understatement. The community in France is the actual Taizé; what happens in the small groups and large gatherings around the world is something a little different. These groups are part of an informal network that circulates the resources of music, prayers, and inspiration in general from the community. Some involve participants who have visited the French community, and some do not. Although many of the groups were started by Taizé pilgrims, others were established by people who first attended a large Taizé service that brought area churches together in their own countries, then decided to spin off a more intimate prayer group in their own homes or churches. These areawide pilgrimages started in 1978 in major cities in Europe and spread to the United States by 1980.

Although the brothers would like to have some contact with or knowledge of the groups using their prayers and music, this is increasingly difficult, particularly in far-off countries. In the United States, they have more or less given up attempting to keep track of Taizé groups. In fact, they have a problem even calling such groups by the Taizé name. "It's really just different groups using our music," says one brother visiting the United States.

Even at the community, the brothers do not see the visitors as joining the group as much as "sharing our space of prayer." As several participants I interviewed pointed out, the brothers never sat down and planned to have thousands of young people converge on their quiet monastery every summer. People just started coming to pray and ask questions about the faith. As word spread about the "strange" ecumenical order, it became a phenomenon, particularly in Europe.

But it is not fully the case that the brothers are uninterested in spreading the Taizé message. Taizé brothers have written books on spiritual topics. They have videos to send to groups and church leaders around the world interested in coming to the community or starting a Taizé group in their own area. The Internet has spread Taizé prayers and music around the world, as well as introducing seekers to the community in France and to the prayer groups and services held regularly around the globe. The Taizé Web site contains daily meditations, and the brothers correspond with many seekers via e-mail.

News stories and other publicity about Taizé highlight the usual earmarks of these services: silence, darkness, candles, songs, prayers chanted in different languages, and, of course, the young age of those who attend these events.

A 1998 *Wall Street Journal* article was similar to other popular reports in calling Taizé "trendy" and seeing its approach as blending "in with the eclecticism and consumerism of Generation Xers."[11] One newspaper article even described Taizé as a new religion, something that would disturb the brothers and participants alike. Meanwhile, the prominent New Age community of Findhorn in Scotland adds Taizé chants into its syncretistic mix of practices from several spiritual traditions—from Zoroastrianism to Judaism. A leader of the community says she would "never go to Taizé. It's far too Christian." But the community has no problems with adding Eastern meditative *oms* to Taizé chants. Writer Eldred Willey speculates that he was "witnessing the paganization of Christian music. This was Findhorn learning the art of inculturation."[12]

The news of Taizé's popularity and adaptability comes as something of a surprise to the Taizé brothers. "We probably can't avoid it, but it won't last," says Brother Pedro, a Taizé brother visiting New York for mission work for several months. Both Brother Pedro and his fellow Taizé member, Brother John, speaking at their residence in Manhattan, stressed again the ordinary nature of Taizé.[13] The brothers saw themselves as just entering a monastic order, albeit an ecumenical one, when they joined during their twenties. Each had journeyed to Taizé as one of the thousands of pilgrims and came away inspired by the simple yet profound vision of Brother Roger and the commitment of the other brothers. It is this common life and the call to seek reconciliation with God and others that led the two brothers out of the community in the 1970s to live in New York's Hell's Kitchen section with the poor and the homeless.

Brothers Pedro and John also led larger Taizé gatherings in different cities, bringing their community's style of prayer and music to ever-larger audiences. But the brothers never intended to start a phenomenon or a trend, says Brother John, a native Philadelphian. He admits that the community of brothers was uneasy as different groups started using the Taizé name; they did not want their style of prayer to become a movement. For that reason, the brothers discouraged others from using the name *Taizé* in conjunction with their prayer services. This effort to short-circuit replications of the Taizé community in other parts of the world arose partly out of a concern not to compete with churches. Aside from the community's desire not to become a movement, the attempt to downplay the Taizé name also stems from the prospect of groups and churches using Taizé for their own purposes, such as teaching doctrines that run counter to the ecumenical Christianity espoused by the community.

Taizé and Youth Spirituality

Although I was looking for alienated Generation Xers when I visited a Taizé gathering at a Lutheran campus ministry at a large university in New England, I found mostly young people who seemed to maintain a balance between their involvement in congregational life and their newfound appreciation for Taizé. The campus minister had started using Taizé prayer on an alternating basis with other services and, at first, some of the students had problems with the silences, chanting, and visual symbols such as icons.

Diana, a twenty-year-old student says, "It was a different style than I was used to. I come from a fairly conservative church. It took adjustment. But [Taizé prayer] became a time to sit there and just open myself to God. It's different in church. You don't have that period of silence. Just when you might be getting into prayer, it stops; the service changes." Diana and some of the other students went with the campus pastor to the community in France and, like other visitors, felt they encountered the heart of Taizé. In attending the prayer services three times a day and rubbing shoulders with pilgrims from around the world, Diana says she and her friends experienced a deep sense of spirituality. When it came time to pray around the cross, she hesitated. "You had to kneel and touch [the cross]. I didn't think I could do it. It was very weird. But the last night there, I gave it a try. It was really a very emotional experience. There were all these people around me kneeling and praying, and some were crying."

Another student, Vicky, says that her visit to Taizé and subsequent involvement in Taizé prayer has "renewed my belief. It's renewed my faith in being Lutheran." But she added that she is also "more accepting of other views and what we can learn from them." The group of students went to France as part of a Lutheran-Catholic dialogue team and came away from the trip believing that, in one participant's words, there "was more that united us than divided us." All of the students I interviewed found three components that made Taizé different and valuable: the diversity of people, the personal dimensions of prayer, and the unity of people praying together. They tried to recapture the experience by participating in Taizé prayer on campus, as well as in personal devotions. Another student says that Taizé prayer "adds an inner dimension to prayer . . . a stillness." During the day, he might recall a Taizé song and start singing it.

The matter of silence was often difficult for the students to accept at first but became the most valuable practice. Sarah says that, like Diana, she "always had silences at my home church but never used them productively. Now I'm getting used to it. Every time I'm having lunch or doing something alone, I use it for reflection and prayer. I don't use [silence] for worrying like [before]."

Pastor Carla, the Lutheran campus pastor, says that Taizé does tend to make certain Protestants uneasy. She does not agree with the Taizé brothers' position on the importance of the pope serving as a universal pastor for a reunited church. She said that this view has "never been emphasized" during visits to Taizé or in talking with the brothers. In fact, many Taizé participants had never heard of Taizé's ecumenical positions. She recalls that German Lutheran visitors at the French community were very critical about the lack of preaching in Taizé services. She counters that the services are based on singing and praying the biblical texts even as they introduce other more foreign elements, such as silence and chanting. She adds that Taizé may be too "passive for what young people need and what they should do. But it's not a movement. What it does is give people a plunge experience and then lets them go. They leave things nebulous. . . . The [community] leaves it to me to take the next step" in conducting ministry among the students. In her experience, "young people are not taken seriously enough [in the church]. In Taizé, there is a seriousness in their welcome and invitation for young people to explore the faith. They're saying that young people matter."

Taizé Goes to Church

The sanctuary of Holy Trinity Church in the suburbs of Chicago was packed, even though it was a hot and humid Friday night in August. People of all ages joined in the Taizé songs, holding aloft candles that had been lit from a huge torch at the entrance to the sanctuary. After a long period of silent prayer, the participants brought their candles to the front and planted them in pots of sand. The huge bed of light, the festive banners, the numerous icons, the chants, and the many people kneeling created a portrait of fervent devotion. "It really gives you a sense of community and mysticism," said Julia, an active Catholic involved in student ministries who was a first-time visitor to a Taizé service. "It seems more reflective than one might find in a [typical church service]," she added.

Taizé prayer at Holy Trinity was started seven years ago, and the gatherings already have an average attendance of seven hundred to eight hundred—more people than attend Sunday services. The service started out with just a few people from the parish. The parish's music director had been to the Taizé community in France and wanted to introduce its style of prayer to the suburban parish. By word of mouth and mailings to area congregations, the participants increasingly began to represent the community— Lutherans, Methodists, and Mennonites. Today, the service has an equal representation of Protestants and Catholics, drawing people from across the Chicago area. Participants have started Taizé services at their own churches; every week in the month there is a service taking place in the Chicago area.

Phillip, the music director who leads the Taizé service at Holy Trinity, said he knows of participants who view this as their primary spiritual community. "Some are disenchanted with their local communities. At Taizé, they're not preached at—that's an attraction to some people." The pastor of the congregation agrees that many attending the gatherings "get more out of it" than out of the Sunday services that "don't give them extended periods of quiet." But he finds that most of his parishioners attending the Taizé service also go to church on Sunday. The real value of the Taizé services, he adds, is the ecumenical dimension. "Many stay after the services, and it build ties and good spirits" among different believers. Taizé has also found a place in different programs at the parish. Taizé music is sometimes used during Sunday services, and the church day school is using the Taizé-based periods of quiet for its devotional services.

In other churches, the relationship between Taizé prayer and parish life is even more intimate, though not in the way one might think. St. Phillip's, a small Episcopal church in Pennsylvania, started a Taizé service with the arrival of a new pastor. Pastor Gail first learned of Taizé when she was at seminary. When she got involved in campus ministry, her introduction of Taizé services found a welcome reception among students. In moving to parish life, she joined with the organist to start a monthly Taizé service for evensong, an Anglican prayer service held on Sunday nights. "We really built a whole new community. It drew people from across the board, including quite a few musicians from other churches who wanted a time to worship, and most of them weren't members of the parish," she said. Eventually the service was expanded to twice a month.

"I think it was the chants, with the combination of community without the church doctrine and church politics that made it meaningful, including for me," Pastor Gail adds. She views Taizé prayer as part of her parish rather than something external to it. The services are listed in the parish bulletin and on the church's answering machine message. "I see Taizé as an extension of our community. It offers a form of prayer to people who aren't comfortable with the Episcopal service and the Book of Common Prayer. It's [making] us wonder, What is the church community? Who are members? It's pushing us away from a strict definition of parish life." In the same way, she says that her denomination and denominations in general need to recognize and appreciate how Taizé prayer leads people to get more involved in the life of the church. "The denomination needs to be open to it. Episcopal structures are no longer meaningful to many people. I view Taizé as indistinguishable from St. Phillip's. It's the ecumenical part of the parish, and that's fine."

Discovering Prayer Through Taizé

Aside from the music, prayer and contemplation are the mainstays of Taizé that keep people coming back to its services. When asked about its appeal, most of those I interviewed said they felt a strong sense of peace and spirituality upon coming across Taizé prayer. At the same time, they readily admitted that some people, including friends they have brought to the services, have felt unmoved by the liturgies and prayer. One of the common observations, and criticisms, concerns the repetition of the prayers, responses, and songs during the services. To regular Taizé participants, this repetition is an instrument that gives an inner depth and meaning to prayer and worship.

James, a thirty-year-old journalist, said that he understands praying the Taizé prayers "like praying the rosary. The point is not to focus on every word but to let a spiritual awareness flow beneath that, while occupying a part of your mind with the cognitive part. It's waiting for God." Jonathan, a twenty-seven-year-old executive, says that Taizé "uses words like pictures. The repetition lifts one out of constraints. You forget the word in your mind and grasp it in your soul—that's where the liberation comes." Some of the participants valued the use of foreign languages in the prayers and chants, making the words they did not understand function as a mantra, a repetitive word or sound that aids meditation. Jonathan readily adds that such a prayer and meditation technique is similar to "almost every other religion. It's a psychological fact."

As Linda, an active Catholic businesswoman in her forties, got more involved in a Taizé prayer group, she found the weekly gathering at a local college chapel a way of "reinforcing her spirituality." Now when one of her coworkers remarks that he is going to his weekly Buddhist meditation group, "I say that I'm going to my own meditation group. There's a definite similarity there." Although Linda finds much of her religious identity in the Catholic Church, she finds the regular prayer services at her parish not very inspiring. "The prayer groups mainly center around reciting the rosary. They're a little dry. Taizé allows for more creative expression." Linda's involvement in Taizé services shows an interesting similarity to the growing number of people involved in some form of Buddhist and Eastern spiritual practices. They may be Catholics or Jews who would not for a moment surrender their religious roots, but at the same time they see Eastern meditation as an important supplement to their faith. They find little of the mysticism and experiential religion in their home congregations and look for spiritual renewal outside the bounds of their traditions.

Although attending Taizé prayer services is not as exotic or foreign for a Catholic or Protestant as is turning to the East for enlightenment, both kinds of spiritual practice also share in mystical and contemplative traditions. The practices and prayer found at Taizé meetings often serve unintentionally to generate new interests and connections between many of the participants and other forms of meditative spirituality. "There is an overlap between those attracted to Taizé and those drawn to Zen," says one longtime Taizé participant and coordinator. "There's a similarity in the emphasis on being still as opposed to doing."

A segment of the Taizé participants said they are interested in Eastern spiritual techniques and practices. It seems that an appreciation for and interest in the practices of monasticism sometimes accompanies a serious involvement in Taizé prayer. This leads to an ecumenical and even interfaith openness based on monastic and meditative practices. "Taizé was a door into the broad monastic experience. It allowed me to have a relationship with [such practitioners], even those in Buddhist monasticism," says Jason, a twenty-eight-year-old consultant in New York. Although as an evangelical Christian he would have seen such non-Christians as unsaved, "I wouldn't say that anymore. I believe that Christ is present with all people, whether they know it or not or whether they call it that or not. It may be Christ in different masks." By contrast, a Taizé participant in Chicago found that the Christ-centered emphasis of Taizé services actually helped move him away from a universalistic belief—holding that all will be saved regardless of whether they believe in Christ—and gave him more appreciation of Christ's role in salvation.

Taizé as a Spiritual Community

Most participants seem to see the Taizé experience as comple-
menting their religious lives. But for some, the services and gatherings also served as a form of spiritual community. Kathryn, a
thirty-year-old graduate student, was raised in a nominal Methodist
home in South Africa. During high school, she became involved
with an evangelical group. Although drawn to the figure of Christ,
she increasingly disliked the dogmatism and narrowness of the
group with which she was involved at school. At the same time, she
was drawn to the social activism that was developing against
apartheid in her country. Eventually, she found herself attending
Anglican church services. "There was more room for reflection
there, and there was less dogma. It was less exclusive." She found
these same features in the Taizé service that her university's campus ministry held.

Both the Anglican Church and Taizé prayer "give one space
and the sense that God is love without dogma. The lack of judg-
ment was helpful." When Kathryn moved to England, she kept in
touch with the Taizé community and attended their services.
Spending a week at the community in France gave her a greater
appreciation of the unique nature of the group. She liked the fact
that the services and other activities were not directed. "It wasn't
like 'now we ought to stand.' Things are just there, and you can
choose to participate or you don't."

The emphasis on simplicity in the music and prayers was also
important. "The fact that it's simple, just a single line of lyrics, is a
meditative aid. There's less emphasis on performance." Kathryn
took the Taizé experience with her when she moved to New York,
where she located a Taizé group. In this group she finds a sense of
support and community, as well as responsibility, as she helps plan
and perform the singing for the service. Not having similar success
in finding a parish, she added that she attends church services only
about once a month. The Taizé group "provides a kind of identity"
for her even though she acknowledged that Taizé stresses that one
should work within existing parishes and not view its prayer services as a primary religious community.

For James, the Taizé group also came to be much like a congregation. Brought up in a Presbyterian home where his father was a

leader in the denomination, he drifted into agnosticism in his youth. When James went to France to study, he recalled mention of Taizé in church circles while growing up, and he decided to look up the community. He had not expected to be overwhelmed by the experience. "I remember just getting [to Taizé] when the bell rang for prayer and everything stopped. At the service, there were a few songs and the Lord's Prayer and then the silent prayer. I wasn't prepared for that, coming from my Protestant background. I was waiting for someone to get up and preach. It was this experience of being alone with prayer that is the genius of Taizé. The way it is structured makes it very accessible. The gospel and Christian message is right there. It astonishes people who imagine that [this kind of prayer] is complicated and that you have to receive training. But at Taizé they find themselves right in the middle of it."

James ended up living with the Taizé community for a year and has returned for long visits between assignments as a journalist and human rights worker in Latin America. When he moved to New York, he began to attend the local Taizé prayer group as his most regular form of Christian support, forgoing a traditional parish. Today, when he travels for his job around the world, he finds a network of fellow believers and prayer groups that draw on the Taizé experience.

Taking Taizé to the Streets

I did not expect to find the influence of Taizé at Phillips House, a Christian community in inner-city Philadelphia. The ecumenical community, located in a distinguished-looking brownstone next to boarded-up tenement buildings, is made up of members who have committed themselves to share a common life of prayer and involvement in the neighborhood; some live on the premises, and others do not. Gwen, a social worker and one of the founders of the community, sees the work of Taizé as an important inspiration for and encouragement of the difficult task of community building. When she helped start the group in the 1980s, it was part of an Episcopal parish in the neighborhood. But after a few years, things were getting more difficult. A new priest who had come to the parish was not as interested in the community as the priest who had helped found it. During this time of uncertainty, Gwen visited the Taizé brothers who had taken up residence in New York. She was impressed by the simplicity of the service she attended.

When she later visited the community in France, she was struck by the way the brothers listened to people. "It wasn't about giving answers but helping to create a space for you to hear the answer from within you. It's refreshing because so many groups will say they have the answer. But Taizé [says,] 'We don't have an answer, or we'll accompany people in the quest to figure one out.' A lot of times, we want to rush to a resolution. Especially in America, the [urge is] to demystify. We're not comfortable with mystery."

The Taizé philosophy of not providing answers, of "just being present and listening," helped reaffirm Gwen's vision for living in community in the inner city. "It taught me not to go in with an agenda. Not to have to fix a neighborhood, but just to be there. Then the problem can solve itself." The community became more ecumenical. Taizé prayers were used in the group's daily prayer gatherings that are open to the wider community. The Taizé service known as prayer around the cross was particularly useful in the community's life. As Christ is seen as bearing humans burdens on the cross, the service is intended to give people the space to share and lay their burdens and struggles on God, usually symbolized by venerating and praying before the cross or an icon of a cross. The prayer draws participants to kneel next to the cross and sometimes stretch out their arms with palms open, a symbol of letting go of their burdens and placing them on the cross.

The service has drawn people with AIDS as well as caregivers and provides something that Gwen thinks is missing in many churches. "There's not a lot of places in [many churches] where burdens are held." Several participants said that Taizé prayer allows people to trust their spiritual lives. Gwen says, "There's not a lot of trust that a person can come to answers about God and ourselves. In our society there's a tradition of distrust. Taizé plants little seeds of trust that lead to big things."

Taizé, unlike many other spiritual renewal groups, carries a significant social action component, even if such a social agenda is not spelled out for participants by the Taizé brothers. Kathryn views Taizé as "less overtly political" than much of religious social activism, but "it is also outward looking. It inspires people to respond to their own situation and then act." But it is the Taizé tendency of not being explicit about particular causes that draws both criticism and praise from observers. James, the journalist and activist, thinks that Taizé should be more open to the discussion of some issues that young believers face in their daily lives. For instance, for a young woman who journeys to visit the community in France, or is introduced to the meetings in the United States, and who feels called by God to the full-time ministry, the Taizé community's silence on the role of women in the church may be difficult to understand.

Because of Taizé's concern to be a reconciling force in Christianity, the community knows that a determined stand on an issue like women's ordination could cause a rift with Orthodox and Catholic members and supporters. For Helen, a Taizé leader who has organized services and visited the community in France many times, it is just this unwillingness to focus on the divisive and controversial issues of the day that makes Taizé unique and important for the renewal of Christianity. "Everywhere you go, there are groups talking about these issues. It's easy for churches to express these viewpoints. It's all part of the ego. Taizé prayer is the place where I shut up and God speaks."

Other Taizé participants also reported a shift in their approach to social concerns and activism as a result their involvement in the group. "It made social concerns less a matter of [following an] agenda and more based on a variety of relationships. It was more impersonal before," said Matthew, a college professor. Before participating he was cochair of a social action committee in his church. Today, he is just as involved in the church, but now he is involved in spiritual formation instead; both he and his wife serve as leaders of the catechumenate program.

Gary, age sixty, was at first unimpressed by the Taizé services he attended. As a Lutheran who had returned to the church from a strong social activist background, he said he thought the Taizé rituals might lead to self-absorption. "I also thought it was a white phenomenon; it wasn't multicultural. It represented the quiet side of Christianity" rather than the social activism he valued. He eventually came to appreciate the way the Taizé service got him "centered and focused on worship." He also liked the way "one can be anonymous in a group" in the Taizé services. At his Lutheran congregation, "passing of the peace" takes ten minutes, with socializing taking up an important part of church life. While he values the close ties of fellowship, the Taizé liturgy is "more private; you can be inside yourself, and I find that very helpful." He was so impressed with Taizé prayer, particularly the way it drew in young people, that he helped start a monthly service at his own congregation. But still, something about Taizé "bothers" him in the way it can "become a distraction to social concern—and I still wish it wasn't so white."

Taizé—Postmodern Christianity?

Taizé has been hailed as representing a postmodern form of Christianity particularly relevant to Generation Xers. In an article in *Re:Generation Quarterly,* the magazine for Christian Generation Xers, Nelson Gonzalez stresses that Taizé emphasizes the theme of pilgrimage in its work with young people. "The searching of the young is never trivialized. At Taizé, there is never condemnation for not having 'arrived.' Yet searching is not aimless. Rather, it leads the pilgrim to abandon him- or herself with a 'yes' to Christ's invitation to follow him that lasts a lifetime. . . . The Taizé call for reconciliation—with God and one another—provides an answer to the alienation among youth."[14]

Taizé's use of the visual arts appeals to a postmodern generation influenced by images more than text and is another example of the postmodern nature of the community. The pilgrimage spirituality that visitors bring to Taizé is part of the phenomenon of seekers finding spiritual solace at religious shrines and holy places around the world—from the grotto at Lourdes to sacred burial grounds in the American Southwest. A direct experience of the sacred rather than adherence to creeds or moral living is the galvanizing force behind the idea of pilgrimage as a spirituality, and it seems to hold a special appeal to the young.

The noninstitutional, rootless, and questioning characteristics of younger generations, such as Generation X—at least as suggested in many polls—seems to fit the spirituality and practices of Taizé. Similar groups and movements are appealing to youth, and their practices—such as labyrinth walks, *lectio divina* (chanting of Scripture), and Ignatian spiritual exercises that entail visualizing encounters with Jesus from the New Testament gospels—are even being put to use by churches. All of these practices are rooted in particular communities and traditions but have increasingly been retrieved—and sometimes reworked—to appeal to more consumeristic and individualistic yearnings. The modern use of ancient rituals, silence, images, and repetitive music also bears close similarities to elements of popular youth culture, particularly as expressed in the trance and rave dance phenomenon. In Western culture, in which Gregorian chants, Kabbalah mysticism, and dizzying varieties of meditations thrive, Taizé prayer seems to speak to the youth culture even in its silences.

Sociologist Robert Wuthnow writes that Americans have moved from a spirituality of dwelling to one of seeking. Whereas forty years ago a person would have attended church or synagogue to get in touch with the sacred, today there is more a sense that spirituality and even religious practices can exist and flourish outside of formal congregations. When religion is separated from institutions, it can be packaged and repackaged, mixed and matched to meet consumer preferences. According to Wuthnow, this consumerization rides the crest of trends and fads that often are short-lived, solitary, and shallow. But he notes that the same seeking can lead to more committed and enduring spiritual practices. These practices, often involving such contemplative disciplines as meditation and prayer, provide a sense of roots and spiritual sustenance that may or may not lead to regular involvement in a congregation.[15]

This stress on the importance of spiritual practice rather than belonging to an institution resonates with several of the Taizé participants I interviewed. The Taizé brothers Pedro and John believe, often from their own experiences in working with young people, that involvement in Taizé prayer and music often leads to other forms of religious involvement; they admit that a weekly or monthly service of chanting and silence is not enough to fortify the Christian life. They may be right. Taizé prayer often complemented rather than substituted for regular religious involvement and worship, even among the supposedly alienated Generation X college students I interviewed. But the interviews and surveys of church attendance in general suggest that some people may choose to keep their ties to institutions informal and loose.

Taizé services formed a primary spiritual community for participants like James and Kathryn, even as they attempted to get more involved in church life. Individuals highly influenced by religious consumerism can assemble their spiritual practices and beliefs from a variety of sources: self-help books, meditation centers with fairly fluid clienteles, and church services they may attend on a weekly or monthly basis. The loose ties and lay-based, do-it-yourself nature of Taizé services and similar practices may well serve as the Christian counterpart to the Buddhist meditation centers and yoga classes that have become so prevalent in recent years. Both serve as nonthreatening entry points for seekers and the disaffiliated to begin some form of spiritual practice or awareness, even if they do not lead to the formation of full-fledged religious communities. In this regard, Taizé has the advantage of never claiming to be a congregation or movement and thus is willing and able to direct participants to other Christian communities. Donald Miller finds interesting similarities between what he calls the "new paradigm" congregations and Taizé. The emphasis on spiritual experience and bodily prayer and worship in both charismatic churches and in Taizé may hint at why they appeal to the younger generation.[16]

All this may not be what Brother Roger and the other Taizé brothers envisioned for their monastery in France. The community's vision of reconciliation between Christians and within the world still burns brightly in the chants and prayers of Taizé gatherings. Some of Brother Roger's and the other Taizé brothers' ecumenical concepts, such as the role of the universal pastor in a unified church, may fall on unreceptive ears in the United States. Researcher Sally Ross found in her interviews of visitors to Taizé and her study of the theological writings of the Taizé brothers that visitors had views on doctrine that did not often coincide with the official community's views. Where the official writings emphasize doctrines stressing God's transcendence—such as the Trinity, the resurrection of Christ, and the reality of sin—many of the visitors tended to view faith in terms of immanence—that God was part of organic matter. They viewed ecumenism in terms of non-denominational and small group meetings between different Christians, whereas the Taizé writings stressed formal recognition and intercommunion between denominations and other larger institutions.[17]

One Taizé coordinator in the United States says that even Brother Roger is no longer stressing specific visions of church unity as he once did (visions that can prove to be divisive in themselves), but rather emphasizing the mystical encounter with God. The brothers I interviewed say that the questions of today's young Taizé visitors have turned from practical issues of social action and church unity to the more existential questions of the meaning of life and faith. Many lack literacy or even familiarity with basic Christian teachings. Taizé chants, prayers, and other forms of contemplation and meditation may serve both as a simple introduction to the Christian life for the uninitiated and as a supplement of spiritual sustenance for those already in the faith.

5

A Progressive Vision
Call to Action

Soldiers, athletes, and politicians can testify to the thrill of the battle—the rush of adrenaline and concentration that comes from intellectual and physical challenge and opposition. The same penchant for confrontation and debate may have something to do with the existence and growth of Call to Action (CTA), a liberal Roman Catholic reform group. Sociologists say that successful religious groups often operate with a certain degree of tension in relation to the wider society. Such tension serves to create loyalty to the faith and to provide a sense of mission and identity. Perhaps some tension with one's denomination may also help energize reform groups. After interviewing participants and leaders in the various reform and renewal groups, I often came away thinking that life would be easier for them if they could remove themselves from all the conflict and take up membership in a more congenial church, synagogue, or denomination. But a degree of friction between those on opposing sides within the same institution may drive the reformers and renewalists as much as does the prospect of tangible change and success.

In its ten years of existence as a national organization, CTA has had tension to spare, dealing with excommunications of its members and being locked out of parish buildings and dioceses across the country. But from their offices in an old monastery in a Chicago neighborhood dotted with factories and small houses, CTA leaders Dan and Sheila Daly seem remarkably sanguine and good-humored about their struggles.[1] They admit that their plans for radical change in the Catholic Church are no longer novel;

they seem more distant today in the face of an increasingly conservative church leadership than they did just twenty years ago. But the Dalys are in the church reform enterprise for the long haul and refuse to give up hope. After all, they point out, the Second Vatican Council was convened unexpectedly, and it ignited a series of remarkable changes that are still reverberating in the Catholic Church.

In mapping American Catholicism, most observers would place CTA well to the left of the Catholic mainstream represented by most bishops and other official channels of the church. CTA's membership of twenty thousand is a drop in the ocean of the some sixty million souls in the Catholic Church in the United States. Yet CTA's story and concerns share many themes with the overall plot of American Catholicism. The effort to find a place in U.S. society while maintaining a distinct religious identity has marked recent church history. Because much of U.S. Catholicism was shaped by immigrants, the drive for assimilation and acceptance in a Protestant nation has shaped Catholic organizational life well into the present. Vatican II was an international event with clear theological foundations, but in the United States the council's most visible effect was bringing Catholicism out of the ghetto and into the mainstream of American life. Changes such as celebrating Mass in the vernacular, allowing closer ecumenical relations, and encouraging a greater appreciation of democracy and religious freedom were all direct results of Vatican II.

But there was less certainty about the council's other purposes and achievements. Some interpreted the Vatican II documents as suggesting that greater democratic equality should be enacted within the church, with the laity taking up some roles once reserved for clergy. All this jibed with the social liberation movements of the 1960s. Many Catholic nuns and laywomen saw the changes wrought by feminism in the wider culture as complementary to the council's call to renew religious life and parishes. The sexual revolution brought the issue of priestly celibacy into the discussion, even though the council did not seek to change this requirement.

CTA emerged during this time of ferment in the mid-1970s. Other groups also sprouted up during this period, such as the Women's Ordination Conference and Catholics for Free Choice (on abortion), which sought substantial change in the Catholic

Church. Similar liberal or progressive groups were also emerging in other religious bodies starting in the 1970s. Movements and organizations have formed within conservative denominations as disparate as the Southern Baptist Convention, the Church of Jesus Christ of Latter-day Saints (Mormon), the Greek Orthodox Church, and Orthodox Judaism, seeking greater freedom and theological and social innovation in their traditions.

Some of these liberal reform groups consisted of individuals who held considerable influence under leaderships that approved or permitted changes in teachings or structure; some ascended to prominent positions in seminaries and other areas of denominational life. When new conservative leaders came into power, however, this liberal presence found itself under pressure. These liberals felt that protest and organizing was the only way to preserve the innovations and other gains they felt they had made in their denominations. Such is the case in the Southern Baptist Convention, where a growing conservative trend has spawned at least two moderate movements: the Alliance of Baptists and the Cooperative Baptist Fellowship. These groups' advocacy of women's ordination, biblical criticism, and other modern theological currents has placed them on the edges of Southern Baptist life, requiring them to build their own structures and ministries, such as seminaries, missions, and educational literature.

An organization called the Mormon Alliance was formed in the wake of a series of excommunications of theologians, historians, and other members who had questioned official views on the veracity of the Book of Mormon and church doctrines in the mid-1990s. Other liberal renewal and reform groups also emerged in response to perceived crises, scandals, or simply tendencies toward stagnation in their denominations and traditions. The most dramatic recent case of this kind of group forming and wielding considerable impact in a denomination took place in the Greek Orthodox Archdiocese of North and South America in the late 1990s. A group calling itself Greek Orthodox American Laity helped force the resignation of the presiding Archbishop Spyridon. The archbishop was widely viewed as a hard-liner who was out of touch with more democratic U.S. church procedures. Unique about this reform effort was the dissidents' use of the Internet to energize protests across the whole church.

Mainstream Beginnings

CTA began as an unprecedented nationwide conference that would lay the groundwork for CTA as a movement. In October 1976 the bishops convened a nationwide consultation on Catholicism in Detroit to be known as Call to Action. From all historical and journalistic accounts of the gathering, the bishops received more input than they asked for. Things were unusual about CTA from the beginning. In preparation for the event, Catholics gathered in parishes and religious communities and were asked to hash over the issues that they felt were most important in their lives as Catholics and Americans. In a short history of the movement, theologian Bernard J. Cooke writes that more than 800,000 responses were received from across the country. Such a request for local input was not common in the church and tended to increase the expectations of many liberal Catholics that the CTA convention would introduce wide-reaching changes in the church. These expectations were often based around church issues, such as the teachings on birth control, celibacy for clergy, the ordination of women, as well as the social issues of war and peace, capital punishment, and economic justice. Cooke recounts that during those three days of gathering in October, the candor of the participants grew along with the expectations of change. The 1,340 delegates made unprecedented proposals, including making priestly celibacy optional and ordaining women. "At that point, however, the bishops, who until then had been supportive of the process, were startled by it, and, probably because they found 'more action than they called for,' felt the need to halt the momentum of the Detroit meeting," writes Cooke.[2]

The delegates' more liberal proposals were squelched by the bishops. The laity involved in shaping this novel deliberative process in the church were understandably disappointed; some gave up hope of extensive lay-based changes to the church after Vatican II and subsequently dropped out of church life. But much of the convention's social action agenda was translated into diocesan CTA centers set up by bishops who attended the Detroit convention. Eventually, many of these centers, which had spread to twenty dioceses, were closed by bishops who had second thoughts about their support for the organization and some of its proposals. Only in the relatively liberal Archdiocese of Chicago was CTA continued, largely because it was independent of the archbishop's control. Organizers believed that a permanent organization was needed to keep the ideals and proposals alive, at least in Chicago, if nowhere else. The local association of liberal Catholics moved toward a national expression after Catholic activists attended a 1987 Vatican synod on the role of laity and realized that they would not have much of a role unless they started organizing.

CTA gained national prominence—or notoriety, in the eyes of the church hierarchy—when it published its Ash Wednesday advertisement in the *New York Times* in 1990. The ad reiterated many of the issues and positions upheld during the 1976 Detroit convention: optional celibacy for priests, ordination for women, and freedom of conscience on sexual matters. The group then held a national conference on the future of the U.S. Catholic Church in Washington, D.C., where renowned liberal theologian Hans Küng championed a manifesto drawn up by CTA, thereby attracting the attention of liberal Catholic activists across the country.

Both social activists and those working on church reform issues were drawn to the 1990 conference because CTA—both in its conference and movement phases—has always sought to combine a liberal (some may say radical) social vision calling for economic justice and world peace along with its progressive view on theological and church issues. The link between politics and theology was nothing new in American Catholicism. The church, even before Vatican II, never blended in with conservative Republican political life. Catholic social teachings criticized the unfettered free market and supported labor unions and a living wage—all measures traditionally championed by the Democratic party. The optimism of the early 1960s and the call for sweeping changes in church and society that took place during Vatican II convinced many American Catholics that the church was on the side of liberal political change, if not on moral and sexual issues then at least on issues of poverty, war, and peace. The growth of liberation theology—which made the link between social justice and salvation explicit—in the late 1960s in Latin America, as well as the civil rights and antiwar movements in the United States, only amplified the call for a radical Catholic social message.

The belief that democratization in the church was around the corner seemed to complement the vision of worldwide social justice and peace. The post–Vatican II church in the United States was also experiencing a changing of the guard in the 1970s. New bishops, such as Rembert Weakland in Milwaukee, Joseph Bernardin in Chicago, and Raymond Hunthausen in Seattle, espoused a clearly liberal social vision that energized lay activists who had been shaped by the turmoil and protests of the 1960s. The U.S. bishops' pastoral letters on disarmament and economics during the 1980s helped foment among a segment of the laity and clergy a de facto resistance movement to the policies of President Ronald Reagan and the politically ascendant Republican Party. On these issues, CTA attained official recognition in 1986, when it was awarded by then-Cardinal Bernardin for its dramatic and musical presentations on the themes of the pastoral letters on peace and the economy, even performing before the U.S. bishops conference.

The original CTA was also influential in shaping the consultative style of the bishops' pastoral letters of the 1980s. The pastorals, like proposals drawn up during the 1976 convention, were the result of input from a wide variety of specialists and laity on pressing issues of public policy. But what really caught the attention of the media and U.S. Catholics in general was how the fledgling national organization expanded its agenda to include (and increasingly to stress) modern notions of democracy and human rights within the ancient Roman Catholic Church itself. CTA became a sharp critic of the conservative papacy of John Paul II and the resulting change in the hierarchy in the church as the pope named conservatives to key positions in dioceses around the country.

The new media attention to CTA was also due to the publicity surrounding the national conferences the group has held since 1990. Attendance at the event has grown annually—from four hundred at the first nationwide conference in 1990 to over four thousand by the late 1990s. As the most visible expression of CTA, the conferences serve as annual think tanks on how best to enact reform and renewal in the Catholic Church. The speakers are the main attraction, with the organizers selecting both the most popular and controversial in liberal Catholic circles. In fact, CTA conferences typically bring speakers to the podium at the height of their respective controversies and conflicts with the church hierarchy. Thus, Sister Jeanne Gramick was a highlighted speaker in 1999, just as she was in the process of being disciplined by Rome for her ministry to homosexuals and ordered to cease speaking on the issue. Another favorite is Sister Theresa Kane, who publicly and unexpectedly confronted Pope John Paul II on the question of women's ordination during his 1979 visit to the United States.

The emphasis on openness both to the culture and other spiritual traditions is evident in much of CTA's work, particularly in its national conferences. The 1999 event's lineup, for instance, is typical. A workshop on labyrinth prayer—a popular phenomenon of walking labyrinths for contemplative prayer—a Jewish-based Sabbath service, body prayer, feminist prayer services invoking the feminine aspects of the sacred, and a seminar entitled "Encounters with a Disabled God" show the diversity of CTA conferences. They are a kind of Woodstock—or shopping mall—of progressive Catholicism.

Among the popular speakers and seminar leaders at past conferences were Charles Curran, who was expelled from the Theology Department of Catholic University in America for his liberal views on sexual ethics, and Bishop Samuel Ruiz Garcia of Mexico, an influential leader in the Zapatista revolt in Chiapas. The 1999 conference featured a panel on another heated subject: entitled "Women Celebrating Eucharist: Path to Transformation," it explored the forbidden practice of women presiding at Eucharists in private settings.[3]

Most of the CTA people I spoke to who had attended an annual conference said the high intellectual fare laid out by the speakers was a major draw to the event. But they also valued the networking and sense of community they found with fellow reformers. Anyone attending the event can find ways to link up with fellow members and start chapters and other attempts at reform and renewal where they live. CTA has also been strongly involved with other liberal and left-leaning Catholic groups, particularly through Catholics Organized for Renewal, a loose coalition of thirty-four Catholic organizations. The coalition, including such progressive Catholic groups as Pax Christi (a Catholic peace group) and the Association for the Rights of Catholics in the Church, serves as a clearinghouse for the coordination of projects and the sharing of information. Protest groups that formed in Europe during the mid-1990s to call for church reform have also linked up with CTA for interchange and a sense of unity.

Perhaps the landmark event, if not achievement, for CTA was the excommunication of members of its Lincoln, Nebraska, chapter in 1996 by Bishop Fabian Bruskewitz. The excommunication generated immense publicity about the group, leading it into a new period of growth. CTA remains a lay organization, though it has a large representation of clergy and church workers. Dan Daly says that two-thirds of the approximately twenty thousand members are laity and one-third are religious, with nuns making up the majority in this category. A 1999 survey of Catholic small groups and communities, such as the Catholic charismatics and Hispanics, by William D'Antonio of Catholic University of America found that CTA members are often the best educated and most affluent in those groups. The study also found that the majority of these small-group members are over age fifty and many are women.[4]

Memories and Hopes of Reform

If the Catholic University study suggests a typical CTA member, then Jack and his wife, Barbara, seem to fit the bill. Jack, fifty-five, attended parochial schools and a Catholic college and has always been active in parish life. Both were enthusiastic supporters of Vatican II, although they felt the council's reforms should "have gone further" on matters such as ecumenism and the role of women in the church. Jack, particularly, says he is not concerned with reforming Catholicism from the fringes of the church and enjoys the diversity of his suburban parish, where both conservative and more liberal members interact, though somewhat uneasily. He appreciates the fact that his priest grants parishioners considerable freedom and does not "micromanage" the parish. He and Barbara are involved in a small group in their parish that gathers for Bible study, prayer, and discussion; the group is free to discuss controversial issues and views. But Jack fears that if a bishop appoints a conservative pastor to the parish, the change would bring division and splintering into smaller groups.

A member of this small community gave Jack and Barbara some tapes of a CTA conference, and they were favorably impressed. They liked the way the conference brought the "great minds of the church," such as Richard McBrien and Hans Küng, to its podium, while also being a "very prayerful and joyful" environment. From their subsequent involvement in CTA national and local chapter meetings, they see the movement as a "place where the church acts like it's in the twenty-first century. People [at CTA] tell you what they believe and why and let you make up your own mind about the issues."

In his parish work, Jack tends not to talk about his CTA involvement, thinking that it may "rock the boat." He and Barbara agree, however, that the local CTA chapter should provide more than "intellectual discussion," including more opportunity for prayer, reflection, and social action. Although they see many priests and nuns at the national conference, they bemoan the lack of involvement by the religious on the local level. But the couple supports having laity preside at the Eucharist, believing it reflects the simplicity and freedom of the early Christian church.

It is in their attachment to the church that Jack and Barbara have their differences. When asked whether he would ever consider leaving the church if conservatives gained more power, Jack answers that he refuses to be pushed out, since it is "my church too." Although he sympathizes with the people and priests who left or were forced out of the church, he hopes schisms do not multiply among Catholics. Barbara says that she feels more alienated from the church, particularly as she sees women excluded from the altar every Sunday. "I resent it. It's not just about the ordination of women but also the cultural patriarchy of Christianity as a whole." Where Jack wants to reform the papacy, Barbara sees the institution itself as the "opposite of Christianity." Inspired by feminist theologians, she sees the early Christian communities as radically egalitarian, "telling each other Jesus stories and eating together," with little need for ordained priests and the other structures that have grown up around the church.

Barbara looks back to simple gatherings of equals in the early church as her ideal of the church, whereas Jack harkens back to Vatican II and the church's effort to update its teachings to better influence modern society. Barbara has considered leaving the church several times, but she stays on because of her faith community. "I have the comfort of a small group with like-minded people that rings true for me. It's how I remain in the larger church."

Father Ralph, a fifty-year-old priest in a moderate-sized inner-city parish in the Northeast, still displays a glimmer of enthusiasm when he speaks about the early days of Vatican II. He was just coming out of seminary when the reforms were unfolding in the United States. When he took his first assignment at a parish, he felt like he was "riding the waves of reform" that would eventually change the face of the church. But as time went on, his frustration and impatience about what he saw as the slowing and even reversing of the program of change inaugurated by the council grew. He was involved in housing and other social issues at his parish and never had the opportunity to get involved in the fledgling groups seeking reform in the church. But in the early 1990s, he was becoming increasingly resentful at the way his diocese locked out "some of the best minds in the church," forbidding them to speak in church facilities.

It was during this time that he started attending conferences where he learned about CTA. He went with a group of laypeople to the national event and has gone ever since. After one of the conferences he got together with other attendees from his area and started a CTA chapter. He says that although priests and even a few bishops attend the CTA conferences, most of his contacts and relationships from the group have been with the laity. Today he finds CTA appealing because of its "empowerment of the laity. It treats them as adults who have much to bring to the table and to the church's ministries." The pastor at his parish followed him in becoming a member of CTA, though he is less active. Although Father Ralph has not run into much opposition from his bishop or other church officials, his style of ministry, such as inviting all Christians to communion, does clash with that of the new priest at his parish, a young man who is more conservative than his two older colleagues. Other than that, Father Ralph does not feel his priestly style pushes the envelope in radical ways. But he finds that such innovations as letting the laity lead at worship, even presiding at the Eucharist, are important, even if difficult to implement in many parishes. "There's more than enough for priests to do. It's not as if we'll lose our importance," if the laity take up such functions, he says.

Like other CTA members, Father Ralph finds he is often frustrated by the lack of change in the church. "It's disillusioning, and it eats away at morale," he says. That's why he feels it is important that CTA keep its gadfly, progressive identity. He also echoed the views of other members in his belief that change in the church will come inevitably, as a critical mass of reformers takes things into its own hands, with the hierarchy following. Even if he is limited in the reforms he can enact, Father Ralph stresses that CTA should remain out in front with its "prophetic stands. It has to stay true to its ideals and not compromise too much. It's been strong about justice in society and never backed off on that. I hope it won't be afraid to take chances that might distance it from the institutional church and do things without waiting for approval."

Margaret, a fifty-two-year-old artist and architect, sees CTA as unique in that it has a comprehensive agenda and reach and is not bogged down on any single issue. She is a veteran in social justice and peace activism—from the Vietnam War to animal rights. Brought up in a traditional Catholic family, she still remembers her early yearnings to be a priest—until her sister told her that girls are not allowed in such a role in the Catholic Church. She dropped out of the church during her teen years and avidly explored other spiritual traditions and philosophies—from the Baha'i faith to secular feminism. After she had children, she realized they should be exposed to some religious tradition and started "shopping around different parishes."

She knew she had found her parish when the priest stood up during one Mass and apologized to the women there about how they had been treated throughout history by the Catholic Church. She developed a strong relationship with the priest and eventually became active in parish life. She started a parish meditation group and brought her feminist identity and activism into parish life by starting a feminist study group. Her liberal Catholic parish supported her to the extent that they sent her to seminary, even if her study could not lead to the priesthood. In class at seminary, she tries to exert a strong feminist presence to counteract what she sees as a male-centered and male-controlled church. The sense that the church excludes not only women but others who are outside the hierarchy was driven home to her when a priest was transferred out of her parish for his liberal views and leadership. "They just pulled the priest out of the parish. [The bishops] don't know anything about relationships," Margaret says. The members withheld money from the offering plates and raised enough dissent that a vicar was sent to the parish by the bishop for a discussion. But although the protest forced a delay in removing the pastor, it did not prevent his removal.

That incident and others have changed Margaret's mind about the importance of women's ordination and reform in the church in general. "I've come to believe that if women were ordained tomorrow, there would still be the same system there. Having women ordained is not a guarantee of anything. I know women who were ordained in other denominations but still have secondary status in their churches." It was this concern with changing the system of the Catholic Church that drew her to CTA, particularly as the group embraces social reform as well as greater gender equality and justice in Catholicism.

Although Margaret had long heard about CTA and wanted to have a chapter in New York, she realized the potential of the movement only when she recently attended her first national conference. At the conference she found close to four thousand like-minded Catholics worshipping, learning, and discussing church and other spiritual issues. "I had a lot of preconceived ideas about Catholics from other parts of the country. But everyone was so open and friendly." The CTA liturgies were particularly impressive to her because they spoke to her yearning for an inclusive vision of Catholicism, in which both men and women presided at the altar. Many in CTA feel that this kind of liturgy could not be condemned by the church hierarchy because ordained priests stand at the altar along with the other participants.

The improvised and unapproved liturgies of CTA are nothing new to Margaret. She has participated in feminist Masses in which the Eucharist was celebrated by women without a priest present. For several years she has regularly attended a women's Eucharist in New York. At first, she had doubts about the authenticity of the Mass, aware that the church teaches that a priest is necessary to confect or make Christ present in the bread and wine for them to be sacraments. But during one of the Eucharists, as the women were gathered in a circle, passing the bread and wine around, one of them dropped a piece of bread and then, in Catholic fashion, promptly picked it up and consumed it. "Something clicked when that happened, that what we were doing was real." One of the problems she has with CTA liturgies is that they sometimes use noninclusive language, such as saying that Christ was "made man" rather than "made flesh."

Organizing the Struggle, and the Struggle to Organize

Building and sustaining a CTA group is a difficult enterprise. Several of the people I interviewed expressed frustration about the time involved in creating and nurturing a group or community and the lack of interest and support they encountered. A good number of chapters—some of which were listed in CTA's newsletter and other literature—had ceased meeting or showed stagnant memberships, and most experienced a struggle in staying alive. Difficulties come both from the outside, as when a diocese restricts CTA activity, and from the inside, with inactivity and discouragement among members and burnout among leaders who may not see clear results from their reform efforts.

Carol and her husband, Ben, were leaders of a small chapter in New England during the late 1990s. The group was not very large, and the going was difficult from the beginning. For one thing, the diocese to which most of the people belonged would not permit the group to use any church buildings. They had to travel about an hour to another diocese for their meetings. Although a former pastor supported the couple's involvement in CTA, the new parish leadership sees it as taboo. "CTA is a no-no word. I'm not even considered Catholic if I mention I was involved," Carol says.

As at many CTA chapter meetings, discussions were a big part of the gatherings. Members discussed affairs in the church—both nationally and regionally—and speculated on how change might come to the church. Carol and Ben also wanted to bring a social action dimension into the chapter. They had been involved in protests against the operation of the School of the Americas, a U.S. training camp for military involved in Latin American regimes. But they had trouble convincing fellow members of the importance of such activism; "they didn't want to be seen as protesters," Carol says.

Eventually, the group broke apart, but it was more than differences among its members that led to the chapter's end. "The feeling was, after a while, what's there left to do? We accomplished what we could. What could a small group do? I sense this is what happens with other [chapters that have closed]. There's really not much you can change [in the church]. Things seem to going backwards," explained Carol. The growing conservatism of the Catholic Church was enough to drive one chapter member to leave and join a United Church of Christ congregation. Even experiencing the crowds, support, and inspirational speakers at CTA's national event was not enough in the long run. "You go to those national meetings, and you get very high. And then you come home, and you see that change is very hard to generate," Carol adds. She and Ben still support CTA, read its literature, and participate in regional meetings. Even with the difficulties and pressures that come with CTA support, Carol says, "you have to try to make an awareness of it. The problem is that there's no awareness of CTA. No one knows what it's about."

Edward, a community activist in New York City, was drawn to CTA as a way of providing community for his family. He was dissatisfied with parish life, although he continues to attend Mass fairly regularly. Edward particularly felt that the church positions on women priests and homosexuality were wrong. He learned from the CTA office in Chicago about others in the New York area who expressed an interest in the group. Eventually, he was able to organize a small CTA meeting at his home. The group discussed different issues in the church rather than doing any joint social action or worship. "Most of the people were already active in social action. They were looking more for community among those who shared a common perspective," he said.

But then several members moved away, and the group eventually disbanded. Edward has since tried to start a citywide CTA group, but the busy schedules of prospective members and his own reluctance to take on most of the leadership duties when he is unsure of the commitment of others has squelched these plans for the near future. CTA's broad agenda for reform both drew members and made keeping them a problem, according to several people I interviewed. Often a newcomer will come to a local CTA chapter with a specific concern or issue, such as gay rights or women's ordination, and try to make the group a single-issue caucus. If the new member's efforts fail and the chapter moves on to other issues, the newcomer will tend to drift away.

Jeanne, a sixty-seven-year-old CTA member and veteran church activist, says that "CTA is . . . ubiquitous, and many people put their energies into one issue." Another longtime member says the organization has a "revolving-door" problem that makes steady recruitment necessary to replace those leaving. The CTA members I interviewed tend to tell others about their chapters and invite friends to meetings and other gatherings. But as CTA is locked out of many parishes and especially dioceses, it cannot rely on the church's vast official network to spread the word about the organization and its activities. The disapproval that Catholics feel in being involved in CTA also hampers the group's overall strength and ability to build commitment and community. Many members who work in the official church structures have to be careful about their degree of involvement in and identification with CTA. Such caution eventually weakens loyalty and a sense of community in the chapter, not to mention hampering confrontational action and protest on church issues.

Schism and the Limits of Reform

It has happened countless times in North American Protestant churches: a pastor is dismissed by his denomination and he moves across town to start another congregation, taking many of his former church's members with him in the process. But when such a split takes place in a Catholic parish, it is front page news. Corpus Christi Parish in Rochester, New York, was unlike most Catholic churches in the area, if not the country. Women were invited to the altar to consecrate the Eucharist; the unions of gays and lesbians were publicly blessed; and non-Catholics were openly invited to receive communion. In short, the parish was imbued with the liberal reform spirit that drives CTA and the host of other progressive groups in American Catholicism. The priest, Father James Callan, was not only pushing the envelope on contentious issues in the church but also building one of the most influential parishes in the city, drawing in many new members and establishing ministries ranging from a free health clinic to a homeless shelter.

When the bishop of the diocese intervened and demanded that the unorthodox practices at the parish be stopped, Callan found strong support among the lay leaders and parishioners at Corpus Christi for his resistance. The bishop responded by excommunicating Callan and firing the women lay leaders. But this was not the end of the story, at least for much of the parish and its sympathizers, such as CTA. After a few months, Callan returned to Rochester, started his own parish a few blocks away from Corpus Christi, and drew most of the members from his old parish. The new independent church, called Spiritus Christi, soon reactivated many of the ministries that were started at Corpus Christi.

The new church even claimed to be in the Catholic tradition, though it was not a part of the diocese. CTA found itself in the difficult position of upholding its mission as a reform group within the church while also acknowledging that Spiritus Christi shared the "Vatican II vision of a participatory, inclusive servant church."[5] CTA national leaders began a process of dialogue between the remnant of Corpus Christi, the new church of Spiritus Christi, and CTA members in the Rochester area. In its 1999 national conference, the principal woman lay leader of Spiritus Christi was a major speaker on the topic of women celebrating Eucharist. The church also led a morning prayer session at the conference. There are still strong divisions on the matter. Some CTA participants did not think the CTA leadership should lend support to Spiritus Christi, believing it would undercut their own efforts at staying in to reform the church. CTA has attempted to reconcile its members with Spiritus Christi members by organizing a new chapter in Rochester, but the tensions and divisions remain, according to Don Wedd, a spokesman for CTA in Chicago.[6]

Most of the CTA members I interviewed expressed strong support for Father Callan and the Spiritus Christi community. A priest said that for CTA to exclude Spiritus Christi would be going back on everything for which the group has stood over the years. "I'm encouraged by what's going on there [at Spiritus Christi]. All you have to do is be there to see that the Holy Spirit is there. They can be seen as a model [for Catholics] and prophetic in a new way."

A smaller and, interestingly, younger group of CTA members was uneasy about the whole idea of separating from the church and the implications that may have for the prospects of reform. Ronald, a forty-three-year-old teacher, says that "it probably could have gone a different way," and both sides of the conflict bear some responsibility in what happened. A forty-two-year-old businessman had similar views. "It's like a marriage [breakup]: there was probably a lot of defensiveness and reaction [in the excommunication and resulting split]. It's difficult to hang in there and communicate. The thing is that when splits happen, it's hard to get back together again. Like the Reformation, you still feel the effects of it."

Might CTA members consider joining a like-minded church or denomination in which they could feel less conflict? The frustration of some of the interviewees made me ask this question again and again. Most of the CTA members say they have entertained thoughts of going to greener pastures, usually the Episcopal Church or a similar mainline denomination. But they resisted this option for reasons of upbringing, affection, and hope for the future. Jack, an eighty-two-year-old CTA member, was clearly angry at an institution that he says encouraged him to have a large family and forgo contraception but did not support him in his financial problems nor foster a healthy attitude toward sex. He says that priests and bishops encourage a secretive, dysfunctional church that takes parishioners' money but will not let them have a say in church life.

Yet right after delivering this jeremiad against the church and the Vatican, Jack said he would never consider leaving the church. "It's like Andrew Greeley says, we stay in the church because we want to be Catholic. There's an attachment to the beliefs. You see these people who are so angry at the church, but will they die without wanting the ministrations of a priest? Maybe there's some Irish superstition mixed in there. I also don't disagree with the core teachings. I'm not saying I don't believe in the Trinity or the incarnation, though I don't understand them. It's the management I don't believe in."

It is the long-standing attachment and appeal of Catholicism that keeps most CTA members engaged in both the church and reform efforts. It may be that the old saying "Once Catholic, always Catholic" bears some truth. Many CTA members cited their Catholic upbringing as the main reason that they did not consider leaving the church. It may be that the distinctive identity of Catholicism, with its popes and priesthood, and its elaborate doctrines and rituals, provides a cultural and even ethnic identity as much as a religious one. Most traditions encompass several denominations: if a member disagrees with the conservative positions of the Lutheran Church–Missouri Synod but wants to remain a Lutheran, she can join the more liberal Evangelical Lutheran Church in America. Although some smaller alternative churches that have split from Rome—such as the American Catholic Church on the left and the Society of St. Pius X on the traditionalist right—still consider themselves Catholic, most Roman Catholics, including CTA members, see their church as uniquely embodying this tradition.

Call to Action and the Next Generation

Another problem noted by both friends and critics of CTA is the graying of the movement. CTA itself has recognized the group's shortage of young adults and has started Next Generation, a network of young adults that holds conferences and works to recruit the under-forty crowd to the organization. Most of the CTA members with grown, married children admitted that their children were not strongly involved in the church, with a few in each family completely inactive or members of other denominations. While they may be sympathetic to their liberal parents' concerns, most of the grown children are busy with careers and starting families and have not taken up the activist mantle.

Alice, a fifty-three-year-old mother of five grown children, says that as they become more settled "they will have to deal [with church reform] issues." Jeanne, the veteran activist on church reform issues, adds that the older children of her conservative friends do not necessarily stay in the church. That may be so, but conservative Catholics and active parishioners in general have stronger support systems (one thinks of the many new conservative Catholic colleges that have formed since the 1980s in order to counter "liberalism" in Catholic universities) that can retain and win back straying young Catholics.

The reforms that CTA calls for are deeply rooted in the dreams and hopes surrounding Vatican II. CTA's vision is based on a particular and perhaps nostalgic reading of Vatican II, but nevertheless the movement sees its work as carrying out the unfinished agenda of the council. Jack, unlike his wife, Barbara, says he sees the church portrayed by the Second Vatican Council as the "perfect church." He says he could never leave the Catholic Church and join a Protestant congregation even though he may be more in agreement with the latter.

"I don't see that dream of Vatican II in other churches, liberal or otherwise." By "perfect," Jack seems to mean the emphasis on social justice and world peace found in the Vatican II documents, as well as the attempt to update the church teachings on ecumenism and a greater role for the laity. Because most of the younger baby boomers and Generation Xers were small children or not born yet during the period surrounding the council, it is not surprising that the message of reform based largely on the council that inspired members like Jack has a hard time reaching the ears of the younger generation.

"Among my generation the division is not really between conservative and liberal as much as between conservative and complacent," says Gary, a nineteen-year-old student at an Ivy League university in the Northeast. "Many who don't agree with some teachings just give up. They don't feel any ownership of the church." Because most of the active Catholics on his campus are conservatives, Gary was eager to get involved in CTA, even working to start a chapter in his university town. He has been involved in a CTA e-mail discussion group for young adults and recently visited his first chapter meeting an hour and a half away from campus. His parents passed their liberal Catholic views on to Gary early, and these stayed with him through much of his twelve years of parochial education. Even before he arrived at college, he visited CTA's main offices in his hometown of Chicago to find communities and contacts to sustain him in his new setting.

Gary is involved at the Catholic center on campus, although when discussions there turn to church teachings, he tends to keep his views to himself, not wanting to get into arguments with the other students and priests, most of whom are conservatives. He values CTA because it allows him to meet people with similar views and provides him with a place where he can discuss and express his views on controversial issues without feeling scrutinized or criticized. He says he does not want to criticize or insult conservatives, but he cannot understand how they come to their positions if they are looking rationally at the church and its teachings. Gary adds that the conservative students' unwillingness even to discuss the issue of women's ordination is one example of how they do not use reason when talking about the church.

Anne, a twenty-five-year-old graduate student at the same university, recently became involved with her parish young adult group, where she, like Gary, also encountered dominant conservative views. She had attended Catholic schools and had "amazing teachers who encouraged us to think for ourselves, to do [our] own research." Her interest in feminism and dissent on such issues as women's ordination and contraception led her to CTA. She learned of the group by searching the Internet, a common medium for learning about CTA among almost all the young adults I interviewed. Anne says the freedom to explore issues at CTA and the fact that chapters are not required to hold a party line on the issues are the most appealing features of the group.

I found that the younger CTA members (under age fifty) tended to be more conservative and were hesitant about taking actions that might be considered too radical. Jeff, a forty-three-year-old businessman, said that he was pleasantly surprised when he attended his first CTA meeting. "I had heard that they were troublemakers and that they were not sophisticated in how they dealt with issues in the church. So I was anxious when I first went. I was impressed with the depth of knowledge the people had. They didn't strike me as reactionary."

Jeff has doubts about CTA liturgies that do not have a priest officiating. "I never felt attracted to that. I wouldn't call it a Eucharist. It would be just the breaking of bread. I still see a role for the priest [in celebrating the Eucharist]." He is active in his middle-of-the-road parish, where the priest lets him put announcements about CTA in the bulletin. Jeff serves in the Rite of Christian Initiation for Adults, a catechism program that initiates prospective members into the life of the Roman Catholic Church. "There's a lot we can do. Like the liturgy—God, when it works, it really works. It's good stuff; the theology is right on and has a lot of richness." Although he would like more Bible study and prayer in his chapter, Jeff tends to see CTA as providing an open forum where ideas about the church and how it could change are openly discussed.

Visions of a New Church

The more Edward is involved with church reform, the more he sees how different it is from his work in community organizing. "In community organizing, you try to deal with winnable issues. But when you talk about church reform, you have to have long-range goals. The reform group provides community for people who want change and, like community organizing, they have to share the struggle. But it's much tougher. You just don't get small victories for women's ordination in the church." He sees the job of a group like CTA as "expand[ing] the dialogue" in the church.

Edward stresses that rules and some basis of authority in the church are important. He does not want to see factionalism grow in the church. "All religions have holy people who have to keep the tradition. I have no problems with that. But to make that a litmus test is the problem. On sexuality, there's a lot more room for discussion and acceptance of theologies that are not heretical. All this would imply some change in what it means to be Catholic. But it can't just be change. I mean, not everything someone says is Catholic is [automatically] Catholic. There has to be some norms [to run the church by]. At this point, the need is to open up the process. There may be ten-year period of listening and making changes. But then we would have to decide on things. There's still original sin. There'll be a [need] to keep everyone honest."

In reading the literature and talking with CTA members, I speculated that the visions and dreams of reform might also have an exclusivist effect on the church, although this time it would be the more conservative and traditional Catholics who might feel unwelcome. It is a charge that the CTA members I interviewed have heard before and are rather sensitive about. "We don't squeal about the conservatives. They're the ones who report [to the bishops and the Vatican] everything about us. The church should embrace everything, conservative and liberal. If you want to teach the Baltimore Catechism, the pre–Vatican II guide to church teachings, in your parish, that's fine. As someone said, as long as you end up with Jesus. If following almost every word of the pope brings you to Jesus, it shouldn't matter," says Stephen, a sixty-five-year-old CTA member.

In fact, several of the CTA members felt that they were targeted by conservatives, though CTA itself spent little time attacking such Catholics. They said that CTA takes a "common ground" approach that welcomes everyone. In other words, the failure in dialogue and communication with conservatives is not CTA's doing. But this view fails to take into account the degree to which the confrontational approach of CTA rankles the hierarchy and more conservative Catholics. By taking opposing viewpoints from church leaders and the pope and riding the waves of the most publicized controversies in the church, most evident by the roster of speakers at their national conferences, CTA has become a reliable target for attack by conservatives. The conservatives' frequent charge that anti-Catholicism is alive and well in American society often is accompanied by the view that liberal Catholics are disloyal and are actually abetting this rising tide of prejudice by consistently opposing the hierarchy.

Pressing for Reform in Centralized Institutions

How does an activist seek to change things in an institution in which power is held in the hands of a few leaders? CTA seems to have figured out early on in its existence that significant reform of the church will not happen anytime soon, and thus the organization set about creating interim plans. Serving as an open forum on church matters is an important function, particularly in its local chapters. CTA provides the space for dissenters to remain in the church while criticizing and envisioning alternatives to many of its positions. CTA participants often cited diocesan restrictions on outside speakers whose orthodoxy was in question and the Vatican's determination to end the discussion on the prospect of women's ordination as clear indicators of the need for free space in the church. For many of its participants, this venting function in itself is justification for CTA's existence. But a group based mainly on open-ended discussions, protests, and brainstorming for visions of change when such transformations seem far off will have trouble sustaining itself. As one former chapter leader recognized, talk of reform tends to go flat against the weight of a centralized structure like the Catholic Church.

Although CTA emphasizes democracy and freedom of expression within the church, the group clearly has a distinct identity and ideology of change. Not every view is given equal time in CTA meetings; a distinctly liberal view of social change, human rights, and feminism marks the discourse. This is seen in the strong support of CTA members and leaders for inclusive language, including balancing feminine with masculine language for God, and other feminist innovations. These views may hold relevance for many baby boomers, but they can elicit blank stares and shrugs among the younger generations, who have no memory of a strict Catholic culture and a golden moment of opportunity and drastic change that Vatican II seemed to herald. Younger Catholics are more likely to drop out of the church to do political organizing or espouse views on changes in gender relations in a secular context.

A group working for broad change also has to give members an identity and practices for the periods between inertia and reform. Since its beginnings as a national movement in the early 1990s, CTA has toned down its use of satire and criticism of church figures, such as Pope John Paul II and Cardinal Joseph Ratzinger, the Vatican official in charge of maintaining orthodoxy, to make its points. Today, the emphasis is more on the issues than on the personalities, and on creating community among CTA participants. CTA's annual national conference, with its mix of lectures by renowned speakers, Bible studies, and liturgies, not to mention the camaraderie generated among thousands of others reform-minded Catholics, provides this sense of community and purpose for many liberal church activists and laypeople. CTA leaders appear to recognize this and are trying to bring the energy of the national conference to regional and state gatherings. It is the CTA liturgies and other forms of spiritual practice and the sense of community they generate that seem to attract members and keep a chapter on the path of stability.

But it is CTA's tendency to push the envelope on controversial issues, such as the celebration of the Eucharist by laypeople and specifically women, in these conferences that seems to draw the most criticism of the movement from the church hierarchy; these issues are likely to remain a stumbling block for working for reform within the Catholic institution. In the same way, there may well be deeper issues beyond the acceptance of women's ordination and married priests, but pushing for more radical changes can alienate church leaders and fellow church members who do not subscribe to the whole CTA agenda. That CTA has also formed ties with dissenting groups that have left the church may be a reason for concern for those who view the movement as a force for internal reform. A 1998 CTA directory of resources of other church reform organizations lists parishes of the breakaway American Catholic Church as well as independent "ecumenical Eucharist fellowships," usually home-based groups seeking to draw all Christians together in worship.[7] CTA's supportive relationship with the breakaway Rochester group Spiritus Christi is another example of the organization's postdenominational outlook. Yet the CTA members adamantly claim that they belong to the Catholic tradition. In her research on liberal Catholic reform groups, sociologist Michelle Dillon finds that members use language and a value system derived from the Catholic tradition (including belief in the Eucharist and the universality of the church) to express their dissent and lifestyles that may conflict with official church teachings. Dillon argues that their engagement with church doctrine forces the hierarchy into a dialogue on issues that would otherwise remain neglected.[8]

The Catholic Church, like any ancient and centralized structure, changes slowly. Historian Paul Johnson has compared the church to an iceberg; it moves slowly and its changes are beneath the surface and not easily seen. The most effective reform of the church, and of other religious institutions with centralized structures, may come from those reform groups that are in for the long haul, adapting themselves to the grind of change at a slow pace. In explaining how the Catholic Church changes, sociologist David Martin writes that Catholicism should be viewed as a system "assimilating impulses from a worldwide net and then redistributing those impulses once again to a worldwide net."[9]

There is no doubt that Catholicism has been influenced by forces both Catholic and non-Catholic—from Pentecostalism to secular and grassroots religious social justice movements, reflected in the church's social teachings. In assimilating these impulses, the church often repackages them and, in Martin's terminology, redistributes them to the vast church networks throughout the world. The Vatican's current view of the charismatic movement as a vehicle for the "new evangelization" of the church is a prime example of this repackaging and redistributing. To one degree or another, this pattern of assimilating and redistributing is present in other centralized organizations, including the Church of Jesus Christ of Latter-day Saints (Mormons).

As we have seen throughout this chapter, in the formal sense, CTA is out of the loop of the Catholic system. The local chapters are shut out of parishes and dioceses in many parts of the United States, and the national movement is stigmatized by church hierarchy. Although this situation is less dire outside of the more conservative Northeast, where I conducted my interviews, even more liberal dioceses are feeling the effect of the Vatican appointing conservative bishops. This will make it difficult for CTA to get a hearing in the American church and, more importantly, in the Vatican in the years ahead. Yet in such sectors as universities, colleges, and in the opinions of the Catholic populace, CTA's message of dissent has found a following. Of course, the majority of U.S. Catholics may agree with some CTA stands, but they do not necessarily buy into the group's confrontational style or its liberal positions on other issues such as gay rights or lay-led Eucharists. Surveys have shown that American Catholics do not line up strictly on the conservative or liberal ends of the spectrum. They may question the Vatican's teachings against contraception and yet be pro-life and enthusiastic about Pope John Paul II.[10]

The younger generations in CTA may be the ones who move beyond the sentiment and drama surrounding the hopes of Vatican II and the dashed dreams that followed that tend to form the mind-sets of most current members and leaders. The younger members tend to view Vatican II as history and to search instead for areas of church life where they can have an impact, as well as find things worthy to preserve in the tradition. The future of groups like CTA will be decided by their ability to create a counterculture that can both provide identity to its participants and keep alive the hope that its ideas and innovations will reach the mainstream.

6

Spiritual Intimacy in an Ancient Faith
Jewish Renewal

As she stands at the head of a small circle of worshippers in a large room at a Quaker meeting house in New York, Rabbi Goldie Milgram's chants seem to capture both a sense of awe and everyday life, with some humor thrown in. In leading the congregation in a prayer for those who have been hurt or insulted, she counsels that the problem often lies with the perpetrators and then chants, "In other words, it's not about you, it's about them."[1]

The rabbi led the group in guided meditation, using chanting and visualization. Her language was a blend of the psychotherapeutic, the mystical, and the traditional, as she spoke of the "shadow side" and of forgiveness as being a liberation "from negative energy." She described prayers for the forgiveness of transgressors after they have died as dispelling bad "karma" so that the transgressed can get on with life. Milgram describes God more often as the "source of life" that is a part of the world than as a transcendent judge and lawgiver.

Yet the rabbi constantly returned to the sources, to the Torah and the interpretations and applications of the holy text found in the Talmud, even if its teachings and practices are reframed in more popular style. One of the blessings was a new one for this synagogue, although ancient in its origins. A ceremony for those who have come into contact with the dead or dying and need to be cleansed and healed of its spiritually draining effects was practiced

in the temple in Jerusalem. The rabbi said this healing and blessing should be revived and asked participants to recount their own
stories of such experiences. One man told of viewing his deceased
parents when he was younger and the harrowing effect it had on
him. At the end of the service, Milgram invited anyone present to
come forward and receive a blessing. By the end of her call, most
of the participants had gathered at the front of the room with
prayer shawls wrapped around them to receive blessings for a
desire to live a more holy life.

"It creates a spiritual intimacy," Milgram says of her unique
approach of leading a service.[2] She is one of a growing group of
rabbis teaching in line with the Jewish Renewal, a loosely based
movement that tries to imbue a mystical and modern spirit into
Jewish rituals and teachings.

Countercultural Beginnings

The Jewish Renewal still has a youthfulness and enthusiasm about
it, even though most of its veteran members and leaders are deep
into middle age. Much of the renewal was born during a period of
disillusionment and rebellion against both the religious and secular establishment among Jewish young people during the late 1960s.

The *establishment* is a term commonly used by Jewish renewalists to describe the Jewish mainstream in which they and most U.S.
Jews were raised. As with Christianity, Judaism grew considerably
more diverse after it was transplanted to U.S. soil. Aside from
traditional Orthodox Judaism, the Reform movement, begun in
Germany in the mid-1800s, attracted an early following among a
segment of Jewish settlers in the United States. Its attempt to
update and modernize Judaism in worship, laws, and customs,
struck a chord with an assimilating Jewish community. Conservative Judaism, established toward the end of the nineteenth century,
represented a more modified break with traditional Judaism
(retaining the use of Hebrew and dietary laws) but also attracted
many immigrants and their sons and daughters. Reconstructionist
Judaism later reinterpreted Judaism as a civilization or a people-
hood rather than a divinely revealed religion.

These attempts at modernization, whether intentionally or not,
fit in with the process of Jews becoming Americanized. The period

of the 1950s and 1960s—just when baby boomers were growing up—saw a growth of new congregations, mainly Reform and Conservative, sprouting up in the burgeoning suburbs. But these synagogues were largely unable to retain the allegiance of the younger generations. By the 1960s, the previous decade's upsurge in synagogue attendance had ended. By then the Jewish community had to face the new challenge of intermarriage, as Jews intermingled with gentiles in public schools and universities. As Jewish ethnicity has diminished over the last few decades, synagogues and other institutions have had to find alternatives to fill the vacuum. Jewish renewalists were in the vanguard of those proposing that Judaism had to reinvigorate its spiritual traditions and practices and make them relevant to seekers if it hoped to bring back its disaffiliated and keep its young people.

Although there are contested versions of how the renewal emerged, most accounts agree that youth dissatisfaction with the synagogue system in the United States played a leading role. Some observers see the Conservative and Reform youth movements and summer camps of the mid- and late 1960s as incubators of the renewal. Many youth experienced the contrast between the spirituality, energy, and fellowship of these events and programs and the more somber and formal environment of a typical assimilated Jewish synagogue.

The most prominent strand of the Jewish Renewal came from the havurah movement in the late 1960s. This represented a clear break from synagogue Judaism, as young Jews decided they could worship and celebrate their Judaism on their own terms. This early anti-synagogue posture was evident as participants claimed that rabbis and cantors were not needed to hold meaningful Jewish services. Instead laypeople gathered in living rooms to pray and study, holding discussions about the Torah and its relevance to everyday life. Relevance was the watchword of the movement, as there was an attempt to join political action and a critique of American materialist society with a return to a more holistic Judaism that addressed everyday life. Through rituals, celebration, folk songs, dance, discussion, contemplative prayer, and meditation, the havurahs sought to create a Jewish body, mind, and spirit.

The mystical nature of the renewal can be traced to its two prominent leaders, Rabbis Shlomo Carlebach and Zalman Schachter.

They were both trained in the Lubavitcher Hasidic tradition, in which fervent and mystical prayer, study, and outreach to fellow Jews are wedded to traditional observance. In fact, Schachter and Carlebach toured the country for the Hasidic community known as the Chabad, working with college students. In the late 1950s, Schachter felt limited by Chabad Orthodoxy in part because of his study of the psychology of religion. His exploration of the youth culture's use of psychedelic drugs, particularly LSD, as a form of spiritual seeking effectively cut the ties with the Chabad, though not with Hasidic mysticism.

Though Chabad leaders condemned Schachter's experimental views, the rabbi created a synthesis of mystical teachings taken from the Kabbalah, medieval mystical Jewish texts, and the quasi-spiritual youth culture of the 1960s. The Kabbalah contains writings on the mystical nature or manifestations of God and provides direction as to how one can experience God's presence and achieve holiness. In short, Schachter attempted to universalize and popularize a form of Judaism that had rarely escaped the confines of the tightly knit Hasidic worlds of Eastern Europe and Brooklyn. The fact that Schachter was a student of the Lubavitcher Hasidic leader Rabbi Joseph I. Schneersohn has provided renewal participants with a link to tradition and an authenticity that they felt was lacking in their Americanized and assimilated Jewish upbringings.[3]

Schachter eagerly translated his mystical work into the practical arena of the burgeoning havurah movement, viewing it as a sort of laboratory in which to try out his ideas. He was instrumental in founding one of the pioneer havurah–Jewish Renewal communities in the United States, the Aquarian Minyan in Berkeley, California. In a wide-ranging interview during the twenty-fifth anniversary of the minyan in 1999, Schachter recounted that the convergence of the drug culture, the sexual revolution, and the rise of Eastern spiritual groups in the San Francisco Bay Area during the late 1960s and early 1970s set the stage for the creation of a unique synagogue. Actually, the founders and early participants did not think they were creating a synagogue, let alone one that would last for over twenty-five years. Schachter said that the ragtag group of students, professors, political activists, and dropouts from Orthodox Judaism could best be described as "a floating crap game. Floating crap games don't have permanence. What it felt like to me was like I needed to infect people—with a bug, as it were—to say that Judaism can be ecstatic, can be exciting, deserves attention, can get you high."[4]

There was a good deal of mixing and matching spiritual traditions and practices in those early days. The early Aquarian Minyan met in various households and was composed of Hindu swamis and Buddhist meditators, among others. One Friday night Sabbath service featured a Sufi choir, with African American preacher Cecil Williams delivering the sermon for worshippers gathered at Glide Memorial Church in San Francisco. The underlying assumption of such borrowing from many traditions was that all the religions had a common mystical core, even if their rituals and methods of accessing this spiritual dimension were very different. The Kabbalah offered Jews such a body of mystical teachings, but these were obscured by, on the one hand, an assimilated Judaism that valued the ethical and social dimensions, and on the other hand, by an Orthodox Judaism that stressed doctrine and ritual.

So the first task of the Aquarian Minyan and of the fledgling movement in general was to research these missing mystical meanings and rituals and integrate them into a modern Jewish consciousness. As Rodger Kamenetz notes, this attempt was different from the modernizing of tradition that Reform Judaism sought. The modernist approach was "editing halakhah [Jewish law] on the basis of personal preference." In its place, Schachter proposed a "psycho-halakhic process," which says that "everything we have done in halakhah is important but we have to ask, What function did it fulfill in an earlier time and what's the best way to fulfill that function in our current situation?" In other words, what may have been kosher in an earlier time may not be kosher today if it does not serve the original purpose of stewardship and care of the earth and its creatures. For example, finding out about the harm of insecticides may be as important as knowing the conditions under which a certain kind of food is prepared.[5]

But there is an element of choice and selective retrieval of tradition in Schachter's writings and teachings. Schachter is critical of the traditional Jewish distinctions between purity and impurity, and the natural and the supernatural. He maintains that such teachings undervalued the role of the natural in understanding God. God is understood as being part of the rhythm of life, not wholly transcendent but also immanent, the source or "wellspring" of life. In revising the traditional roles of the sexes and upholding a strong egalitarianism, renewal leaders claim that the Orthodox refuse to acknowledge the "possible holiness of our present understanding," that might challenge such laws, according to Kamenetz.[6] From the start, Schachter held that he and fellow renewal leaders were helping bring Judaism into a new encounter with modernity, and with its innovations in feminism, science, ecology, and particularly psychology. He is credited with translating kabbalistic concepts into a modern psychological framework.

But all of this was not uppermost in the minds of the many unaffiliated and unbelieving Jews who made their way to the Aquarian Minyan and the other havurahs and communities that were appearing during the 1960s and 1970s. It was the revamped rituals with their wide-open sense of participation and new translations of ancient texts stressing inclusivity and equality (especially between the sexes) that most strongly attracted seekers. Participants in holy day celebrations were allowed input into the form or style of the services. Everyone was allowed to comment on a text of Torah, and the distinctions between teacher and student were relatively porous, at least at first. Participants in services stood in a circle, eschewing the pews and podium where the rabbi was usually stationed. The high level of participation gave minyan members a sense of ownership and, in the process, created strong bonds of community.[7]

The mixture of ecstasy and short-term and improvisational planning made the Aquarian Minyan unique and popular in the counterculture. Mostly, though, it was the ecstasy—Sabbath services with strobe lights and throbbing music by Carlebach and others who wrote original songs and chants blending pop, spirituals, and Jewish folk melodies—that drew people. One early participant recounted that "I don't know how to explain it or even understand it. It feels like we're transported to another dimension. The joy is so intense that the only thing I can do is to sing, or shout, or dance for hours, or hug everyone, or just close my eyes and cry. It feels like the tears and the laughter of a hundred generations of our people are exploding in a wave that carries us all the way to God's revelation at Mount Sinai, or to the beginning of creation itself.

Once you have this experience, your nervous system is changed and your soul is changed, and you can never go back."[8]

The creation of other havurahs and renewal communities that functioned as alternative synagogues in the 1970s and 1980s gave Jewish Renewal a distinct place in American Judaism. But what gave the renewal its growing influence in mainstream Judaism was the building of institutions that would not be viewed as competing with the synagogue. For instance, the Havurah Institute, an adult education center on emerging forms of Jewish community and practice, was increasingly attended by those in more mainstream synagogues. A spate of popular books unlocking secrets of the Kabbalah for uninitiated seekers, and the increase of teachers who studied with Schachter and Carlebach all helped to bring ideas into synagogues and Jewish associations far from the cultural environs of the Aquarian Minyan. Renewal ideas also strongly influenced Reconstructionism, a denomination that teaches that Judaism is a civilization rather than strictly a religion. The effort to bring the renewal communities and the various education and social action programs into a larger cooperative arrangement resulted in the creation of Aleph, the largest renewal organization, in 1993.

The predecessor body of Aleph was P'nai Or, a congregation founded in Philadelphia in 1962. In 1975, Schachter moved to Temple University as a professor in the Religion Department and became the leader of P'nai Or. Philadelphia, already the home of Reconstructionist Judaism, became the center of the renewal when Arthur Waskow founded the Shalom Center, an organization of Jewish peace and environmental concerns. Jewish activist and writer Waskow started the journal *New Menorah* in 1985, which became P'nai Or's quarterly publication. The Shalom Center merged with P'nai Or in 1993 to become Aleph (today, P'nai Or is the name given to most of the renewal synagogues affiliated with Aleph), and since that time the organization has continued expanding with new departments, networks, and affiliated associations to extend the work of the renewal.

Many of these programs were once freestanding organizations that merged or affiliated with Aleph, such as the Network of Jewish Renewal Communities, a worldwide association of renewal congregations, and Ohalah, an association of rabbis from both mainstream and alternative Jewish institutions supporting Jewish renewal. Aleph also has sister organizations that work with its programs, such as the Jewish Renewal Life Center, a year-long training program in Jewish spirituality, and Elat Chayyim, a retreat center focusing on shorter-term education in upstate New York. All of these organizations aim to reinvigorate Judaism by inculcating it with a distinctive brand of spirituality, community life, and social action. Aleph has also created its own prayer book, *Or Chadish*. The book carries gender-inclusive language for God and humans, and instructions on spiritual practices, including yoga exercises with traditional morning blessings.

Being Jewish and Mystical

It was the Sabbath service before Passover was to begin, and the renewal synagogue was doing what renewalists do best. The lay leader that morning was teaching about how God delivered the Israelites from what the Torah calls the "narrow places" during their captivity in Egypt. And then he turned the tables on the congregants and asked them what kinds of problems and narrow places they would like to be freed from for Passover. Within a few minutes the congregation had broken up into pairs of members sharing their personal trials and hopes.

"Jewish renewal tends to link inner spirituality and emotional liberation. It puts the Torah on a personal plane [as well as] seeing it as a historic story," says Douglas, a sixty-something member of the synagogue.

"If I don't make it personal, then it's just a story. I have to get into the history and make it relevant to me," says Stuart, a fifty-two-year-old social worker who helped lead the service. It was this personalizing of the faith that drew many people to the Jewish renewal. Several of the people I interviewed said the renewal was the only place where they could feel some connection to their Jewish roots and identity.

Mitch, a sixty-year-old artist and writer, grew up in a secular Jewish home where religion was not an issue. When he was taken to a Reform Jewish Sunday school during his youth, he found "nothing in it" and decided that he was an atheist. As a budding artist in New York, he explored Zen Buddhism and existentialism and eventually gained an interest in Hasidic Jewish writings. He investigated these teachings as a matter of intellectual curiosity, but several brief encounters with Rabbi Zalman Schachter between the 1960s and the 1980s changed things. By that time, Mitch had been practicing yoga and was knowledgeable about other forms of meditation. When he attended a Sabbath service given by Schachter in New York, he found the teachings and practices "foreign but familiar." The service and Schachter's teaching were also "distressing— it [went] directly to my life. It wasn't like doctrine that goes somewhere else. The impression was that this was made for me."

Mitch eventually joined a small renewal group that later organized into a synagogue. He has become increasingly interested in Jewish meditational practices and teachings since then, even leading the Sabbath services on occasion. But he has not become more observant in the traditional sense, restricting activities on the Sabbath or adopting a kosher diet. His two children have not taken up any form of Jewish practice. He says that, unlike younger Jews who have taken up Judaism, he does not "need religion to guide [his] behavior," as he developed a sense of ethics from his secular life and involvement in Eastern philosophy. Instead, he sees his Jewish practice as giving him a direct encounter with the sacred and the true nature of the universe. In the other nonrenewal synagogues he has visited, he finds a "cool, liberal Protestant atmosphere. There's not much of the intensity of experience that got to me [as in the renewal]." He finds that his Jewish spiritual practices have "coincided with yoga. I didn't feel that I was going to anything sectarian, but rather going to the next level [of spiritual practice]."

Adam, a forty-three-year-old general contractor, has also been involved in yoga and other Eastern practices. Unlike Mitch, however, he has not gradually switched to engaging only in Jewish spiritual practices as he has become more involved in Judaism and his renewal synagogue. "If I miss the Sabbath service, I may go to a yoga class. I have a composite view of religion. The ideas of all the religions have something valuable to teach Judaism. You can [view] different teachings through a Jewish framework and heritage." For instance, the Kabbalah's teachings on the sefirot, which relates the names or manifestations of God (such as wisdom and beauty) to parts of the human body, are similar to Eastern teachings of chakras, acupuncture, and similar techniques that locate divine energies in the body. Both the kabbalistic and Eastern techniques seek to translate the presence of the divine into human experience. Adam particularly appreciates the way his synagogue "retraces the mystical roots of all Jewish practices."

For Adam, this mystical emphasis of the renewal clashes with the approach of those who follow a strict observance of Jewish law. "I take a pick-and-choose approach to observance and restricting things like Sabbath observance. I think a lot of Jews [drop out of Judaism] because it gives them impossible things to do. I have too many things to do in life already. [Judaism] should have an ease and grace to it." Even as he appreciates the esoteric teachings and rituals of his synagogue, Adam praises the Jewish Renewal for its inclusive, welcoming approach. "The renewal brings to the consciousness of Jews [the message] that you are welcome, that it's okay to join at any level. There's no qualifications; you don't have to know Hebrew. A non-Jew can come to the synagogue and would be able to participate." While most participants in the renewal did not become strictly observant, several spoke of a newfound appreciation for ancient observances. Barry, a fifty-year-old lay leader at one renewal synagogue, says that he now cherishes the Sabbath because it creates a zone of sanctity and timelessness in the world as an anticipation of the way things will be in the kingdom of God.

Almost no interviewee associated with the renewal, whether participant or rabbi, failed to mention some contact with Rabbi Schachter. Either they had heard some of his tapes or public teaching or had received individual instruction from him for a short period of time. Other prominent teachers were often cited as imparting special wisdom and knowledge that would be difficult to find anywhere else. This one-on-one teaching method has close associations with the guru-student relationship found in Eastern religions. These spiritual teachers in the renewal are often called rebbes, a title previously reserved for the teachers in Hasidic Judaism. There was even a good deal of controversy about the power these teachers might have over their students in the renewal. As with Eastern spiritual groups during the 1980s and 1990s, some renewal participants charged that they had been sexually or emotionally abused by teachers in the renewal, with the public allegations particularly swirling around Schachter's associate Schlomo

Carlebach. The controversy was threatening enough for Aleph to draw up guidelines for teachers forbidding them from initiating sexual relationships with students.[9]

Schachter was instrumental in bringing the role of the rebbe to the non-Hasidic world, and he has since tried to expand the role of the rebbe to laypeople. Teaching what has been called a "rebbetude of believers,"[10] Schachter holds that all Jews should be able to impart the wisdom and teaching of the Torah to one another. This was demonstrated at one service at a renewal synagogue when everyone was invited to discuss the Torah reading. While valuing esteemed teachers in the renewal, most of the participants I spoke with said the teacher-student relationship was not central to their Jewish practice. They credit the renewal with providing them with a sense of ownership and participation that contributes to their Jewish identity. For instance, Adam had his share of guru-student relationships in his involvement with Eastern religions; he came to the renewal synagogue for a more communal experience with strong lay involvement.

Like Mitch and Adam, almost all of the renewal members and participants whom I interviewed either had engaged in or still engaged in non-Jewish spiritual practices, particularly Eastern spirituality. Most tended to view Judaism as a spirituality rather than a religion; several recoiled from describing themselves as religious. Picking and choosing spiritual practices was not frowned upon, though respondents acknowledged the problems with a consumer approach to faith and spirituality. This does not mean that individualism alone defined their spirituality. There were close ties in the small synagogue I visited and a strong sense of community among its members. But the tendency among members of the renewal synagogues to view Judaism as a spirituality rather than a religion makes the personal seeking of spiritual truth and experience as important as adhering to common revealed teachings that can unify a congregation.

The importance of the personal search was brought home in the account of Steven, a forty-two-year-old computer programmer. He moved away from his "marginally Conservative" Jewish upbringing during high school. He dropped out of college after a few years and became involved in communal living experiments. He moved to Israel and lived in a kibbutz but was turned off by the attitudes of Jews he met there. After studying Christian writings, he embraced Christianity, though not for long. A more dramatic conversion was in store for Steven when he came in contact with Lubavitcher Hasidism, the Orthodox movement that stresses mysticism with strict observance. "It was the first place where the people seemed authentic; they knew what they believed and tried to live it."

Steven devoted eighteen years of his life to the Lubavitcher Hasidim, but he grew disillusioned with the way the rebbe or leader of the community was viewed as God's ordained leader, an oracle to whom the followers had to submit. When Steven got divorced, he found himself labeled a troublemaker in the community. After he left the community, he attended a service of a Jewish renewal synagogue and was favorably impressed. "What seemed to hold the community together was a love [of members] for each other. They supported each other as truth seekers. The emphasis was not on accepting doctrine or waiting for the answers from a book, but on awakening your own center of wisdom."

This view that seeking the truth and spiritual wisdom is an ongoing process that continues even after joining a community was common among Jewish renewalists. This kind of "seeking in place" means that one can be true to one's Jewish community even while valuing spiritual practices from outside this tradition—such as Eastern meditation.

Of course, such flexibility was not interpreted only in a positive light. Rabbi Milgram said that renewalists who take on both non-Jewish and Jewish practices at the same time often experience a "spiritual traffic jam. When you use an eclectic mix of spirituality, you only experience 20 percent of what is possible on one path. You need a coherent system in order to experience [spirituality]."

The Renewal and Social Action

The fact that the participants had similar backgrounds in alternative spiritualities as well as similar liberal social and political backgrounds may have contributed to the camaraderie at the two renewal synagogues I visited. As Adam said, "If I was going to a service and worshipping with people and then later found out they were all Bush Republicans, I would be bothered by it. There's very little narrowness [here]. We're culturally connected . . . most agree with progressive politics, and the freedom of choice." Almost all of the members and participants are baby boomers or older. A few younger people have attended the services but have not become regular participants or members.

Along with mystical spirituality, social action is a major part of the Jewish Renewal. The movement was born in the late 1960s and still reflects the liberal and in some cases radical politics and social concern of that period. Much of the renewal's social action agenda is tied to its spiritual teachings on egalitarianism and the immanence (or nearness)—as opposed to transcendence—of God to nature, which leads to environmental concern, and, most importantly, *tikkun olam,* or "repair of the world." Tikkun olam is manifested by doing good works and acts of social justice, whether it be working in a soup kitchen or engaging in political protest. The egalitarian emphasis is present in renewal gatherings as women and, more recently, gays and lesbians fully participate in Jewish life. This stress on inclusiveness is a reflection of the renewal's liberal social activism and is intended as a model that participants should seek to carry over to the wider society.

Kamenetz reports that the feminist presence in the renewal has only grown in recent years. Jewish feminist scholar Judith Plaskow says that the early havurot were often male-only institutions. But "almost immediately they were influenced by feminism. Many women, myself included, had our first experiences of egalitarianism in the context of the havurot."[11] The issue of women davening (praying publicly) and being counted in a minyan (traditionally a gathering of men) served as a test as to whether the renewal and havurahs would follow Orthodox halakhah or endorse the full inclusion of women in the community.

This endorsement of women's concerns allowed further innovations to be launched, even as it excluded the involvement of Orthodox Jews in the havurahs and much of the Jewish Renewal in general, Kamenetz notes.[12] The next phase of feminist influence in the renewal was through translation and creation of inclusive liturgy and other texts. Prayers that may have used the terms *Father* or *Lord* or the pronoun *He* when referring to God are changed or balanced with gender-neutral or feminine imagery. The traditional *Adonai* (Lord) often becomes the gender-neutral *Yah* (for the

Hebrew *YAVH* or the unknown name of God) in renewal services, particularly for chanting and meditation. Feminists and other renewal Jews have also used immanent rather than transcendent terms in worship, replacing *Lord* with the *wellspring of life*.

This effort to make liturgy accessible and relevant has also led to the revitalization of Jewish music. The belief in the presence of the sacred in nature likewise spurs renewalists on to ecological concern. Maintaining an eco-kosher diet, which entails avoiding foods processed through means that harm the environment, is often recommended in renewal literature as one Jewish approach to ecological concerns. All of these social concerns have been taken up by such activist renewal leaders as Arthur Waskow, whose interest is particularly in ecology, and Michael Lerner, in his magazine *Tikkun*. Lerner, a rabbi trained and ordained by Rabbi Schachter, has argued that the spirituality dimension is in danger of overshadowing social action in the renewal.

Lerner writes that it is difficult for many in the renewal to integrate "spirituality and transformative politics. Many people turn to spirituality for comfort and escape the very distorted realities of life in a materialistic society, so they don't want to be dragged back into these realities by a religious or spiritual community." On the other hand, "progressive politics continues to ignore their spiritual dimension, and social change movements rarely try to incorporate a spiritual dimension into their daily activities."[13] The people I interviewed all reported that they had been involved in social activism in the past and were currently concerned with various issues. They came to renewal activities more as a way of adding a neglected spiritual dimension to their lives than seeking a synthesis of spirituality and social action or a Jewish rationale for activism. In other words, they had little problem getting involved in social issues throughout most of their lives; finding spiritual value and involvement in Judaism was more of a challenge.

Judy, a forty-two-year-old TV producer, was something of an exception to this pattern. She was raised in a liberal Jewish home where social issues were discussed. But she grew up uninvolved in either Judaism or social action. When Judy was in her late thirties, a friend invited her to a Conservative synagogue that had been influenced by the Jewish Renewal. She recalls that she was struck by the spirited music and contemplative atmosphere of that first

Sabbath service. "I couldn't stop crying. I was blown away by it—by the number of people, especially young people, there, and what the rabbi had to say. The inspiration of all that was incredible." Judy became a member and soon learned that the synagogue offered many social action programs. She found in the synagogue a way to get involved and have the support and interest of a large community behind her. She helped organize an AIDS walk and was eventually assigned to be coordinator of social action. "There's a richness in spirituality at the synagogue, but you also should be socially involved. It doesn't want to be an ashram. The rabbi teaches the three pillars of Judaism—prayer, study and tikkun [social concern]." She is concerned that the inward-looking approach of contemplative and meditative spirituality at the synagogue not discourage members from engaging in social action.

Carol, sixty-six, another member of the synagogue, says that as a social worker she has long been involved in activism and social concern. But her study of the Torah and participation in the spiritual and community life at the synagogue during the past few years have had a strong effect on her work. "I work with seriously disturbed children. I find I'm more open to them now; I hear them more, and I respond to them differently. I think I have a different perception of myself, viewing myself as a spiritual person now." Most of the participants in the renewal and in synagogues influenced by the movement said that deciding to take part in social action was a deliberative step that was separate from their practice of Jewish spirituality.

Bringing the Renewal to the Mainstream

"When the Jewish Theological Seminary organizes a spiritual retreat for its seminarians, you know things are changing," says Rabbi Milgram with a sense of wonder. Milgram, forty-four, was not always so sure herself that Judaism and spirituality had much to do with each other. She was raised in a Conservative Jewish home and was a leader in various Jewish youth groups, but grew disillusioned with the religion. She remembers being aware even when she was in high school that women and Jewish spirituality were rarely discussed together. Things did not change when she converted to Orthodox Judaism in her twenties. "The forms of Judaism had been held intact, but whatever gave it energy and meaning was not there," she says. She was considering taking an alternative spiritual path but decided to give Judaism another try.

Milgram then found herself working with the elderly, many of whom were Holocaust survivors. She found that although many in her parents' generation were still deeply wounded from their involvement in the Holocaust and World War II in general, they had no relation with God and could not find any healing from their religion. From this experience and subsequent study of the Jewish tradition, Milgram grew convinced that Judaism had both the resources and traditions to address much of the "wounded-ness" she saw, even though it had not responded to modern crises and dislocations. Milgram's comments were similar to those of other renewalists I interviewed. Many shared the view that they grew up in a form of Judaism that lacked vitality and spirituality, saying that the Judaism they inherited was "freeze dried": the content and form may have been there, but it had to be cooked up for its nutrients and flavor to take effect and be enjoyed. But Milgram is critical of attempts to label certain innovations and practices as "renewal. It's not something that can be marketed like a product. I want to empower the process of desired growth within expressions that people determine for themselves."

In visits to different parts of the world to teach renewal Judaism, Milgram says she has to adapt these teachings to the local context. In the Ukraine, where most are learning Jewish basics for the first time, it may be implausible to think that the feminist thrust of the renewal will be entirely acceptable to such Jews; she adds that they are often uncomfortable about invoking *Yah,* the renewal's gender-neutral term for God. In the same way, some American Jews may not be ready or willing to embrace all the teachings and rituals of renewal Judaism.

That is one of the reasons Milgram does not think that the prayer book issued by Aleph will be an effective agent for renewal within the mainstream. "Our purpose is the unfolding of Judaism and to become part of the streams shaping Judaism and the future, and then someday to be invisible. We'll serve when we're needed, but new needs will emerge. We serve best when [we are] helping people apply the spiritual principles of renewal in their own cultural contexts. Our job is not to replicate Jewish Renewal but to help Jews in finding holiness and the presence of God in their lives," says Milgram.

She finds that Jewish renewal is most effective and desired in times of crisis in people's lives. Many of the baby boomers are encountering such situations as they reach middle age and experience serious illness and family problems. The earlier wave of participants in Jewish renewal were those Jews who had been seekers in other religious and spiritual traditions. Today, the "third wave" is mainly made up of more average Jews who have stayed in the religion but want to experience spirituality and Jewish practices. "I'm speaking today to Hadassah members, mainstream synagogues. Ordinary people are looking for comfort in Judaism." At the end of our interview, Milgram added, however, that she was looking forward to leading holy day services at Esalen, a California center of New Age and alternative spirituality.

Both critics and supporters of the Jewish Renewal acknowledge that the various parts of the movement are finding a growing appreciation and acceptance in more mainstream Jewish circles. The key word here is *parts* of the movement; the Jewish Renewal as a whole is unlikely to be exported from its bases in renewal synagogues, havurahs, and retreat and learning centers into synagogue life. Rabbi Daniel Siegel, the director of Aleph, says the organization is based on a "research and development" model, in which different services and programs relating to the renewal are offered to the whole Jewish community.[14]

This resource model describes much of the renewal movement in general. Aleph and kindred renewal groups produce a repertoire of practices and teachings that are selectively taken up by a wide range of individuals, synagogues, and other Jewish institutions. Kamenetz finds that the havurah movement in particular has gained wide currency in many Jewish institutions. Reform and Conservative synagogues have established their own havurahs, where laypeople lead services. Other older freestanding havurahs have formed networks and associations with Jewish federations and established synagogues. Liberal Jewish philanthropic organizations, such as the Nathan Cummings Foundation, have supported Aleph and other renewal organizations like the Metivta Institute, a school of Jewish meditation in Los Angeles. The music coming out of the renewal, blending traditional, folk, and more contemporary genres, is also now found in a wide range of synagogues, as are feminist-inspired translations and other texts.

In describing how the renewal affects mainstream synagogues, Siegel says the "first step is usually to adjust the product to a congregation's sensibilities. Then the question is, Will it stay that way or will it change? A lot of this stuff is coming in but without the user's manual." For instance, chanting is becoming more common in many synagogues, but the chants are often used as songs. "They don't understand the practices and meditation" behind the chanting, he adds. Siegel says that the next phase of the renewal is for Jewish denominations and other institutions to become more "porous," allowing for greater diffusion of renewal innovations into Jewish life.

Rabbi Jonathan, leader of a prominent New York synagogue, has gradually integrated many renewal practices into his congregation: meditation classes are offered weekly, and healing services are held regularly. The contemplative dimension of Judaism is found in the synagogue's prayerful Sabbath services, punctuated with long periods of silence, as well as in the music by popular renewal composers. Rabbi Jonathan stresses that renewal is only one influence on his diverse and growing congregation, but the signs of the renewal are evident enough in the participatory nature of the services and in the several havurahs that meet in members' homes.

Whereas the rabbi and cantor, each in his designated place, once led the synagogue in formal prayers, today's service is one in which participants clearly experience and participate in their religion. "It's the experience of the divine; it's not only an idea. We have a completely different approach from when prayer was offered at the center of synagogue by the rabbi. The rabbi is not the master of ceremony, but it's the people who are praying," says Rabbi Jonathan. The participatory style is also seen in the forty social action committees and projects and adult education programs that regularly enlist over five hundred congregants—almost half the synagogue's membership. But he has problems with the downplaying and sometimes rejection of the role of the rabbi in some renewal circles. "There is a place for the rabbinate that shows leadership, without creating an us versus them [scenario]," he adds. Yet Rabbi Jonathan appreciates the avant garde approach of Aleph and the way it challenges the mainstream with new ideas.

The Future of the Renewal

In a way, Rabbi Michael Strassfeld's varied life in the Jewish community personifies the changing nature of the renewal. He grew up in an Orthodox home, the son of a rabbi. As a young man in the early 1970s, he became involved in the havurah movement. Strassfeld is best known as the coeditor of the *Jewish Catalog: A Do-It-Yourself Guide.* Modeled after the *Whole Earth Catalog,* the Bible of the youth counterculture, Strassfeld's book sought to show young people that Judaism concerned the whole of life and that it could be practiced and celebrated without the assistance of synagogues and rabbis.

Later in the 1970s, he was part of an effort to revive Anshed Chased, a dying Conservative synagogue on Manhattan's Upper West Side. Eventually, Strassfeld found his way to seminary. After graduating and being ordained, he was appointed rabbi at Anshed Chased. Today, the synagogue has over five hundred families and is a center of Jewish intellectual and spiritual life in the neighborhood.

Strassfeld sees the future of the Jewish renewal in cultivating Judaism as a spiritual practice. The danger in Judaism is "that it becomes rote, saying the same liturgy every week. Making Judaism a spiritual practice gives you a reason to do it on a regular basis—you want to do it. The halakhic system is made to bring people to an awareness of the holy and God all day long, to pray three times a day."[15] By integrating meditation and spirituality into observance, it provides the why as well as the how of practicing Judaism. The Kabbalah may well provide the language for Jewish spiritual practice, though these texts' complex and esoteric teachings will not have a wide impact, Strassfeld adds. He cites the example of the wide usage of tikkun olam, a complex mystical Kabbalistic concept that has been translated to mean doing good deeds and social action.

In writing an updated version of the *Jewish Catalog,* Strassfeld has struggled with the question of what aspects of the renewal will endure. He thinks the havurah movement will likely have a wide impact even for its small numbers because it creates new forms of community life. Likewise, Jewish meditation will have a notable influence, particularly because the retreats run by such teachers as

Jonathan Omer-Man of the Metivta Institute are drawing rabbis from diverse backgrounds to this new paradigm of viewing Judaism as a spiritual practice.

The future of flagship renewal groups like Aleph are a little harder to figure out. Strassfeld asks, "Is Aleph the cutting edge, having an impact on the Jewish community, or is it just the edge? [Aleph doesn't] see it as the edge because a lot of the people [that it] deals with are at the same place [on the Jewish spectrum]." Aleph's mystical orientation, drawing directly from the Kabbalah and borrowing from other esoteric traditions, as well as its revising of Jewish law, can seem threatening to more traditional Jews. The challenge is "how to influence the wider group and avoid not being seen as a threat," Strassfeld adds. Anyone concerned about renewal in synagogue life will have to respond to the differing needs of Jews. "When some people go to the synagogue they want to feel like they're coming home. Others come to a synagogue because they want to be challenged," he says.

The way that Jewish Renewal may serve as an entry point into greater involvement in mainstream Jewish life is illustrated in the account of Andrew, a fifty-year-old social worker. He was involved in his Reform temple in the New York suburbs, serving on various kinds of committees. But he felt the services were abstract, with sermons and rituals that did not seem connected to everyday life. "Attending board meetings, you kind of feel cut off from things. It seemed fund-raising and social life just kept things going," he says. Reading Michael Lerner's book *Jewish Renewal* served as a wake-up call for Andrew. "It was an eye-opener. He was able to put forth Judaism as a radical belief system that challenges the status quo. The Torah is a radical document." After looking into other Jewish renewal teachings and eventually coming into contact with a small renewal synagogue, Andrew was impressed with the way Judaism could "push for evolution of consciousness—how it connects to everyday life." Although he too was long involved in "smorgasbord spirituality," practicing several kinds of meditation, his Jewish practices and involvement are now his only form of spirituality. He has also found that he is more interested in studying the Torah and now also has restricted his diet to mainly kosher food. Andrew is bringing his new Jewish spirituality back to his Reform synagogue, which he notices has also become a more spiritual place, stressing spirituality as well as ethics and social action.

Those Jews who became involved in spiritual renewal practices within a more mainstream context, such as Conservative synagogues not connected with Aleph, were likely to become more observant, restricting activities and attending synagogue on the Sabbath and maintaining a kosher diet. This is in contrast to those who participated in Jewish spiritual practices in the retreat centers and synagogues that are more directly related to Aleph. Most, though not all, of the participants in the renewal synagogues tended to report no greater rate of observance after becoming involved in Jewish spiritual practices. Most of these members said they kept an eco-kosher vegetarian diet, although they acknowledged that it might differ in some small ways from traditional kosher eating.

This pattern is easily explained by the different teachings on observance of Jewish law found in many centers of the renewal, such as Aleph and its affiliated synagogues and communities. The renewal synagogues' observance of an eco-kosher diet and the critique of traditional observances and other Jewish laws as being outdated naturally influences participants. Rather than becoming observant in traditional ways, these participants locate their awakened Jewish commitment in the experiential and practical benefits of Jewish spiritual practices, in their deepening social concern and interpersonal relationships.

Schachter himself does not rule out the importance of traditional Jewish practice: "Jewish Renewal doesn't try to make the whole thing completely new as if nothing before existed. Rather, the goal is to take everything a Jew does—kashrut [the kosher diet], holy days, daily davening [or prayer], Shabbat—but to do it with a different consciousness."[16] But it seems that developing such a different consciousness through spiritual practice and worship takes priority over traditional kosher and Sabbath observance for many renewal synagogue participants. As suggested by Andrew's account, a participant in Jewish renewal who is also connected to a mainstream congregation tends to deepen his or her commitment to Judaism in more traditional ways. Involvement in the renewal sparks a new or renewed interest in Judaism that is carried over to and influenced by mainstream Jewish life. Those who were connected with mainstream synagogues also reported more involvement in concrete social action projects than did the participants in the renewal synagogue. This may mean only that mainstream synagogues have more resources—volunteers, funds, and denominational support—to channel committed members into social action work than the more freestanding and less connected renewal institutions. The strong mystical bent of renewal synagogues may also draw those seeking sprituality rather than social outreach. The same pattern holds for passing on Judaism to the next generation. The participants in the renewal synagogues said their interest in Judaism did not often influence their children or spouses to embrace the religion. Those tied to more mainstream synagogues were more actively concerned about interfaith marriages and their children's involvement in Judaism.

Separation or Infiltration?

What is the best way to foment and spread renewal and reform? Is it through well-defined structures that draw in and form participants with distinctive teachings? Or is a more ad hoc, decentralized strategy better, one that creates and presents resources to its host denomination or congregations and then lets them take it from there? The groups we have looked at throughout the book have varied takes on these questions, mostly related to the religious environments in which they are working. Most observers agree that the looser ties to historic Judaism among renewal participants point to a need for structure in the movement's future. Rabbi Jonathan says that the importance of structure and balance has not been crucial for Aleph and other renewal institutions because they are led by the strong personality and charismatic force of Rabbi Schachter. The seventy-five-year-old doyen of the Jewish Renewal has been able to steer much of the movement, and Aleph in particular, away from a vague syncretism and conflict with other Jewish groups. But once Schachter passes from the scene, it may be more difficult to keep that balance. That is where the two thousand years of structure and experience of the more traditional synagogue may become more important, says rabbi Jonathan. "We're better able to handle the tensions that you have to live with. The fact that the renewal draws on the spiritualities of other religions [means] that it has to be very grounded and close to the [Jewish] texts and tradition," he says.

A topic of frequent debate in renewal circles and specifically in Aleph's journal *New Menorah* is the future of the renewal. This concern is particularly pressing as the children of the renewal pioneers are near the point of deciding whether to continue in Judaism. In a far-reaching article in *New Menorah,* Burt Jacobson and Abigail Grafton write that "for the most part, we are in our forties or fifties, and we have made no significant commitment to building the institutions and structures that will carry the movement into the twenty-first century." Part of the reason for this hesitancy, they write, is that many in the Jewish Renewal are indifferent or opposed to building structures that could serve the unaffiliated and allow for growth.[17] Most of the renewalists I interviewed are opposed to the renewal becoming another branch of Judaism alongside the Reform, Conservative, Orthodox, and Reconstructionist branches, believing that building another institution would prevent the renewal from reaching all Jews with its teachings and practices. But a clear division exists in the renewal between those who see the movement as representing a new brand of Judaism and others who see the renewal as exactly that—a revitalization of existing Jewish institutions and theology. The former position was most forcefully stated by Rabbi Rami Shapiro in an article in *New Menorah.* He states that the renewal is creating a "new foundation myth" that redefines the Torah, Jewish law, and God.[18]

As Jacobson and Grafton point out, the renewal is most effective among unaffiliated Jews turned off by the conservative, impersonal, and formal expressions of Judaism. Yet it has not developed the mechanisms to recruit the discontented and those who have dropped out. Jacobson and Grafton quote Judy Petsonk, who notes that for the renewal to continue "we will have to distill our best insights and make them available and relevant to a generation shaped by very different forces (from those that were generated by the counterculture of the '60s). The renewal movement has to discover how our idiom translates to the 1990s."[19]

The Jewish Renewal faces a fork in the road similar to that of the Catholic charismatics we discussed in Chapter One (and to a lesser extent, that of Call to Action in Chapter Five). Most of the

Catholic charismatics decided fairly early on that they would seek to integrate their practices and teachings into the church structure. The formation of separatist covenant communities was an exception to this strategy and did not become the dominant pattern in the Catholic charismatic renewal. The Jewish Renewal faces a far more complex situation mainly because American Judaism itself is highly diverse and decentralized. The research and development model favored by Aleph and most others in the renewal works effectively in the pluralistic Jewish world, which takes for granted the guarded and selective approach that many synagogues and denominations take toward the unruly movement.

The movement also accepts and takes advantage of the post-denominational environment in which many synagogues operate today.[20] The renewal synagogues that I came into contact with often did not have a clear denominational identity; they had rabbis, staff, and members from Reconstructionist, Conservative, and Reform educational and professional backgrounds (not to mention Orthodox childhoods and young adulthoods). If the renewal were to create its own schools and denominational structures, it might lose its flexibility in dealing with the shifting and localized allegiances of many Jews. Aleph's creation of a new prayer book appears to be a step toward forming a more separate renewal identity and even affiliation apart from the other branches.

The renewal synagogues and retreat centers serve as important laboratories for creating and testing new practices and teachings that later filter—often in changed, toned-down forms—into the mainstream. In many regards, the renewal groups resemble the "new paradigm" charismatic churches—a similarity that has been recognized by Jewish writers.[21] They are reluctant to form hierarchies and bureaucracies, are strongly experientially based, stress informality and spiritual intimacy, and have high rates of lay participation and leadership. Although the renewal synagogues are liberal in many areas and the new paradigm congregations are conservative and evangelical, both tend to attract the seekers, those more uprooted and alienated from traditional congregations. As demonstrated by the large numbers of disaffiliated—and some affiliated—Jews who have experimented or continue to experiment with non-Jewish spiritual forms, a ready-made market exists for the renewal mission, even if it needs to be newly fitted to the needs of the young.

Thus the Jewish Renewal may be caught between a rock and a hard place. On the one hand, it must maintain connections and credibility with the mainstream if its participants are serious about the work of renewal rather than seeking to build a new denomination. On the other hand, the renewal has a mission to provide a Judaism that seems authentic to the spiritual seeker who has little interest in the Jewish mainstream and its baggage. A more optimistic way of putting all this is that a two-pronged approach of both infiltrating the mainstream and building a distinctive movement may be necessary in providing a future for the Jewish Renewal.

Conclusion

Trusting the Spirit
Principles and Strategies
of Renewal and Reform

Attempting to renew religious institutions is thankless work. Renewal and reform groups experience uphill struggles recruiting members and maintaining support among their own, but they have no trouble finding criticism and outright opposition from those within the institutions they are trying to change. And the trouble is not visited only on the renewalists. What about the congregations or denominations that have dealt with groups seeking change and revitalization and come away from these encounters with more questions and problems than inspiration? Every case study we have looked at shows that the work of these groups can generate unintended (and sometimes intended) consequences of division, resentment, schism, or even abuse in institutional religious life.

Renewal and reform groups will face a persistent revolving-door problem. The difficulty of this work is compounded by the plethora of alternatives that renewalists and reformers encounter on the religious landscape. When some participants in these groups become so involved in and drawn to particular spiritual practices and beliefs, they may decide to go straight to the source and escape from the pluralism and clash of beliefs that most renewal groups face every day. Hence, the Catholic charismatic may leave her prayer group to find what may seem a more pure experience of the Holy Spirit in the Pentecostal church. Or the evangelical catholic Lutheran pastor may come to value the common sacramental understanding found in the Roman Catholic

Church, where the stronger authority of bishops and the papacy attempt to safeguard these teachings.

Yet looking at bad effects and defections in renewal and reform efforts gives us only a partial picture. These organizations and movements have created new institutions, practices, teachings, means of outreach and education, and other innovations that have benefited individuals, congregations, denominations, other religions, and even wider society. It may take years until many of these contributions are acknowledged and put to use, but history shows that renewal and reform is worth the effort and disappointment. Ever since I started writing this book, the interviewees and leaders of these various groups asked whether I had arrived at any general conclusions about renewal and reform. I often tried to turn the question back to them. I wanted to know what they liked best about their particular organization or movement. What really grabbed them about their involvement in such efforts?

I knew I was on to something when I heard the word *trust* in more than a few people's responses. These groups tended to display and generate high levels of trust among participants. They felt that the leaders of their groups were people whom they could trust with their support. Participants viewed the literature and other material issued by the renewal and reform groups as trustworthy. They also said that they, in turn, felt trusted by their leaderships as well as by fellow participants and practitioners. The more intimate environments and simplified and decentralized structures of renewal and reform groups accounted for a good deal of these perceptions of trustworthiness. Leaders were directly in touch and accessible to members and participants, and they could be removed or criticized much more effectively than in larger, less personal institutions. But I also think that their answers had something to do with the spiritual nature of renewal and, to a lesser extent, reform groups.

Because of the relatively simple structures of these groups, participation and the importance of using one's spiritual gifts are highly valued. Some interviewees could not believe they were trusted with the various responsibilities they were given in their particular groups. Lack of family or career connections or formal education were not barriers to involvement as they might have been in the more official precincts of denominational life. The lack of material resources in some renewal and reform efforts tend to turn leaders and participants toward a greater reliance on what could be called spiritual capital, values and practices such as trust, generosity, discernment, prayer, and reflection. Just the fact that these groups and individuals are striving for spiritual renewal or religious reform tends to make them more open (and sometimes more vulnerable) to people, intuitions, and ideas that may not find a place in more efficient, bureaucratic environments.

Strategies of Reform and Renewal

Of course, these groups are not merely about providing a place to cultivate new spiritual gifts. Ideally, they want to change things in their larger institutions, as well as on the local level. Each group we have looked at presents different dilemmas and challenges in the work of renewal and reform. The Catholic charismatics started out as a movement that was viewed as foreign and outside the perimeters of traditional Catholicism. But in the process of being accepted by and assimilated into the church, the movement may be losing the energy and distinctive identity that appealed to so many Catholics in the first place.

Moving in the opposite direction, the evangelicals who gathered around the Biblical Witness Fellowship (BWF) in the United Church of Christ originally sought to be the catalyst for evangelical reform in the denomination but came to question the value of the denomination and its structures as they moved to the margins of church life. The evangelical catholic Lutherans seeking confessional renewal within their respective churches encounter a new pluralism that challenges their vision of an orthodox and united church. The Taizé community emerged with expectations of encouraging Christian unity and helping believers act as a force of reconciliation in their churches and society. But the community's practices and style of spirituality have been swept up in the currents of the spiritual marketplace, making them susceptible to individualism and consumerism.

Call to Action started out intending to reform the Catholic Church but along the way also discovered alternative ways of ministry and worship. Will these new patterns of ministry hinder the group's effectiveness as a force for reform in an increasingly conservative church? Jewish Renewal seems to be stalled at a fork in the road: it could go in the direction of becoming a distinct Jewish movement, with its own ideology, teachings, and structure, or it could remain a loosely based coalition of groups and teachers that seek to revitalize institutions and individuals in existing Judaism.

Studying each of these efforts in light of the others suggests some similar themes that apply to most renewal and reform groups, movements, and activists. They all ask the practical question of how to enact renewal and reform in a rapidly shifting religious landscape. Is it through confrontation and pressure from outside the church or subtle influence from within the institution? When is it best to retreat from institutional life and create a group with its own distinctive teachings, practices, and traditions, in the hope that these innovations will filter into the mainstream? And when is it more advantageous to travel light and eschew teachings and styles that may erect barriers between the renewal or reform group and the host institution?

The case studies suggest two ways of carrying out renewal and reform in today's religious environment. One type of group serves as a resource center providing information and services: alternative ways of giving and benefits, pastor referrals, means of protesting and addressing concerns with the larger body, and new forms of cooperation with like-minded congregations. The boundaries between resource centers and denominations are not clearly defined, and the centers generally have few or no requirements for membership. Congregations can use the services of this type of organization—subscribing to its newsletter or finding a pastor through a referral network—without necessarily joining or accepting its agenda.

The other category of reform and renewal groups is the affiliation fellowship. These groups and movements tend to have clearly defined memberships, maintain a strong identity, and often show a greater degree of tension with the wider denomination. The members are more likely to seek religious identity from these groups than from their denominations. These fellowships are more likely to take part in schisms and splits from their respective denominations than the resource centers, probably because members experience enough solidarity and support in the group to consider alternatives to the denomination. The fellowships represent more than just isolated individuals and congregations and can, if necessary, band together to create a separate existence outside of the denomination or affiliate with another body.

The American Lutheran Publicity Bureau is a resource center serving a diverse group of confessional and evangelical catholic Lutherans from different church bodies, even though it is at odds with the denominational leaderships. The Society of the Holy Trinity, like any religious order, is clearly in the affiliation fellowship camp. Taizé is an example of a resource center that emerged from a very strong affiliation fellowship—a monastery—as it sought to minister to visitors and then impart its spiritual practices and teachings among church members and seekers. Some Taizé prayer participants would like to make the group a close-knit fellowship, but the Taizé brothers continue to resist such institutionalization.

BWF and the Catholic charismatic renewal started out as affiliation fellowships, creating separate identities for members. But the more recent history of both groups shows a change in strategy; the local chapters of BWF were discontinued, and the covenant communities of the Catholic charismatics fell upon hierarchical disfavor. Today, the Catholic charismatics have tried to integrate their practices and teachings into the institution, and BWF and other evangelical renewal groups are riding the wave of decentralization in mainline Protestantism, creating new networks with like-minded Christians outside of their respective institutions.

Call to Action (CTA) originally sought to appeal to the whole church, eliciting the early support of bishops during its 1976 gathering. But the hierarchy distanced itself from CTA as its liberal reformist agenda became clear; CTA became a pressure group in the church. As the leadership of the church became increasingly conservative during the 1980s and 1990s, CTA adopted a strategy of resistance. Because the group is restricted within the official church, it does not have enough leeway to act as a resource center. Instead, it has become a haven for fellowship, distinctive spiritualities, and practices, as well as a free space for discussion among dissenters.

The Jewish Renewal is unique in that it serves, if uneasily, both as a resource center and an affiliation fellowship. For a segment of participants, the renewal provides a primary religious affiliation; other Jewish institutions and individuals outside the renewal select practices or teachings from its menu that suit their needs and pass over those that do not. It remains to be seen whether Jewish Renewal can continue to cater to its core supporters (and help them keep their children in the movement) and attract a younger population while making its practices and institutions (particularly its retreat centers) accessible to mainstream Judaism.

Both ways of carrying out renewal and reform offer promises and present problems. Affiliation fellowships answer the need of congregation members looking beyond religious individualism for a sense of community. These groups will play an important role in denominations that restrict members and congregations from giving input into the leadership structure and its decision-making process and from engaging in debate. They will provide leverage for a degree of change, free space for discussion, and a testing zone for new forms of religiosity and spiritual practice. Their informality, lack of bureaucracy, and high rate of participation will serve as models for denominations, even if the spiritual intensity and uniformity of these groups' views will make their dynamism difficult to replicate in complex and pluralistic denominations.

The resource center model, however, appears particularly compelling in a period of growing consumerism and decentralization in religious institutions. This model is flexible enough to make room for the multiple loyalties and attachments evident among leaders and members of congregations today. It accepts the possibility that members concerned about renewal and reform may borrow some of an organization's innovations and yet also sign on to other causes and efforts that take varied approaches to denominational change. For instance, a Presbyterian congregation may support an evangelical renewal organization's work in missions, hold Taizé prayer services, and join the AIDS ministry of a liberal Presbyterian caucus. These activities and agendas may or may not conflict, but such varied causes and concerns are typically found among congregation members who have become increasingly pluralistic in background and belief.

The resource center model is also in sync with recent insights on how organizations function and flourish in a decentralized environment. This postmodern approach tends to work through coalitions rather than through hierarchies, holding that organizations succeed by widening relationships, or forming networks, with other groups and individuals. The Alliance of Baptists adopted this approach in its attempts at reforming the Southern Baptist Convention. Sociologist Nancy Ammerman found that the group focused on "forging alliances for the purpose of pursuing specific short-term goals." Although the alliance has helped start a seminary and publishes alternative Baptist literature, it has not kept these initiatives as the exclusive property of the organization; it offers them to participants in other liberal and moderate Baptist bodies.[1]

Business expert Peter Drucker sees the formation of partnerships as the defining characteristic of the new business culture, an observation relevant to religious institutions influenced by new organizational models. He adds that "in a partnership one cannot command. One can only gain trust."[2] We have seen how renewal and reform groups also operate on the principle of trust, suggesting a close fit with postmodern organizations.

Principles of Reform and Renewal

In their successes and shortcomings, the case studies in this book point to principles that renewal and reform participants and supporters, as well as leaders of religious institutions, may wish to consider.

1. Effective groups were intentional about reform and renewal. Leaders and participants did tend to speak a little too softly about their involvement in groups and movements working for change in their respective religious bodies and traditions. In other words, they did not try hard enough to get recruits. Some were understandably concerned about their careers and future opportunities in ministry should they appear too radical or reactionary in criticizing the powers that be or engineering change in their respective congregations and religious bodies. But I sensed that there was room for creating more support for these groups among congregants. Those who feel that the controversies and divisiveness surrounding renewal and reform groups might detract from the spiritual emphasis they wish to instill in their sermons or liturgies could use other avenues, such as open forums, home Bible studies, and discussion groups, to engage these concerns.

2. Effective groups work within the existing pluralism in American religious institutions. In turn, denominations should realize that suppressing dissent and the formation of new groups may cause more problems than it solves. This is another touchy issue because it challenges religious boundaries that seek to protect truth from error. Every denomination has to set some limits, to define what is beyond the pale of official teachings, policies, and practices, and what is allowable. But the tendency in many denominations—both liberal and conservative—has been to try to create uniformity where usually none exists. The formation of the many special interest groups and renewal and reform movements testifies to this de facto diversity in American denominational life. The challenge for denominations is to open more lines of communication, decision making, and cooperation with these groups, even if they are strongly critical of official positions. In short, as Rabbi Daniel Siegel of Aleph noted, the denominations must be "more porous" in filtering in and sending out innovations and resources.[3]

Lyle Schaller, a specialist in church growth, recognizes this possibility in his call for a "big tent"–style structure of denomination. In addressing the serious divisions within the United Methodist Church over sexual and ministry issues, Schaller writes that the "older style of trying to impose order and seeking consensus or common ground and the highly centralized polity of the denomination, built on a high level of distrust of local leadership, is incompatible with ideological pluralism." He adds that a model of this kind of structure would be the Methodists holding several different annual conferences, rather than one, for each of its constituent groups: Korean-American congregations, large downtown churches, self-identified theologically liberal churches, and self-identified evangelical congregations. The United Methodist Church would thus become more of a federation of linked annual conferences than a centralized denomination.[4]

Though such inclusiveness increases the possibility of chaos and theological and moral relativism as well as cooperation, it also addresses some of the dilemmas facing renewal and reform groups. In such a decentralized scenario, renewal groups would have greater input into denominational affairs even if their plans of broad reform might be stymied by the new diversity. Even if Schaller's proposal might seem unlikely to succeed, a measure of denominational decentralization would compel religious institutions to look at renewal and reform groups more as resources for revitalizing denominations than sources of competition and conflict.

By allowing these groups to work closer to the center of denominational life, a new process of organizational growth and competition could be set in motion. Those groups that gain strong support and commitment by congregations and members would rise to prominence and greater influence within the wider institution. Groups that fail to find support and participation among the grassroots would naturally move toward the margins of the institution or go out of existence altogether. Hence, although the early stage of such a decentralized denomination might well look like an example of ideological pluralism, the finished product might actually show more cohesion and unity than many centralized denominations do today. The cycle of birth and death through which many religious movements travel also applies to renewal and reform groups and movements. As has happened in the past, renewal groups and movements within declining bodies may well be the seedbeds from which new religions and denominations emerge.

3. *Getting caught up in culture wars or other ideological battles may distract both participants and critics from the vital issues involved in renewal and reform, although a certain amount of tension may be useful.* Taking an us-against-them stance or using battle imagery does not help in winning arguments, particularly as it may give weight to charges that renewalists and reformers think themselves superior to their leaders or the average congregation member. By focusing on the divisive issues, groups may run the risk of alienating the very people they are trying to reach. Although both renewal groups and reform organizations seek to engage denominations with their concerns, the renewal groups have the advantage of more easily avoiding political rhetoric because they specialize in spirituality. Seeking spiritual and transcendent principles that can unify differing parties helps in moving the arguments and conflicts toward a higher level of dialogue.

Of course, conflict is the fuel for many renewal and reform efforts. The tension between a renewal group and the wider denomination tends to spur activists and participants on to greater levels of commitment. Sociologists such as Rodney Stark and Roger

Finke have found that religions exhibiting a certain degree of tension with the wider society are found to generate greater group loyalty and higher rates of growth.[5] The same may be true for renewal and reform groups standing in tension with their denominations, although our case studies suggest mixed results. It is possible to have too high a level of tension between a group and its host denomination. One thinks of BWF and CTA, in which disengagement and burnout are the results of too wide a gap between reformers and their denominations. In contrast, the Catholic charismatic renewal, particularly as expressed in the work of the National Service Committee, may have reduced too much of the tension between the movement and the church, leading to a loss of identity on the renewalists' part.

4. *The use of ritual, music, magazines, liturgies, and other forms of "material religion" gives a tangible expression to the message of renewal and reform.* When I was asking one of the leaders how best to get an understanding of the Jewish Renewal, he advised me to "listen to the music." When CTA was doing musical presentations on Catholic social teachings, they were asked to perform for the American bishops—something that is unlikely to happen in their more serious and cerebral reform mode. The music, songs, and hymns emerging from reform and renewal groups have their own sound and sensibility and have had a significantly positive effect on those who may not yet be receptive to the formal teachings and practices of these groups.

The prayer books published by the American Lutheran Publicity Bureau, the chants circulated by Taizé, and the more bodily worship style of the Catholic charismatics are a few examples of these groups' innovations that have been welcomed by the mainstream. Renewal and reform groups can change things and find a hearing just by being true to their own particular gifts and callings. These tangible expressions both serve to create an identity for group participants and introduce others to the group's teachings and practices.

5. *Widening the circles of connections and contacts with believers and sympathizers in other groups and traditions can assist in the work of renewal and reform.* It was surprising how often members and leaders of the groups I interviewed were not aware of renewal efforts similar to their own. Yet even the groups with strong doctrinal and

theological identities often acknowledged that denominational labels no longer have the significance they once did and were interested in coming into contact with like-minded groups. For instance, the evangelical catholics of the Evangelical Lutheran Church in America who participate in the American Lutheran Publicity Bureau and the Society of the Holy Trinity are attempting to retain their close ties to the Lutheran Church–Missouri Synod, even as these bodies move further apart officially.

Such groups as BWF, Taizé, and Jewish Renewal accept that they are functioning in a postdenominational environment; they make their services and resources available to a wide constituency, and accept groups, leaders, and members from other traditions. Even if reformers do not agree that we live in a postdenominational world (many members of the largest denominations—from the Catholics to the Mormons—have strong denominational identities), they should seek out allies in other bodies and avoid limiting their renewal and reform activities strictly to their own denominational structures. Individuals in similar traditions could probably benefit from the experiences and lessons that renewal and reform groups outside their denominations could offer.

6. *Education and particularly youth formation are key to insuring that the next generation will carry on renewal and reform work.* The graying of renewal and reform groups was a common phenomenon throughout my research. The generation that was young in the 1960s and 1970s seemed much more likely to form and get involved with renewal efforts than subsequent generations. The interest in renewal and reform is usually based on an early involvement in traditional congregations and parishes and a basic religious literacy. Because many young people lack these fundamentals, their lack of involvement is not surprising; without a personal investment and background in the faith, they feel no need for reforming the religion. That is why many renewal and reform groups (as well as all congregations) are focusing on educating youth and encouraging their participation and eventual leadership. The larger structures of denominations and religious schools can play a part in helping renewal and reform groups reach out to younger generations by making a priority of educating the next generation.

7. *Congregations and larger religious institutions that encourage "religious virtuosity" among their members, young and old, will be crucial to*

the future of renewal and reform. I began this book by noting how religious virtuosi are the life force of renewal and reform movements. Whether endowed with a supernatural gift or a natural talent, these individuals have a knack for trusting the spirit and conveying that spiritual dimension to others. It is in the interest of religious institutions to cultivate and put to use spiritually gifted individuals because they are the ones who reenergize religious life. But, unfortunately, that is not always what these institutions do, especially in denominations and congregations in which permitting separate groups and movements to form would conflict with the concept that all members are spiritually equal. Sociologist Patricia Wittberg writes that "if a church fails to provide such an outlet for those who feel called to do more for their faith, it runs the risk that its more committed and fervent members will desert it for 'holier' churches. Recent studies have shown that this is precisely what is happening to the various mainline Protestant churches in this country."[6]

We have seen that, beyond their other functions, reform and renewal groups serve as outlets for spiritual fervency and commitment. Along with religious orders, monasteries, and parachurch groups, reform and renewal organizations and movements are the places where religious virtuosos are valued and others have the opportunity to develop their own gifts. The difficult part is encouraging these movements while avoiding their tendency to foster elitism and divisions within congregations.

Conflict between renewal and reform groups and religious institutions should not be the last word. The flexible nature of these groups allows participants to devote their full energies to them or to borrow their resources and practices in more partial ways. Even if many of these organizations' strategies and plans for institutional renewal do not come to full fruition, groups seeking renewal and reform will continue to be born, ebb, and flow, demanding our attention.

Appendix A
The Research Methods Used in This Study

The case studies in this book were conducted through a mixture of journalism and sociology. In-depth interviewing and reporting were joined with ethnographic research and observation of group activities and gatherings. I interviewed fifteen to thirty participants and leaders in each of the groups and movements profiled. The interviews were conducted from December 1998 to June 2000. I also conducted content analyses of the literature issued by various groups and consulted studies and other accounts concerning each of these organizations and movements. Here are more details about the interviews and other research methods conducted for each case study.

Chapter One

Charismatic Catholic Renewal. Interview with National Service Committee Director Walter Matthews, Fredericksburg, Virginia. Interviews with fifteen leaders and other laypeople in the charismatic renewal. Observation of four prayer meeting sessions in the New York area.

Chapter Two

Biblical Witness Fellowship (BWF). Interview with BWF Director David Runion-Bareford, Boston. Interviews with fifteen pastors and laity involved with BWF and congregations related to the group in New England, New Jersey, and Pennsylvania. Content analysis of BWF publication *The Witness,* 1997–1999.

Chapter Three

Evangelical Catholics, American Lutheran Publicity Bureau (ALPB), *and Society of the Holy Trinity* (STS). Interviews with ALPB officials Reverends Frederick Schumacher and Glenn C. Stone, in New York. Interview with Reverend Phillip Johnson, Senior of STS. Interviews with thirty clergy and laity involved with this movement and groups in New York City area and Chicago. Content analysis of *Lutheran Forum*, 1970–2000.

Chapter Four

Taizé. Interview with Taizé Brothers Pedro and John, New York City. Interviews with twenty participants in Taizé in New York, Boston, Chicago, and Philadelphia. Attended and observed six Taizé services.

Chapter Five

Call to Action (CTA). Interview with Dan Daly, Sheila Daly, and Don Wedd, Chicago. Interviews with fifteen CTA members in New England, New York, Philadelphia, and New Jersey. Content analysis of CTA newsletters, 1992 and 1998–1999. Attended and observed one CTA meeting.

Chapter Six

Jewish Renewal. Telephone interview with Aleph Director Rabbi Daniel Siegel. Interviews with fifteen Jewish renewal participants in New York and Philadelphia. Content analysis of *New Menorah*, 1985–1999. Observation and attendance at three services of three synagogues (two renewal congregations and one Conservative synagogue).

Appendix B
Resources on Renewal and Reform Organizations

Although my case studies can give the reader some indication of the diversity of renewal and reform groups today, this resource guide shows the proliferation of these organizations on the religious landscape of the United States. Each entry profiles the background and identity of the renewal and reform group, as well as citing its activities and providing contact information.

Acts 29 Ministries. This is the fellowship for charismatics in the Episcopal Church. Formerly called Episcopal Renewal Ministries, the organization publishes a magazine and holds national and regional conferences. Contact: Acts 29 Ministries, 1900, The Exchange, Bldg. 100, Ste. 170, Atlanta, Ga. 30339. Telephone: (800) 299-6324. Web site: (http://www.a29.com).

Aldersgate Renewal Ministries. This group is the organization of the charismatic renewal in the United Methodist Church. Since 1974 the group has held national conferences as well as seminars and retreats seeking to introduce and strengthen United Methodists in spiritual growth, including use of spritual gifts such as healing and speaking in tongues. ARM also encourages regional fellowships to provide opportunities for worship, learning, and fellowship. Contact: Aldergate Renewal Ministries, P.O. Box 1205, Goodlettsville, Tenn. 37070. Telephone: (615) 851-9192. Web site: (http://www.aldersgaterenewal.org).

Aleph. The Alliance for Jewish Renewal. The alliance is the principal organization of the Jewish Renewal. The group runs seminars and programs in Jewish mysticism and learning, as well as social action. Aleph publishes the journal *New Menorah* and serves as a resource center for synagogues and Jewish organizations that are usually on the more progressive or liberal side of the spectrum. Contact: Aleph, 7318 Germantown Ave., Philadelphia, Pa. 19119-1793. Telephone: (215) 247-9700. Web site: (http://www.aleph.org).

Alliance of Baptists. The alliance serves as a reform group for the movement of Southern Baptists who have been pushed to the margins of denominational life since conservatives gained control of the Southern Baptist Convention during the 1980s. In supporting alternative seminaries, publications, and missions organizations, the alliance is less interested in forming a new Baptist denomination than in providing resources to dissidents and networking with like-minded Baptist groups. Contact: Alliance of Baptists, 1328 16th St., N.W., Washington, D.C. 20036. Telephone: (202) 745-7609. Web site: (http://www.allianceofbaptists.org).

Alliance of Confessing Evangelicals. Although evangelicals are the ones forming most of the renewal groups to influence their mainline denominations, the Alliance of Confessing Evangelicals is attempting to reform evangelicalism itself. The group, started in the mid-1990s, targets the growth of consumerism and church growth techniques in evangelical churches. The alliance calls for a return to classical Christianity that is in line with Reformation theology. It publishes the magazine *Modern Reformation.* Contact: Alliance of Confessing Evangelicals, P.O. Box 2000, Philadelphia, Pa. 19103. Telephone: (215) 546-3696. Web site: (http://www.allliancenet.org).

American Anglican Council. The council is one of the largest and most inclusive conservative renewal groups in the Episcopal Church. It attempts to bring together all orthodox Episcopalians, including both those opposing and those supporting women's ordination, in order to present a united front for renewal in the denomination. The council holds regular conferences. Contact: American Anglican Council, P.O. Box 180159, Dallas, Tex. 75218.

Telephone: (800) 914-2000. Web site: (http://www.episcopalian.
org).

American Baptist Evangelicals (ABE). Started in 1992, ABE seeks
evangelical reform in the moderate to liberal American Baptist
Churches, particularly on issues of scriptural authority and sexuality. The group publishes a journal and provides other services
for member churches. Contact: American Baptist Evangelicals,
P.O. Box 128, Library, Pa. 15129. Telephone: (877) 233-8264. Web
site: (http://www.abeonline.org).

American Lutheran Publicity Bureau (ALPB). The ALPB publishes the
Lutheran Forum and *Forum Letter,* the foremost publications for evangelical catholics, who stress the importance of the sacraments,
liturgy, and historic confessions in U.S. Lutheranism. Along with
tracts, books, and worship material, the ALPB also organizes occasional conferences. Contact: American Lutheran Publicity Bureau,
P.O. Box 327, Delhi, N.Y. 13753-0327. Telephone: (607) 746-7511.

Association for Church Renewal (ACR). The association represents an
attempt by various evangelical renewal groups to come together to
find a stronger and more unified voice in confronting their
denominations and larger structures. One example of such unified action was a petition organized by the ACR in 1998 to restore
doctrinal orthodoxy to the World Council of Churches. Contact:
Association for Church Renewal, 1521 16th St., N.W., Ste. 300,
Washington, D.C. 20036-1466. Telephone: (202) 986-1440.

Biblical Witness Fellowship (BWF). As the strongest voice of conservative evangelicals in the United Church of Christ (UCC), BWF provides several services for its members and supporters. BWF runs a
mission network, linking conservative UCC churches to evangelical missionaries, and publishes its newspaper *The Witness* (sent to
every UCC church in the country). Contact: Biblical Witness
Fellowship, P.O. Box 102, Candia, N.H. 03034-0102. Telephone:
(800) 494-9172. Web site: (http://www.biblicalwitness.org).

Call to Action (CTA). CTA is a liberal reform organization in American Catholicism. Such issues as women's ordination, optional

celibacy for priests, greater lay involvement, and democracy in all segments of the church are key issues in CTA. The organization runs a national conference and has chapters across the United States. Contact: Call to Action, 4419 N. Kedzie, Chicago, Ill. 60625. Telephone: (773) 604-0400. Web site: (http://call-to-action.org).

Catholics United for the Faith (CUF). Unlike Call to Action, CUF believes that the Catholic Church in the United States has been derailed since Vatican II, supporting liberalism and relativism. Originally concerned with monitoring liberal directions in the church and reporting them to the Vatican and to its constituency, CUF has taken a more positive approach of strengthening American Catholics' allegiance to church teachings. The organization publishes *Lay Witness* magazine and holds regular conferences. Contact: Catholics United for the Faith, 827 N. 4th St., Steubenville, Ohio 43952. Telephone: (800) 693-2484. Web site: (http://www.cuf.org).

Center for Evangelical and Catholic Theology. While the ecumenical center cannot formally be described as a renewal or reform group, it is playing a similar role to many of these groups as it teaches a more catholic or sacramental approach to Christian faith and practice. The center publishes the theological journal *Pro Ecclesia* and holds conferences. Contact: Center for Evangelical and Catholic Theology, 1070 South Lake Shore Dr., No. 13, 2-A, Lake Geneva, Minn. 55057.

Confessing Christ. This group was started by centrists in the UCC who agreed that renewal was important in this liberal denomination but at the same time were uncomfortable with the more conservative and aggressive efforts of BWF. Confessing Christ stresses the importance of classic Christian liturgies, theology, and creeds, as well as social action. The group publishes a newsletter and has chapters throughout the United States. Contact: Confessing Christ, P.O. Box 435, Deforest, Wis. 53532-0435. Telephone: (608) 846-7880. Web site: (http://www.execpc.com).

Confessing Movement. This United Methodist group seeks to return its denomination to greater fidelity to historic Christianity and the

Wesleyan tradition. The group also carries an emphasis on liturgical as well as theological renewal. Contact: Confessing Movement, 7995 E. 21st St., Indianapolis, Ind. 46219. Telephone: (317) 356-9729. Web site: (http://www.confessingumc.org).

Cooperative Baptist Fellowship (CBF). The CBF is a moderate reform group similar to the Alliance of Baptists, although the CBF has taken a more independent stance toward the convention, suggesting to some that it may become a separate denomination. The fellowship, with affiliated churches around the United States, publishes literature and supports several new seminaries. Contact: Cooperative Baptist Fellowship, P.O. Box 450329, Atlanta, Ga. 31145-0329. Telephone: (770) 220-1600. Web site: (http://www.cbfonline.org).

Covenant Network. Founded in 1997, this is the leading progressive group in the Presbyterian Church (USA), calling for the inclusion of homosexuals in the denomination, as well as other liberal measures. While calling for unity in the denomination, the network also seeks to counteract the growing conservative influence in the church. The network publishes newsletters and holds regular conferences. Contact: Covenant Network, c/o Village Presbyterian Church, P.O. Box 8050, 6641 Mission Rd., Prairie Village, Kans. 66208. Web site: (http://www.covenantnetwork.org).

Cursillo. Started in Spain by Catholics seeking spiritual renewal, Cursillo has found interest and participation among Protestant churches as well. The movement is based around weekends that stress prayer, Bible study, guided meditation, and discussion. Contact: Cursillo, P.O. Box 210226, Dallas, Tex. 75211. Web sites: for Catholic Cursillo (http://www.natl-cursillo.org); for Episcopalian Cursillo (http://www.go4th.org).

Daystar. This is a loosely based network of Lutheran Church–Missouri Synod members critical of the conservative leadership in the denomination, addressing such issues as women's equality and ecumenism. The group holds occasional conferences. Contact: Daystar, c/o Zion Lutheran Church, 1015 S.W. 18th Ave., Portland, Oreg. 97205. Web site: (http://www.day-star.net).

Disciples Heritage Fellowship. The fellowship attempts to preserve and renew the tradition of the Disciples of Christ stressing a return to New Testament Christianity and congregational autonomy. The group accepts congregations that are part of the mainline Christian Church (Disciples of Christ) as well as other churches claiming the Disciples heritage. The fellowship publishes a journal. Contact: Disciples Heritage Fellowship, P.O. Box 109, Lovington, Ill. 61937. Telephone: (217) 873-5126. Web site: (http://www.disciple-heritage.org).

Edah. This is among the first liberal reform organizations in Orthodox Judaism. The group emerged from conferences for feminists in the Orthodox world, but it currently addresses a wide range of issues beyond the role of women in Jewish life, including Orthodox divorce laws, relations with non-Orthodox Jews, and biblical criticism. Contact: Edah, 47 W. 34th St., New York, N.Y. 10001. Telephone: (212) 244-7501. Web site: (http://www.edah.org).

Episcopalians United. This is another large conservative renewal organization in the Episcopal Church. It draws together a broad coalition of Episcopal charismatics, evangelicals, and Anglo Catholics. The group has local chapters and publishes a national newspaper, *United Voice.* Contact: Episcopalians United, P.O. Box 797425, Dallas, Tex. 75379. Telephone: (972) 381-7374. Web site: (http://www.eunited.org).

Focus Renewal Ministries (FRM). FRM is the voice for charismatics in the UCC. The group takes a more nonpolitical stance than its colleagues at BWF, as it seeks to introduce UCC clergy and laity to charismatic Christianity. FRM publishes a newsletter. Contact: Focus Renewal Ministries, P.O. Box 330, Sassamansville, Pa. 19472. Telephone: (610) 754-6446.

Good News. This is one of the oldest evangelical renewal groups, with its roots in the mid-1960s. Good News seeks to renew the United Methodist Church along evangelical lines through activism and its magazine, *Good News.* Contact: Good News, 308 E. Main St., Wilmore, Ky. 40390. Telephone: (606) 858-4661. Web site: (http://www.goodnewsmag.org).

Great Commission Network (GCN). The GCN represents evangelicals in the Evangelical Lutheran Church in America (ELCA). The network concentrates on evangelism more than conservative activism to change the ELCA. Contact: Great Commission Network. Web site: (http://www.gcnusa.com).

Institute on Religion and Democracy (IRD). IRD can be considered the sociopolitical wing of the conservative renewal groups in the mainline denominations. The institute monitors the social positions and actions of mainline denominations and advocates on such issues as religious freedom, democracy, the free market, and traditional values. IRD publishes a newsletter and has organized committees that work with renewal groups on social issues in their denominations. Contact: Institute on Religion and Democracy, 1521 16th St., N.W., Ste. 300, Washington, D.C. 20036-1466. Telephone: (202) 986-1440. Web site: (http://www.ird-renew.org).

Jesus First. Another renewal group recently formed within the Lutheran Church–Missouri Synod, it includes many of the large Missouri Synod megachurches, large multifaceted congregations. The group opposes the centralization of leadership in the church and calls for greater cooperation with other Christians. Contact: Jesus First, 505 South Kirkwood Rd., Kirkwood, Mo. 63122-5925. Web site: (http://www.jesusfirst.net).

Knox Fellowship. In a denomination brimming with evangelical renewal groups, the Knox Fellowship addresses the issues of evangelism and discipleship in the Presbyterian Church (USA). The fellowship holds regional conferences. Contact: Knox Fellowship, 800 Airport Blvd., #304, Burlingame, Calif. 94010. Telephone: (650) 347-6248. Web site: (http://www.knoxfellowship.com).

Leadership Network. This organization works outside of established church bodies to encourage institutional revitalization among congregations, clergy, and laity. The network, which has been influential in the megachurch movement, sees the postmodern era as posing new challenges to churches and denominations and uses sophisticated technology, publications, and seminars around the country to work for renewal. Contact: Leadership Network, 2501

Cedar Springs Rd., Ste. 200, Dallas, Tex. 75201. Telephone: (800) 765-5323. Web site: (http://www.leadnet.org).

Lutheran Renewal (LR). LR represents the charismatic renewal in the ELCA. The group also addresses areas of concern in the denomination, as well as holding seminars and conferences and publishing a newsletter. Contact: Lutheran Renewal, 2701 Rice St., St. Paul, Minn. 55113-2200. Telephone: (651) 486-2865. Web site: (http://www.lutheranrenewal.org).

Mormon Alliance. The formation of the alliance was the result of a crackdown on Mormon dissenters by the church leadership on such issues as revisionist views of the history of the Church of Jesus Christ of Latter-day Saints, women's role in Mormonism, and the abuse of power in the church. In fact, the alliance calls for members to document cases of "ecclesiastical abuses of power" by church leaders and publishes them in a journal. Contact: Mormon Alliance, 6337 Highland Dr., P.O. Box 215, Salt Lake City, Utah 84121.

National Havurah Committee. This organization is a transdenominational network of Jewish small groups meeting for worship known as havurot. These groups are often lay-led and have a more informal atmosphere than found at most synagogues. The committee holds a summer institute on Jewish life, spirituality, and social issues. The membership of the committee includes havurot that are part of synagogues as well as independent groups. Contact: National Havurah Committee, 7135 Germantown Ave., 2nd floor, Philadelphia, Penna. 19119-1824. Telephone: (215) 248-9760. Web site: (http://www.havurah.org).

National Service Committee for the Catholic Charismatic Renewal (NSC). The NSC, also known as Chariscenter USA, is the main coordinating organization for charismatics in the Roman Catholic Church. The committee organizes conferences, trains leaders, and publishes a newsletter. Contact: National Service Committee for the Catholic Charismatic Renewal, P.O. Box 628, Locust Grove, Va. 22508-0628. Telephone: (800) 338-2445.

Opus Dei. Serving as much as a Roman Catholic religious order as a renewal movement, Opus Dei upholds the philosophy that secular work can be holy and encourages its Catholic members to bring their faith to bear upon their careers. The group's strongly conservative nature has gained the support of Pope John Paul II. Contact: Opus Dei, 524 North Ave., Ste. 200, New Rochelle, N.Y. 10801. Telephone: (914) 235-1201. Web site: (http://www.opusdei.org).

Order of Corpus Christi. The order represents a sacramental and contemplative movement within the UCC. Silent prayer, contemplation, liturgical worship, and appreciation of the sacraments are the touchstones of the organization. Contact: Order of Corpus Christi, 133 Liberty Dr., Oxford Crossing, Langhorne, Pa. 19047-3077. Telephone: (215) 943-7110. Web site: (http://www.occhristi.org).

Order of St. Luke. As with other liturgical renewal groups, the order seeks to generate a more sacramental and contemplative approach to worship and faith in the United Methodist Church. Although it has a Methodist orientation, the order is open to other Christians. The order publishes a newsletter five times a year. Contact: Order of St. Luke, 2683 Carnation Dr., Richardson, Tex. 75082. Web site: (http://www.saint-luke.org).

Presbyterian and Reformed Renewal Ministries International (PRRMI). The PRRMI represents the charismatic movement in the Presbyterian Church (USA) and in other Reformed bodies. Started in 1966, the group presses for both spiritual renewal and conservative reform of these denominations. The organization publishes a magazine and newsletter. Contact: Presbyterian and Reformed Renewal Ministries International, P.O. Box 429, Black Mountain, N.C. 28711-0492. Web site: (http://www.prrmi.org).

Presbyterian Coalition. The coalition is one of several evangelical renewal organizations attempting to reform the Presbyterian Church (USA). The group addresses all aspects of the denomination: missions, seminary education, worship, and policy. As with other evangelical renewal groups, the Presbyterian Coalition has been in the forefront of opposition to the ordination of gays and blessings of homosexual unions. The coalition holds national conferences. Contact: Presbyterian Coalition, P.O. Box 26070, Birmingham, Ala. 35260. Telephone: (205) 979-3313. Web site: (http://www. presbycoalition.org).

Presbyterian Lay Committee. The committee, another one of the older renewal groups with roots in the 1960s, seeks evangelical revitalization in the Presbyterian Church (USA). The group seeks change through both legislation—such as measures against gay rights—and encouraging biblical and Reformed theology and spiritual life in Presbyterian churches. The committee's primary activity is publishing the *Presbyterian Layman,* a newspaper that aggressively critiques denominational actions and reports on evangelical initiatives. Contact: Presbyterian Lay Committee, P.O. Box 2210, Lenoir, N.C. 28645. Web site: (http://www.layman.org).

Presbyterians for Renewal (PFR). PFR is similar to other Presbyterian evangelical renewal groups although it appears to take a more conciliatory stance in the denomination, stressing that it wants to work within (rather than around) the structures of the Presbyterian Church (USA) to restore doctrinal orthodoxy and provide spiritual revitalization. The group publishes a quarterly newsletter and holds conferences. Contact: Presbyterians for Renewal, 8134 New LaGrange Rd., Ste. 227, Louisville, Ky. 40222-4079. Telephone: (520) 425-4630. Web site: (http://www.presbyrenewal.org).

Renewal in Missouri (RIM). As the standard-bearer for charismatics in the Lutheran Church–Missouri Synod, RIM seeks greater acceptance of the renewal among church members and leaders. Under the church's conservative leadership, the charismatics have had less influence—and faced more opposition—than similar renewal groups in other denominations. Contact: Renewal in Missouri, c/o Bethlehem Lutheran Church, 1065 Kings Way, Nekousa, Wis. 54457. Web site: (http://members.aol.com/rimwww/).

Society of the Holy Trinity (STS). The STS seeks to cultivate a life of prayer and other spiritual disciplines for clergy of the ELCA and the Lutheran Church–Missouri Synod. The society, which holds retreats and annual conferences, also attempts to foster a closer adherence to the Lutheran confessions and involvement in spiritual direction and prayer. Contact: Society of the Holy Trinity, c/o St. Paul Lutheran Church, 440 Hoboken Ave., Jersey City, N.J. 07306. Telephone: (201) 963-5518. Web site: (http://societyholytrinity.org).

Taizé. This group is actually an ecumenical community in France, but its influence has been deep and wide in the United States, where groups and gatherings of churches use Taizé prayer, chants, and music. Contact: Taizé, 71250 Taizé, France. Telephone: (011-33) 385 50 30 30. Web site: (http://www.taize.fr).

Witherspoon Society. The society is one of several progressive coalitions and groups that have emerged in the Presbyterian Church (USA) as conservatives have introduced and in some cases passed legislation in this denomination. The society particularly advocates for an inclusive church for minorities and gay and lesbians, and has a strong social activist bent. Contact: Witherspoon Society, 305 Loma Ansco, Santa Fe, N.Mex. 87501. Web site: (http://www.witherspoonsociety.org).

WordAlone Network. The network emerged in 1999 from the heat of battle in the ELCA over the formal agreement to have full communion with the Episcopal Church. Part of that agreement entails that the Lutherans would have to adopt the historic episcopate (the rite whereby bishops are ordained in a supposedly direct line reaching back to the early church), which WordAlone supporters say conflicts with the Lutheran confessions. The network, which organizes conferences and runs a referral service for seminarians and clergy, proposes a more decentralized model of church leadership than the current ELCA structure, even including congregations that have left the ELCA in its ranks. Contact: WordAlone Network, 900 Stillwater Rd., Mahtomedi, Minn. 55115-2267. Telephone: (651) 762-9104. Web site: (http://www.wordalone.org).

Notes

Preface

1. M. Weber, "The Social Psychology of the World Religions." In H. H. Gerth and C. Wright Mills (eds.), *Max Weber: Essays on Sociology* (New York: Oxford University Press, 1958), 450.

Introduction

1. J. I. Packer, "The Future of Renewal," Word and Spirit Conference, June 12, 1999, Dubuque, Iowa.
2. V. Synan, *The Holiness-Pentecostal Tradition* (Grand Rapids, Mich.: Eerdmans, 1997), 30–40.
3. B. Martin, *A History of Judaism* (New York: Basic Books, 1974), 2:419.
4. R. Wuthnow, *The Restructuring of American Religion* (Princeton, N.J.: Princeton University Press, 1988), 22–29.
5. Wuthnow, *Restructuring of American Religion,* 113.
6. Wuthnow, *Restructuring of American Religion,* 120.
7. D. E. Miller, *Reinventing American Protestantism* (Berkeley: University of California Press, 1997), 177–190.
8. N. Ammerman, "New Life for Denominationalism," *Christian Century,* March 15, 2000, pp. 302–307.
9. W. Abraham, "The Logic of Renewal," Word and Spirit Conference, June 12, 1999, Dubuque, Iowa.

Chapter One

1. M. McGuire, *Pentecostal Catholics* (Philadelphia: Temple University Press, 1982), chap. 1.
2. K. Perotta, "The U.S. Catholic Church." In R. H. Nash (ed.), *Evangelical Renewal in the Mainline Churches* (Westchester, Ill.: Crossway Books, 1987), 159.
3. W. Matthews, interview by author, Dec. 10, 1999. All further quotations of Matthews in this chapter are from this interview.

4.   A. Jones, "Communities Falter Under Heavy Hands," *National Catholic Reporter*, Apr. 18, 1997, pp. 8–12.
5.   J. Boucher, and T. Boucher, eds., *An Introduction to the Charismatic Renewal* (Ann Arbor, Mich.: Servant Publications, 1994), 10.
6.   Boucher and Boucher, eds., *An Introduction to the Charismatic Renewal*, 10.
7.   C. Smidt, L. Kellstedt, J. C. Green, and J. Guth, *The Spirit-Filled Movements in Contemporary America: A Survey Perspective, Consultation Proceedings, Pentecostal Currents in the American Church* (Wheaton, Ill.: Institute for the Study of American Evangelicals, 1994).
8.   R. Bord, and J. E. Faulkner, *The Catholic Charismatics* (University Park: Penn State University Press, 1983), 151.
9.   C. Nobile, interview by author, Dec. 11, 1999.
10.   A. Jones, "Small Communities Bear Big Gifts, Study Shows," *National Catholic Reporter*, May 28, 1999, p. 5.
11.   M. P. Lawson, "The Holy Spirit as Conscience Collective," *Sociology of Religion*, Winter 1999, *60*(4), 341–360.
12.   Jones, "Small Communities Bear Big Gifts," 5.
13.   S. Benthal, interview by author, Dec. 11, 1999.
14.   K. McDonnell, and G. T. Montague, *Fanning the Flame* (Collegeville, Minn.: Liturgical Press, 1991), 9–28.
15.   M. McGuire, *Pentecostal Catholics* (Philadelphia: Temple University Press, 1982), 62.
16.   Rev. C. Adrias, interview by author, Jan. 26, 2000.
17.   Msgr. J. Malagreca, interview by author, Jan. 26, 2000.
18.   E. M. Stalcup, "Holy Spirit, Visit Us Again," *Charisma*, July 1999, pp. 62–70.
19.   Nobile, interview.
20.   J. A. Hammond, and G. C. Kinloch, "Denomination and Participation in Charismatic Movements: A Case Study of Two Prayer Groups," *Journal of Social Psychology*, *129*(1), 123–126.
21.   D. E. Miller, *Reinventing American Protestantism* (Berkeley: University of California Press, 1997), 1–26.
22.   Malagreca, interview.

Chapter Two
1.   Rev. David Runion-Bareford, interview by author, Sept. 25, 1999. All further quotations of Runion-Bareford in this chapter are from this interview.
2.   B. Kosmin, and S. Lachman, *One Nation Under God* (New York: Harmony Books, 1994), 295.

3. N. Ammerman, "Challenges to Denominational Identity in Local Congregations" (paper presented at the conference of the Society for the Scientific Study of Religion, Boston, Mass., November 1999).

4. G. M. Sanders, "The United Church of Christ." In R. Nash (ed.), *Evangelical Renewal in the Mainline Churches* (Westchester, Ill.: Crossway Books, 1987), 125.

5. Sanders, "The United Church of Christ," 125.

6. Sanders, "The United Church of Christ," 131–135.

7. D. E. Miller, *Reinventing American Protestantism* (Berkeley: University of California Press, 1997), 1–9.

8. "Church Life in a Post-Denominational Era," *The Witness,* Winter 1998, pp. 16–17.

9. Rev. E. Gussey, interview by author, June 12, 2000.

10. V. Stoop, interview by author, Oct. 12, 1999.

11. T. Oden, "Mainstreaming the Mainline," *Christianity Today,* Aug. 7, 2000, pp. 59–60.

12. A. B. Robinson, "The Procedural Church: At the UCC Synod," *Christian Century,* Aug. 13, 1997, pp. 717–719.

13. R. Stark, and R. Finke, *Acts of Faith: Explaining the Human Side of Religion* (Berkeley: University of California Press, 2000), 266–271.

14. E. Jorstad, "Conservative Anglicans Threatening or Reshaping Anglican Unity?", *Religion Watch,* March 2000, p. 2.

Chapter Three

1. Pr. J. Hannah, interview by author, April 21, 1999.

2. E. Brand, "Worship and the Ecumenical Movement," *Ecumenical Trends,* Oct. 1999, pp. 1–7.

3. Brand, "Worship and the Ecumenical Movement," pp. 4–5.

4. Rev. F. Schumacher, interview by author, Jan. 27, 1999. All further quotations of Schumacher in this chapter are from this interview.

5. A. Graebner, and A. P. Klausler, "50 Years of the ALPB," *American Lutheran,* parts 1–5, Aug. 1963, pp. 14–17; Sept. 1963, pp. 14–15; Oct. 1963, pp. 14–15; Nov. 1963, pp. 20–23; Dec. 1963, pp. 6–21.

6. Rev. G. C. Stone, ALPB secretary and former *Lutheran Forum* editor, interview by author, Dec. 5, 1998.

7. L. Klein, "The Role of *Lutheran Forum,*" *Lutheran Forum,* Advent issue, 1993, p. 4.

8. L. Klein, "Editorial," *Lutheran Forum,* Lent issue, 1996, p. 10.

9. Rev. R. Lee, interview by author, Aug. 9, 1999.

10. M. Meyer, M. Dawn, D. Nuechterlein, E. Yates, and R. Heinz, *Different Voices, Shared Vision* (Delhi, N.Y.: ALPB Books, 1992).
11. Rev. P. Johnson, interview by author, Mar. 20,1999. All further quotations of Johnson in this chapter are from this interview.
12. "Founding Statement of the Society of the Holy Trinity," *Lutheran Forum*, Easter issue, 1997, pp. 60–62. See also *Lutheran Forum*, Winter 1999, pp. 17–40.
13. J. S. Reed, *Glorious Battle* (Nashville, Tenn.: Vanderbilt University Press, 1996), 128–130.
14. P. Hinlicky, "Editorial," *Lutheran Forum*, Reformation issue, 1993, p. 5.
15. N. Ammerman, "New Life for Denominationalism," *Christian Century*, Mar. 15, 2000, pp. 302–307.
16. Reed, *Glorious Battle*, 259.

Chapter Four
1. S. L. G. Balado, *The Story of Taizé* (London: Mowbray, 1980), 41.
2. Balado, *The Story of Taizé*, 41.
3. Balado, *The Story of Taizé*, 65–66.
4. Balado, *The Story of Taizé*, 75.
5. Balado, *The Story of Taizé*, 91–94.
6. Balado, *The Story of Taizé*, 91–94.
7. Balado, *The Story of Taizé*, 91–94.
8. Balado, *The Story of Taizé*, 43–44.
9. Balado, *The Story of Taizé*, 43.
10. K. Spink, *A Universal Heart* (London: SPCK, 1986), chap. 5.
11. L. Miller, "Trendy Taizé Draws Kids with Soft Music and Prayers," *Wall Street Journal*, Apr. 3, 1998, p. B1.
12. E. Willey, "The Spirit of Findhorn," *The Tablet*, June 5, 1999, p. 775.
13. Bros. Pedro and John, interview by author, Oct. 15, 1999. All further quotations of Bros. Pedro and John in this chapter are from this interview.
14. N. Gonzalez, "Postmodern Taizé," *Re:Generation Quarterly*, Spring 1995, pp. 10–12.
15. R. Wuthnow, *After Heaven: Spirituality in America Since the 1950s* (Berkeley: University of California Press, 1998), 168–198.
16. D. E. Miller, *Reinventing American Protestantism* (Berkeley: University of California Press, 1997), 170–190.
17. S. B. Ross, "The Sociological Significance of the Taizé Community as a Religious Phenomenon of Our Time," unpublished doctoral dissertation, Fordham University, 1987.

Chapter Five

1. Dan Daly and Sheila Daly, interview by author, Aug. 14, 1999.
2. B. Cooke, "Call to Action." In M. J. Weaver (ed.), *What's Left: Liberal American Catholics* (Bloomington: Indiana University Press, 1999), 147–154.
3. "Jubilee: Global Justice and Reconciliation," The Call to Action National Conference, Milwaukee, 1999, 1–19 (program).
4. A. Jones, "Small Communities Bear Big Gifts, Study Shows," *National Catholic Reporter,* May 28, 1999, p. 5.
5. "At Old Parish and New, Outreach Ministries Still Thrive in Rochester, NY," *ChurchWatch,* Aug. 1999, p. 4.
6. D. Wedd, interview by author, Aug. 14, 1999.
7. "Renewal Directory," *Call to Action,* Chicago, Ill., 1998, pp. 1–36.
8. M. Dillon, *Catholic Identity* (New York: Cambridge University Press, 1999), 251–225.
9. D. Martin, "Catholicism in Transition." In T. M. Gannon (ed.), *World Catholicism in Transition* (New York: Macmillan, 1988), 4.
10. G. Gallup Jr., and D. M. Lindsey, *Surveying the Religious Landscape* (Harrisburg, Penna.: Morehouse, 1999).

Chapter Six

1. Rabbi G. Milgram, Sabbath service, Feb. 5, 2000.
2. Rabbi G. Milgram, interview by author, Feb. 10, 2000. All further quotations of Rabbi Milgram in this chapter are from this interview.
3. R. Kamenetz, *Stalking Elijah* (San Francisco: HarperSanFrancisco, 1997), 27–29.
4. Z. Schachter-Shalomi, interview by author, "From Reel to Real." In V. Gross, R. Goldfarb, Y. Goldfarb, N. Gross, and M. Stempfer (eds.), *Ancient Roots, Radical Practices, and Contemporary Visions* (Berkeley, Calif.: Aquarian Minyan, 1999), 21.
5. Kamenetz, *Stalking Elijah,* 62.
6. Kamenetz, *Stalking Elijah,* 32.
7. R. Goldfarb, "Open Forms and Closed Forms." In *Ancient Roots, Radical Practices, and Contemporary Visions,* 41–42.
8. A. Coopersmith, "From House to Aquarian Minyan." In *Ancient Roots, Radical Practices, and Contemporary Visions,* 31–32.
9. A. Waskow, "The Shadow Side," *Gnosis,* Winter 1999, pp. 53–57.
10. R. Z. Schachter-Shalomi, "Notes Toward a Field of Rebbetude," *New Menorah,* Winter 5757, pp. 1–18.
11. R. Kamenetz, "Has The Jewish Renewal Made It Into the Mainstream?", *Moment,* Dec. 1994, pp. 42–82.

12. Kamenetz, "Has The Jewish Renewal Made It Into the Main-
    stream?", pp. 42–82.
13. M. Lerner, "Reflections from an Ally." In *Ancient Roots, Radical
    Practices, and Contemporary Visions,* 54.
14. Rabbi D. Siegel, interview by author, Jan. 16, 2000. All further
    quotations of Rabbi Siegel in this chapter are from this interview.
15. Rabbi M. Strassfeld, interview by author, Feb. 27, 2000. All further
    quotations of Rabbi Strassfeld in this chapter are from
    this interview.
16. Kamenetz, "Has The Jewish Renewal Made It Into the Main-
    stream?", 44–46.
17. B. Jacobson, and A. Grafton, "Jewish Renewal . . . Into the 21st
    Century," *New Menorah,* Fall 5754, pp. 3–4.
18. R. Shapiro, "Toward a New Beginning: The Emerging Judaism
    of the 21st Century," *New Menorah,* Winter 5754, pp. 1–2.
19. Jacobson and Grafton, "Jewish Renewal," 4.
20. R. Cimino, "Anti-Establishment Mood Fuels Post-Denominational
    Judaism," *Religion Watch,* Oct. 1998, p. 2.
21. S. Schwarz, *Finding a Spiritual Home* (San Francisco: Jossey-Bass,
    2000), 47.

Conclusion
1. N. Ammerman, "SBC Moderates and the Making of a Postmodern
   Denomination," *Christian Century,* Sept. 22–29, 1993, pp. 896–899.
2. P. Drucker, "The Network Society," *Wall Street Journal,* Mar. 29,
   1995, p. 12:3.
3. Rabbi D. Siegel, interview by author, Jan. 16, 2000.
4. L. E. Schaller, "Is Schism the Next Step?", *Circuit Rider,* Sept./Oct.
   1998, pp. 4–5.
5. R. Stark, and R. Finke, *Acts of Faith: Explaining the Human Side of
   Religion* (Berkeley: University of California Press, 2000), 151–162.
6. P. Wittberg, *Pathways to Re-Creating Religious Communities* (Mahwah,
   N.J.: Paulist Press, 1996), 19–31.

Index

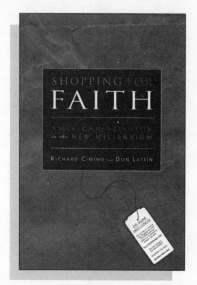

Shopping for Faith
American Religion in the New Millennium

Richard Cimino and Don Lattin

$25.00 Hardcover,

CD-ROM included

ISBN 0-7879-4170-0

"*Shopping for Faith* is as good as it gets in assessing the U.S. religion scene at millennium's end. Cimino and Lattin present a picture of multiple trends headed in often contradictory directions."

—ROBERT ELLWOOD, emeritus professor of religion, University of Southern California

AMERICAN RELIGION flourishes in a consumer culture, and presents us with a bewildering array of choices as we navigate the shopping mall of faith. The authors identify dozens of trends that will shape American religion in the next century and bring together the latest research and intimate portraits of Americans describing their beliefs, their religious heritage, and their spiritual search. With warmth and style the authors document how consumerism shapes religious practice—from conservative evangelical worship to the most esoteric New Age workshop.

Shopping for Faith is more than a book, it is an open line. Its companion CD-ROM enables readers to monitor religious trends via the Internet. Containing the book's entire text, fully searchable and keyword hotlinked, the *Shopping for Faith* CD-ROM connects readers from key terms in the book to resources on the World Wide Web. These web resources—links to related sites and current news stories—are researched and maintained by TheLinkLibrary.com. This innovative feature is sure to keep you apprised of the latest offerings in America's spiritual supermarket well into this new century.

RICHARD CIMINO is editor and publisher of the much-quoted newsletter, *Religion Watch* (http://www.religionwatch.com), which researches trends in contemporary religion. He has worked extensively as a researcher and freelance writer for various publications, including *Christian Century* and *Religion News Service*. He is the author of *Against the Stream: The Adoption of Christian Faiths by Young Adults*.

DON LATTIN is the award-winning religion writer for the San Francisco *Chronicle*. Over the past twenty years he has interviewed thousands of Americans about their religious heritage and spiritual search. He was a fellow at the Program in Religious Studies for Journalists at the University of North Carolina at Chapel Hill and has also taught religion reporting at the Graduate School of Journalism at the University of California at Berkeley. [PRICE SUBJECT TO CHANGE]

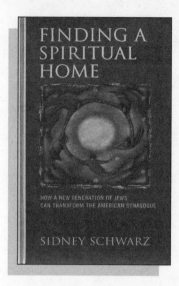

Finding a Spiritual Home

How a New Generation of Jews Can Transform the American Synagogue

Sidney Schwarz
$24.00 Hardcover
ISBN 0-7879-5174-9

"An extraordinary book. A clarion call for spiritual leadership in a post-ethnic age."

—RABBI LAWRENCE A. HOFFMAN, Hebrew Union College, New York; co-founder, Synagogue 2000: Institute for the Synagogue of the Twenty-First Century

"With stories both of individuals and synagogues, Sidney Schwarz shows that old religious structures can indeed become alive with new spiritual meaning, sensitive to generational change. His is an encouraging, beautifully written account of congregations in positive transition—at once inspiring and instructive."

—WADE CLARK ROOF, J.F. Rowny professor of religion and society, University of California at Santa Barbara; author of *A Generation of Seekers: The Spiritual Journeys of the Baby Boom Generation* and *Spiritual Marketplace*

L IKE COUNTLESS others of their generation, many post-war American Jews have abandoned the religion of their birth to search for a spiritual home in other traditions. Some find their way back to the faith of their heritage, but why do so many find that the synagogue has not met their needs?

In this illuminating look at Judaism's future, Rabbi Sidney Schwarz offers a penetrating analysis of the American Jewish community, challenging American synagogues to respond to a generation of seekers and satisfy the spiritual hunger of the "new American Jew." This groundbreaking book not only reveals the possibilities of this new, vital spiritual culture, but also offers strategies for transforming any congregation into a place that the Jews of today can truly call home.

An added bonus in the book is a discussion guide for book clubs and study groups.

SIDNEY SCHWARZ is the founder and president of The Washington Institute for Jewish Leadership and Values, an educational foundation dedicated to renewal of American Jewish life through Judaic study, social justice, and civic activism. He is the founding rabbi of Adat Shalom Reconstructionist Congregation in Bethesda, MD and the author of two books and numerous articles on contemporary Jewish life.

[PRICE SUBJECT TO CHANGE]

BRENDA E. BRASHER

Give me that
ONLINE RELIGION

Give Me That Online Religion

Brenda E. Brasher
$24.95 Hardcover
ISBN 0-7879-4579-X

"Electronic prayer-wheels, cybercast seders, and Heaven's Gate—with more than a million internet religion sites, a critical guide to the phenomenon of cyber-religion is sorely needed. *Give Me That Online Religion* is at once fascinating, troubling, amusing, and provocative—a lively tour through computer-mediated spirituality, presented in terms both the novice and the scholar can appreciate."

—VIVIAN-LEE NITRAY, associate professor, Department of Religious Studies, chair, Asian Studies Interdisciplinary Committee, University of California, Riverside

THE FUTURE of online religion is now! *Give Me That Online Religion* is a provocative exploration of online religion-from virtual monks to millennial fever to spiritual cyborgs—and the profound influence that cybermedia exerts on our concept of God, way of worshiping, and practice of faith.

Increasingly, spiritual seekers are finding their faith communities in cyberspace, creating a metamorphosis of our spiritual environment that is provoking monumental changes within each of us. That's the fundamental argument of this fascinating book. Author Brenda Brasher, a keen observer of media culture and active participant in online religious communities, looks closely at the ways in which the melding of cyberspace and sacred space influences our spiritual needs and aptitudes, our private dreams and public visions, our relationship to our bodies and to our material surroundings, and our emotional palettes and moral sensibilities.

Lavishly illustrating her insights with stories of religious online activity—from the commonplace to the outlandish to the downright frightening—Brasher reveals what people do and experience when they take their spiritual quests online, reviews the spiritual claims made by advocates of computer religion, and demonstrates how online religious activity is inextricably linked to the spiritual crisis of our mass-media society. Detailing the future of faith in the global electric, this compelling book is sure to spark discussion and debate.

BRENDA E. BRASHER is assistant professor in the Department of Religion and Philosophy at Mount Union College in Alliance, Ohio. She frequently serves as a religion consultant to MSNBC and, since 1990, has been documenting and analyzing Web sites of traditional and alternative religious groups.　　　[PRICE SUBJECT TO CHANGE]

Virtual Faith
The Irreverent Spiritual Quest of Generation X

Tom Beaudoin
Foreword by Harvey Cox
$23.95 Hardcover
ISBN 0-7879-3882-3

$16.00 Paperback
ISBN 0-7879-5527-2

"Reveals the deep and pervasive search for meaning that haunts Generation X. This book is must reading for anyone who would understand the spirituality of young people at the turn of a new millennium."

—ROBERT A. LUDWIG, author of *Reconstructing Catholicism for a New Generation*

IN *Virtual Faith,* Tom Beaudoin explores fashion, music videos, and cyberspace concluding that his generation has fashioned a theology radically different from, but no less potent or valid than, that of their elders. Beaudoin's investigation of popular culture uncovers four themes that underpin his generation's theology. First, all institutions are suspect—especially organized religion. Second, personal experience is everything, and every form of intense personal experience is potentially spiritual. Third, suffering is also spiritual. Finally, this generation sees ambiguity as a central element of faith.

This book opens a long overdue conversation about where and how we find meaning, and how we all can encourage each other in this central human searching. Parents and religious leaders of all religious persuasions will gain an understanding of GenX theology in its own terms. And GenXers themselves will find an invitation to a more conscious examination of their own relationship to religion and spiritual experience—and a challenge to take the next step.

TOM BEAUDOIN earned his Master of Theological Studies from Harvard University School of Divinity in 1996 and his Ph.D. in Religion and Education at Boston College.

[PRICE SUBJECT TO CHANGE]